The Blitz Companion:
Aerial Warfare, Civilians
and the City Since 1911

Mark Clapson

UNIVERSITY OF
WESTMINSTER
PRESS

University of Westminster Press
www.uwestminsterpress.co.uk

Competing interests

The author declares that he has no competing interests in publishing this book.

Published by
University of Westminster Press
115 Cavendish Street
London W1W 6UW
www.uwestminsterpress.co.uk

Text ©Mark Clapson 2019

First published 2019

Cover: Diana Jarvis; Images: Courtesy of Library of Congress and
Westminster City Archives.

Print and digital versions typeset by Siliconchips Services Ltd.

ISBN (Paperback): 978-1-911534-48-8
ISBN (PDF): 978-1-911534-49-5
ISBN (EPUB): 978-1-911534-50-1
ISBN (Kindle): 978-1-911534-51-8

DOI: https://doi.org/10.16997/book26

The full text of this book has been peer-reviewed to ensure
high academic standards. For full review policies, see:
http://www.uwestminsterpress.co.uk/site/publish/

Suggested citation:
Clapson, M. 2019. *The Blitz Companion*. London: University of
Westminster Press. DOI: https://doi.org/10.16997/book26. License:
CC-BY-NC-ND 4.0

To read the free, open access version of this book
online, visit https://doi.org/10.16997/book26
or scan this QR code with your mobile device:

Contents

Acknowledgements

I am grateful to the students of my undergraduate Blitz modules at the University of Westminster for their interest in one of the most important events in British history during the twentieth century. Thanks to Andrew Lockett of the University of Westminster Press for encouraging me to write one of the first history publications for the Press, and to my colleagues at the University of Westminster for being such a great team to work with. Katja Seidel kindly helped with the German materials. Thanks are also warmly extended to the staff of the British Library and the other archives I've used in researching the Blitz and reconstruction over recent years, notably the National Archives at Kew, the London Metropolitan Archives and the City of Westminster Archives, Victoria, South of the River.

Some of the chapters below owe a considerable debt to the work of scholars who have already explored the themes discussed, from fear of air raids and preparations for them, to the effect of air warfare on civilians, the post-war reconstruction of the bombed-out cities, and the complex issues involved in commemoration and memorialisation of the victims of the air campaigns in different countries. Here and there, I have been heavily reliant on some key works, but hope that the scope of *The Blitz Companion* is wide and deep enough to provide fresh insights into the local, national and globalised experiences of air warfare on cities and civilians.

Timeline

1937	German air raid on Guernica, Spain
1937	Japanese bombing of China
1937	Air Raid Precautions Act (Britain)
1939–40	Blitzkrieg in Western Europe begins with the Warsaw Blitz
1939	Evacuation from British cities on the eve of British declaration of war
1940	Nazi *Blitzkrieg*
1940	Fall of France; Dunkirk evacuation
1940	The Battle of Britain
1940–41	Blitz over Britain
1940–42	RAF reprisal raids on Germany
1941	Nazi bombing of Eastern European and Russian cities
1942	'Thousand Bomber Raid' on Cologne; RAF bomb Lubeck
1942	The Baedeker Raids on Britain
1943	Area bombing of German cities intensifies
1943	Allied bombing of Italian cities and German and Italian military positions
1944	German V1 raids on London and other British cities
1944	Allied bombing of Northern French cities and German military positions
1944–45	German V1 and V2 raids on London
1944–45	Allied bombing of European cities and German military positions
1945	American atomic bombing of Hiroshima and Nagasaki in Japan
1945	United Nations established
1949	Geneva Convention on the Protection of Civilians in Time of War

1950–53   American bombing during the Korean War
1955   Memorial Peace Park opened in Hiroshima
1958   Campaign for Nuclear Disarmament (CND) launched
           in Britain
1965–73   American bombing of Vietnam
1969–72   American bombing of Cambodia and Laos
1990–91   The Gulf War and American bombing of Iraq
1992   Statue of Sir Arthur 'Bomber' Harris unveiled in London
1999   NATO bombing of Bosnia-Herzegovina
2001   Islamic-extremist terror attack on the Twin Towers in
           New York
2001   US begins bombing of Taliban locations in Afghanistan
           and Pakistan
2002   *The Fire* by Jörg Friedrich published in Germany
2003   American and British bombing campaign in Iraq
2003   Stop the War Coalition formed
2005   Memorial to the Women of World War Two unveiled
           in London
2011   NATO bombing of Libya authorised
2012   Memorial to Bomber Command unveiled in London
2015   Russian bombing of Syria began

Abbreviations

AA	Anti-Aircraft
AAM	American Air Museum
AEF	American Expeditionary Force
ARP	Air Raid Precautions
BCA	Bomber Command Association
BEF	British Expeditionary Force
BFI	British Film Institute
CND	Campaign for Nuclear Disarmament
CPGB	Communist Party of Great Britain
DPRK	Democratic People's Republic of Korea
FRG	Federal German Republic (West Germany)
GDR	German Democratic Republic (Communist East Germany)
HC Debs	House of Commons Debates
HE	Heavy Explosive
HMPP	Hiroshima Memorial Peace Park
HRW	Human Rights Watch
IWM	Imperial War Museum
LCC	London County Council
LMA	London Metropolitan Archives
MO	Mass Observation
NA	National Archives (United States)
NASM	National Air and Space Museum (United States)

NATO	North Atlantic Treaty Organisation
NGO	Non-Governmental Organisation
PPU	Peace Pledge Union
PRONI	Public Record Office, Northern Ireland
RAF	Royal Air Force
ROCAF	Republic of China Air Force
STWC	Stop the War Coalition
TNA	The National Archives (Britain)
UNESCO	United Nations Economic, Scientific and Cultural Organization
USAAF	United States Army Air Force
USAF	United States Air Force
USSBS	United States Strategic Bombing Survey
USSR	Union of Soviet Socialist Republics
UN	United Nations
WFA	World Federalist Association
WRB	War-damage Rehabilitation Board (Japan)

List of Illustrations

CHAPTER I

Introduction: A Century of Aerial Warfare

For many centuries humanity had dreamt of flight, of the wonders of a speedy and expansive mobility above land and sea. This feat was finally accomplished during the early years of the twentieth century, when the Wright brothers and Louis Bleriot took to the air in powered flight. But celebration was soon tarnished by the onset of aerial warfare and its frightening implications. Two bombing events initiated the era of modern air warfare. Both occurred during the Ottoman Wars and before the beginning of the First World War of 1914–18. One was the bombing of Libya by the Italians in 1911; the other was the Bulgarian bombing of Turkey in 1912.

How to cite this book chapter:
Clapson, M. 2019. *The Blitz Companion.* Pp. 1–12. London: University of Westminster Press. DOI: https://doi.org/10.16997/book26.a. License: CC-BY-NC-ND 4.0

The first air raid of the twentieth century was loosely directed at a rural target. In early November 1911, the Italian pilot Lieutenant Giulio Gavotti flew his German-made biplane over the Ain Zara oasis in Libya, dropping four 'grenade-style bombs' onto the desert floor below. Although it was a modest event, killing nobody, this was the beginning of the history of aerial warfare.[1] Italy was engaged in a war against the Ottoman Turkish Empire in North Africa in order to build a little empire of its own to challenge those of other European countries. The following year the Balkan League countries, Bulgaria, Greece, Montenegro and Serbia, rose up against the Turkish Empire in the Balkan War of 1912–13. During this conflict, the Bulgarians perfected the first fit-for-purpose bomb and deployed it on a civilian building:

> The modern aerial bomb, with its distinctive elongated shape, stabilising fins and nose-fitted detonator, is a Bulgarian invention. [A] Bulgarian army captain, Simeon Petrov, adapted and enlarged a number of grenades for use from an aeroplane. They were dropped on a Turkish railway station on 16 October 912 from an Albatross F.2 biplane piloted by Radal Milkov.[2]

The Balkan War witnessed the first bombing runs on enemy targets, the earliest shooting down of an aeroplane, and the first air-naval operation in military history, all part of an early, emergent synthesis of air power with ground and sea forces. In the German strategic bombing campaign during the First World War of 1914-18, Western European countries were bombed from zeppelin air ships, and from biplanes. Military leaders consciously planned for strategic bombing campaigns against military targets, targets that in a rapidly urbanising continent were often situated near to towns and cities.

Bombing was a new and terrible feature of the emergence of 'total war'. During the First World War combatant countries witnessed the militarisation of everyday life. Those who did not don a military uniform and go to fight on the front instead served on the 'Home Front'. Civilians were now essential to the winning of wars, producing food, industrial goods and munitions, and serving in variety of voluntary civil defence, emergency and medical services to minimise the impact of air raids. It is also noteworthy that the St Paul's Watch was formed in 1915, by a team of employees of the cathedral, and volunteers, to ensure the iconic place of worship was not damaged by fire, thus handing a propaganda coup to the enemy.[3]

Following the industrialised carnage in the trenches and battlefields of the First World War, the leaders of Britain, France and the USA met at the Paris Peace Conference in 1919. The Treaty of Versailles established the League of Nations in order to promote international cooperation to prevent war. The Treaty also severely circumscribed the German military, forbidding both an air force and aviation activities from its much-diminished Navy.[4] This 'air disarmament' confirmed that air power was now a threat to everyone involved in national and international hostilities, leading to a new culture of planning for air raids on civilians.[5] As chapter two demonstrates, the leading industrial nations, particularly in the context of growing international tensions in Europe, improved their air forces for aerial warfare, while promoting a civil defence apparatus to minimise death and destruction, and to maintain, as far as possible, civilian morale. In the face of the emerging terror of air wars between 1918 and 1939, millions of people became not only air-minded, but threat-minded. As chapter two also argues, the later 1930s witnessed a number of terrible air raids on civilians which literally brought air war into the home. And from September 1939, the world was pitched into a prolonged global conflict in which air power played a crucial, tragic and yet nuanced role in shaping both civilian experiences in total wars, and in the outcome of the war itself.

Chapters three, four and five cover the first and most sustained global interface between civilian populations and the technology of aerial warfare during the twentieth century. This was the Second World War. Britain is given particular focus in chapter three for the simple reason that it sustained the longest air raid of any European city during the twentieth century, on London from 1940–41. The Blitz has been much debated by historians. How civilians behaved during the Blitz, their collective morale, and the performance of civil defence and emergency services, have been the subject of many controversial and conflicting interpretations. Moreover, contemporary government and media propaganda about heroic tales of civilian endurance and the ultimate triumph over mass bombing, gave rise to a national story of wartime unity and the 'Blitz spirit' that was invoked by the Labour Party in the general election campaign of 1945.

Populations in other countries suffered to a far greater extent than the British, however. The Allied strategic bombing campaign against German cities from 1942–5 was initially viewed, from the perspective of the victorious allies at least, as Germany reaping what it sowed. But recent decades have seen a profound questioning of the morality or otherwise of the bombing of Germany. And countries across continental Europe all suffered air raids that, with the benefit of hindsight, have been criticised as causing unnecessary suffering to innocent children, women and men. Many of those air raids were conducted by the German Luftwaffe, some with support from the *Regia Aeronautica*, the Royal Italian Air Force. Many others were initiated by the Allies, including the Soviet Union, to liberate Europe from fascism. The impact of air raids on civilians across continental Europe is explored in chapter four.

In tandem with Germany and Italy, Japan was the third Axis Power pitched against the Allies. Its decision to attack Pearl Harbor in December 1941 created a powerful nemesis, triggering American entry into the war. Japan would be subjected to heavy conventional bombing by the Allies from late 1944, but the most lethally destructive bombing events of the twentieth century were visited by the Americans upon Japan in August 1945. Victory over Europe or 'VE Day' had been declared by the Allies on Sunday 8 May 1945, but for months afterwards the Japanese continued to fight their American enemies. The decision by US President Harry S. Truman and his military and scientific advisors to drop the atomic bomb on the cities of Hiroshima and Nagasaki was a momentous one in the history not only of warfare, but for human affairs since. Chapter five assesses the scale of the bombing of Japan, the reasons for unleashing the atomic bomb, its terrible impact on the citizens of Hiroshima and Nagasaki, and the debates over the legitimacy of a nuclear catastrophe that brought the flailing but defiant Japanese war to an abrupt end.

Once the war was over, previous conflict areas lay in ruins, devastated by bombing and fire. Millions of people had seen their homes damaged or completely destroyed, while commercial and industrial premises, and road, rail and communications networks were in urgent need of replacement or repair. Pressure to rebuild towns and cities across the world initiated the era of reconstruction, which lasted from 1945 to the later 1950s. Focusing upon Britain, Germany and Japan, chapter six draws upon some highly original and mostly recent scholarship in social, urban and town planning history – as the reconstruction of the built environment was accompanied by propagandist and politicised narratives of national renewal. The war had generated strong myths of national unity across internal class, regional and sectional divides, which were now mobilised by post-war governments to promote a vision of social renewal within the physical reconstruction of the nation. Physical reconstruction, however, was often bedevilled by practical problems and political constraints. Many bold visions for the future were curtailed.

Peace since 1945 proved fragile, and was often disrupted by conflict. The Cold War between the capitalist West and Soviet and Chinese Communism became embroiled with uprisings across former colonial territories of South East Asia. Significant nationalist movements ignited by the Second World War led to further conflict in Korea and Vietnam. Initially these conflicts were challenges to the legacy of imperialism. The United Nations (UN) and communist forces confronted each other in the Korean War of 1950–3. And the United States led the fight against communism in the Vietnam War from 1954–75. Each of these bloody conflicts witnessed strategic bombing campaigns which both drew upon, and ignored, lessons learned by air forces during the previous world war. As chapter seven argues, the Korean and Vietnamese wars brought extensive misery and suffering to civilian populations. Heavy and sustained bombing also wrought profound historical consequences, not simply for those enduring the conflict, but for the history of those countries following the ceasefire. The image and reputation of the United States, furthermore, as the major combatant on behalf of NATO and the UN, was severely damaged. Critics have attacked American bombing policy from the Korean War of 1950–3 to the present century as essentially a demonstration of ruthless imperialism.

The civilian experience of bombing within the post-war context of commemoration is discussed in chapter eight. Warfare has long led to commemoration and memorialisation. For centuries, combatants in military uniform were celebrated in friezes, illustrations, marble or stone memorials, stories, carvings and tombs, culminating in the plethora of memorials erected to the war dead of the First World War in cities, towns and villages across Britain and Europe. Total war, however, involved entire societies mobilising against the military apparatus of other societies. Contemporaneously with the heroic victories or deaths of uniformed combatants, hundreds of thousands of civilians were slaughtered, injured, made homeless and even stateless by the onslaught of mass bombing. How were they to be remembered? Bombed-out cities became sites of memory – *lieux de memoire* – while memorials were erected to the dead of the air raids in the Second World War. Memorials are both sites and carriers of memory, and sources of information about the war. So too are photography, film, literature, autobiographies, memoirs and oral testimony. They evoke the atmosphere of wartime air raids, and images and memories of air warfare on civilians and cities, promoting bombed towns and cities as *lieux de memoire*.

Chapter nine covers the sources and resources available to students and anyone interested in the history of air raids on cities and civilians.

Key Themes and Questions

One hundred years after it was first bombed, Libya was again under attack from the air. Beginning in March 2011, a NATO coalition force involving Britain, France and the United States bombed Libyan cities in order to depose the brutal dictatorship of Colonel Muammar Gaddafi. The Italians joined in soon afterwards. In the short term, at least, the attack on Libya was successful. Gaddafi was brutally killed on 20 October, and for a brief period optimism reigned as democratic forces and a diverse range of young Libyans looked forward to a more affluent and democratic future.

During the years since the 2011 bombing campaign, however, Libya imploded. Many comparisons were made with Iraq, bombed into regime change in 2003 by the USA with assistance from Britain. Initial successes in aerial bombardment were unravelled by the vicious civil war that unfolded in the former dictatorship. This explains the hesitancy in 2015-16, among nervous NATO member countries, about military involvement in Syria, a country wracked with internal conflict under the regime of Bashar al-Assad. Then the Russians began bombing Syrian cities in 2015 in defence of Assad. With the exception of surgical strikes and drone attacks by the USA, NATO members were reluctant to throw air power at the problem until France, reeling from mass murder in Paris by Islamic State (ISIS) militants on 13 November 2015, declared war on ISIS and began bombing ISIS strongholds in Syria.[6] The British government and some of Her Majesty's Opposition, fearful lest they be seen to franchising their defence against Islamic extremism to France, began bombing soon afterwards.[7] Those opposed to the bombing, notably the socialist Stop the War Coalition (STWC), argued that history proved that aerial bombardment was misguided and morally repugnant because it killed innocent civilians and was militarily unsuccessful.[8]

They were only partly right about that. As this book argues, any blanket denunciation of bombing campaigns as essentially immoral and militarily unsuccessful ignores historical realities. While many air raids were indeed notoriously brutal and led to unnecessary civilian casualties, other air campaigns did assist in defeating dictatorships. So for example, while the air raids on London and other major British cities during the Second World War ultimately failed to defeat the British, the atomic bombing by the USA of Japan in August 1945 may be judged to have hastened the end of the war in the Pacific. In other cases the historical judgment is less clear cut. Allied air raids on German cities by the British and the Americans from 1942 have increasingly been criticised for causing unnecessary casualties. Many millions of words have also been written to prove that American bombing campaigns from the Korean War of 1950–3, through the Vietnam War to the recent air strikes in countries in the Middle East, have largely been unsuccessful, and even downright immoral. Yet some critics of American air power remained relatively silent on the bombing of Syria by Russian forces from 2015–17, or about recent Russian expansionism in the Ukraine.

The Blitz Companion assesses the causes and nature of aerial warfare during the last century and the early decades of the present one. Its major theme, however, is the targeting of civilians, and the consequences of air raids upon urban populations. The British experience of air raids forms a significant chunk of the book. When understood comparatively, however, Britain suffered less from air raids than other countries. But it was Britain that hosted the paradigmatic Blitz of the twentieth century, from 1940–1. Across Europe during the Second World War, capital cities and major provincial urban areas were attacked, and Germany sustained many more casualties and significantly greater levels of environmental destruction. In Japan, the conventional and atomic bombing of its main cities eclipsed the magnitude of death and damage in many European urban centres. Hence much of the *Blitz Companion* focuses on air raids and their aftermath in Britain, Germany and Japan, drawing wider comparative conclusions.

The Second World War was the catalyst for the Cold War between Western capitalism and the Communist eastern bloc. During the post-war era, the American bombing of Korea and Vietnam caused widespread death and devastation, within national and historical contexts that were quite different to the popular experience of aerial bombing during the Second World War. And the end of the Cold War in no way brought about the much-heralded 'end of history'. During the 1990s and into the present century, civilians have also been killed and injured in small wars, during the Balkan Civil Wars, in Afghanistan, and in the Middle East, notably Iraq, Libya and Syria. These conflicts were on a smaller scale than the Second World War, but they were a reminder of the cruel lesson learnt in earlier total wars: air power was here to stay, and civilians were going to die.

The bombing of these countries, and of the other civilian populations discussed in this book, leads to some hugely important questions that apply to all air raids on all societies, no matter where or when in time. Among the most important are the following:

- In what ways did sorties over urban centres in previous decades provide dress rehearsals or practical lessons for later air campaigns?
- How did those military and political authorities plan-ning air raids anticipate the effects on civilians of the bombing?
- How did civilians react during air raids? What prepara-tions were made by governments and local authorities to

minimise the impact and consequences of aerial bombardment, and how effective were they?

- Did bombing campaigns, large and small, achieve their
  intentions to degrade or defeat the civilian population?
- How resilient were cities and their residents during air
  raids and in the aftermath of destruction?
- How have societies come to terms with the death and
  destruction caused by the bombing of men, women and
  children?

The focus on civilians and aerial warfare is deliberately chosen for
its emotive and moral dimensions. In the aftermath of the First
World War military strategists and politicians soon understood
that with the onset of air power civilians were no longer marginal
to the process of conflict, but now bound up with it. And in spite
of the Hague and United Nations conventions on military conduct to restrict civilian casualties, the spatial containment of war
from the air to specific theatres of combat was increasingly irrel-
evant. During the interwar years, in the long shadow of the First
World War that had cost so many young lives, pacifist organisations were formed to call for an end to war, and for negotiation
henceforth to become the only path to avoiding war, or for peace
and reconciliation. They were the forerunners of the anti-war
and anti-bomb campaigning organisations of the post-war years.
During the 1950s this was manifested in the formation of the
Campaign for Nuclear Disarmament (CND) in Britain, and in the
rise of peace activism during the Vietnam War. And as conflict in
the Middle East raged following the attack on the Twin Towers in
September 2001, the aforementioned Stop the War Coalition was
formed. Unfortunately, many of the leading personnel of these

global peace movements shared political beliefs that distorted a more balanced appraisal of air warfare. Another intention of *The Blitz Companion*, therefore, is to critically engage with the current range of anti-war pacifist websites, and with critics of air power who fail to do justice to the complex intentions and consequences of air raids.

CHAPTER 2

The Emerging Terror

Introduction

In his poem *Locksley Hall*, written during the 1830s, the decade
that Queen Victoria came to the throne, Alfred Lord Tennyson
imagined the apocalyptic and sublime power of mass human flight.
His 'Vision of the world, and all the wonder that would be' con-
jured up a spectral images of the heavens filled with commercial
vessels, 'argosies of magic sails', and of celestial conflict between
'the nation's airy navies'.[9] The poet was writing during the second
phase of the Industrial Revolution in Britain. The railway network
was beginning to burgeon across the land, speeding up travel time

How to cite this book chapter:
Clapson, M. 2019. *The Blitz Companion*. Pp. 13–35. London: University of
    Westminster Press. DOI: https://doi.org/10.16997/book26.b. License:
    CC-BY-NC-ND 4.0

and bringing once isolated cities and regions into the national infrastructure. Tennyson lived from 1809 to 1892, a lifespan that encompassed the American Civil War of 1860–5 and the Franco-Prussian War of 1870–1. The Civil War involved not only armies and navies of the Union and the Confederacy but the societies of the Northern and Southern states of the USA. Arguably the first modern, industrialised total war in which civilians were mobilised or dragged into conflict, the Civil War also saw the military use of manned air balloons to spy from above on enemy positions.[10] During the Siege of Paris in 1871, air balloons were deployed by the French for communications and propaganda purposes.[11] These conflicts marked the tentative beginnings of airborne vessels in modern warfare. Floating gracefully through the air, balloons were used as tools for disseminating propaganda, unwittingly anticipating the leaflet drops during twentieth-century wars.

Article 25 of The Hague Convention in 1899 on the Laws and Customs of War on Land stated unequivocally that 'The attack or bombardment of towns, villages, habitations or buildings which are not defended, is prohibited.' Article 27 was also explicit about the limitations of offensive military assaults:

> In sieges and bombardments all necessary steps should be taken to spare as far as possible edifices devoted to religion, art, science, and charity, hospitals, and places where the sick and wounded are collected, provided they are not used at the same time for military purposes.

Articles 22 to 28 of the Hague Convention of 1907 made similar strictures about public buildings, arguing that the rights of belligerents to attack the enemy were not unlimited, and prohibiting the bombardment of undefended cities, towns and villages. (The articles are widely available online).

These conventions were drawn up on the eve of aerial warfare during the twentieth century. Civilians had long been casualties of war, or course, as captives, victims of killing, execution and rape, or seen as figures in landscapes torn apart by conventional warfare. Now however they would become directly targeted from the air. During the twentieth century the Hague Conventions were subsequently updated to address the laws and customs of war from the air, and the United Nations Conventions or 'Geneva Conventions' after the Second World War also addressed the problem of minimising civilian casualties. But mass aerial bombardment rendered these stipulations somewhat meaningless: fine words on paper, but easily ignored or negotiated around by belligerent powers seeking to destroy the enemy from the skies.

Fear of the Bomb

Anxiety about the potential of bombing from the air emerged even before mechanised flight was invented, as *Locksley Hall* illustrates. Writers alive to the wonderful opportunities offered by speedier air travel also grasped that air power possessed a hitherto unknown destructive potential. The British science fiction writer H.G. Wells is best known for *War of the Worlds* (1911), an apocalyptic novel about interplanetary aerial conflict which has been made into a number of films. But before hostile aerial bombardment had even happened, Wells wrote *War in the Air* (1908). Portraying mass catastrophe caused by air raids in an industrialised world war, one scene from the novel looked down from a dirigible, an airship, during an air raid on New York:

> He clung to the frame of the porthole as the airship tossed
> and swayed, and stared down through the light rain that

now drove before the wind, into the twilight streets, watching people running out of the houses, watching buildings collapse and fires begin. As the airships sailed along they smashed up the city as a child will shatter its cities of brick and card. Below, they left ruins and blazing conflagrations and heaped and scattered dead; men, women, and children mixed together as though they had been no more than Moors, or Zulus, or Chinese. Lower New York was soon a furnace of crimson flames, from which there was no escape. Cars, railways, ferries, all had ceased, and never a light lit the way of the distracted fugitives in that dusky confusion but the light of burning. He had glimpses of what it must mean to be down there–glimpses. And it came to him suddenly as an incredible discovery, that such disasters were not only possible now in this strange, gigantic, foreign New York, but also in London–in Bun Hill! that the little island in the silver seas was at the end of its immunity, that nowhere in the world any more was there a place left where a Smallways might lift his head proudly and vote for war and a spirited foreign policy, and go secure from such horrible things.[12]

War was no longer somewhere else or far away. Emphasising that modern war, total war, would be 'everywhere', all-encompassing, unavoidable, almost morally and practically unable to differentiate between belligerents and the 'quiet people', Wells waxed upon feminine vulnerability to force home his point:

> There is no place where a woman and her daughter can hide and be at peace. The war comes through the air, bombs drop in the night. Quiet people go out in the morning, and see air fleets passing overhead – dripping death – dripping death![13]

During the First World War of 1914–18, however, the spectre of large grey airships dropping death from the city skies and of biplanes coming in to drop bombs on familiar areas of the city, lent war this fearful new dimension, revealing the realities of mass aerial warfare on civilians for the first time.

The First World War and the New Realities of Air Warfare

Those bespoke bombs dropped onto Libya in 1911 and the subsequent Bulgarian innovation were the flimsiest of historical dress rehearsals for what would occur during the rest of the century. The war from 1914–18, however, more fully defined the nature and implications of aerial warfare for civilians. The first bombs to be unleashed came from Germany on Belgium, France and Britain. Minor raids in 1914 were followed by the first so-called 'strategic bombing campaigns' by Germany from 1915. As Richard Overy argues, there is so singular or clear definition of strategic bombing. It was first used during the First World War to mean long-range bombing behind enemy lines. It can also mean bombing to assist ground forces, the precision targeting of military or industrial installations, or the more generalised carpet bombing of cities and towns in order to degrade infrastructure, destroy key targets and weaken the ability of a nation to wage war, irrespective of ground forces.[14]

During the First World War, German bombing missions over England were aimed at military installations, factories and munitions works, and naval activities in ports. Hence Hull and Whitby in north-east England, and the smaller seaside towns of Great Yarmouth, King's Lynn and Sheringham in Norfolk, were attacked for their mercantile connections, but also because they were on the East Coast, and easier for the zeppelins to reach. Birmingham was attacked, although the zeppelins failed to reach targets

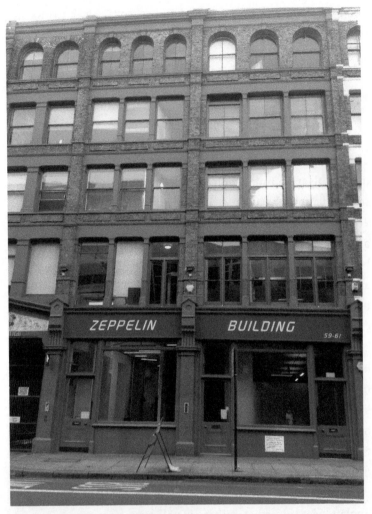

Figure 1: The Zeppelin Building, Farringdon, East-Central London (photograph by author, 2017).

further west. London was an obvious objective for the Germans, however. The air raids in the First World War drew an early pattern of incursion and destruction that would be more widely replicated in the Second World War. Among the first areas of London to be hit were the docks along the banks of the River Thames in East London, and adjacent urban areas. Over the course of the First World War zeppelins raided or attempted raids on Deptford, Greenwich, Hackney, the Isle of Dogs, New Cross, Rotherhithe and Stepney. Towns in the hinterland of London, in the counties of Essex, Hertfordshire and Kent were also attacked.[15]

The air raids on London provided early clues to the behaviour and morale of urban populations under the bomb. As Philip Ziegler argues, when a nightly air raid on East London was imminent, many East Londoners trekked to the relatively safer areas of West London. Many others took shelter in the London Underground tube stations, huddling together on the platforms as the bombs fell above.[16] Others experienced feelings of anxiety, and one 'terrified housewife' committed suicide. By contrast, children were openly thrilled by the spectre of airships coming across the sky. Anger and shock at the casualties and deaths caused by these unprecedented attacks on British cities rarely led to mass panic, moreover.[17] As Susan Grayzel argues, such behaviour anticipated patterns of coping and of self-protection in later wars.[18]

Newspapers reported not only on the air raids but also speculated on the potential changes to everyday life in the event of war from the air. Yet the subject, fearful in itself, also led to humorous and satirical observations. The cartoonist W.K. Haselden, for example, drew an amusing but also insightful portrait of life 'if air raids become a daily occurrence.'[19] While the cartoon is not intended to be an accurate anticipation of the changed contexts of everyday life during air raids, the illustration uncannily hints at some innovations that would be introduced in time for the air raids of the Second World War. Instead of the narrow windows of the house, blackout and storm-proofed curtains were used. The motor car would see its headlamps dipped or turned off, while

Figure 2: 'If air raids become daily occurrences', W.K. Haselden cartoon, *Daily Mirror*, © Mirrorpix.

the cartoon hints at armoured cars for military personnel operating in civilian areas. Protective headwear would indeed be worn by voluntary emergency workers and air raid wardens, and while armoured prams did not materialise, Mickey Mouse gas masks would be introduced for children, for example, alongside normal masks for adults.[20]

If popular culture made light of the implications of total war, highbrow writers made more serious observations. In the years following the First World War, intellectuals grappled with its terrible legacy, encapsulated in the modern spectre of air power. The American-born poet T.S. Eliot had been deeply unsettled by the impact of the war. In *The Waste Land*, published in 1922, and written while he was living in London, a much-debated stanza entitled 'What the Thunder Said' begins with a rhetorical question 'What is that sound high in the air'. The poem goes on to evoke a cracked ancient earth, and the 'falling towers' in such historic cities as Jerusalem, Athens, Alexandria, Vienna and London: 'unreal'.[21] Ancient European cities, bastions of civilisations, are now 'cracked and reformed' in a historically instantaneous moment delivered by modern technology. Furthermore, the sound high in the air and the murmur of maternal lamentation might be viewed as the fear of a mother for her children as the bombers emerge over the far flung landscape, causing the people to flee.

The Waste Land was published almost four years after the Armistice of 1918 and represents an inchoate grasp or fear of the power of airborne destruction. A fuller understanding of the impact of air raids, and of the need to prepare for them in the future, began during the First World War, and continued, albeit in fits and starts, during the 1920s and 1930s. In 1917 the London Air Defence Area (LADA) was established to improve the coordination of British fighter planes when defending the metropolis. And in 1918 the formation of the Royal Air Force (RAF) marked the ascendency of the national air force within the military capacity of Britain. In 1920, in Iraq, the British developed a policy of using the RAF to police the skies above Mesopotamia. The Minister of War and Air, Winston Churchill, and the Chief of the Air Staff Sir Hugh Trenchard, argued that air power could be deployed to support ground forces, to hit relatively remote targets, and to distribute propaganda.[22]

Other countries invested in modern combat air fleets. The United States had created the American Expeditionary Force (AEF) in 1917 when America joined the Allies. The French Air Force, first formed in 1909, was expanded to counter a possible German threat following the Treaty of Versailles. In Italy the *Regia Aeronautica*, or Italian Royal Air Force, was established in 1923, the year after Benito Mussolini seized power. The German Air Force, curtailed following 1919, was reborn as the Luftwaffe in Nazi Germany in 1935. That event accelerated air raid precautions, or civil defence, that had been ongoing in Britain since the 1920s. Other countries also began to assemble air defence measures.

Fear of the Bomb and Preparations for Aerial Warfare, 1918–39

In 1924, a new sub-committee on air raid precautions was added to the functions of the Committee of Imperial Defence in Britain. First formed in 1902, following the ignominious military performance of the British Empire during the Boer War, the Committee for Imperial Defence now began, slowly, to confront the realities of air war for civilian populations. The Chair of the sub-committee was Sir John Anderson, 'an enormously able but uninspiring public servant' whose deliberations and preparations established the civil defence apparatus prior to the outbreak of the Second World War in 1939.[23]

The impact of air raids on innocent civilians during the First World War, and the growing awareness of the terrible potential of bombing in future wars, demonstrated what historians have labelled 'air-mindedness' after 1918.[24] This was evident in the new conceptual understandings of air power in the writings of military leaders notably the Italian Giulio Douhet and the

American Brigadier William 'Billy' Mitchell, 'the most important advocates of assault on the heart of a nation by self-contained, self-defending bomber formations'.[25] In Britain, Captain Basil Liddell Hart, Colonel J.F.C. Fuller and Sir Hugh Trenchard were leading proponents of strategic bombing offensives against enemy nations.[26] In sharp relief, heavy bombing could deliver a knock out blow, rendering civilian populations paralysed, and disrupting or destroying ground targets to allow for successful invasion by land forces. In their study of Liverpool's preparations for air raids, Peter Adey et al. stress the importance of interdependency in Air Raid Precautions (ARP). An attack on one element of the urban infrastructure could have calamitous knock-on effects in a modern state; so joined-up thinking was entirely necessary for holistic preparation for air raids.[27]

The global threat of air power led to international attempts to limit the potential effect of aerial bombardment on civilian populations as far as possible. Article XXIV of *The Hague Rules of Air Warfare*, drawn up in late 1922 (widely available online), was clear that aerial bombardment was legitimate only when directed at a military objective to military advantage; when directed solely at military forces and establishments; and at factories and other centres manufacturing weapons or ammunition. Any bombardment of human settlements beyond the operations of land forces is prohibited, along with the indiscriminate bombardment of the civilian population. Yet the caveats were fluid, to say the least:

> In the immediate neighbourhood of the operations of land forces, the bombardment of cities, towns, villages, dwellings, or buildings is legitimate provided that there exists a reasonable presumption that the military concentration is sufficiently important to justify such

bombardment, having regard to the danger thus caused
to the civilian population.

One of the most important consciousness-raising attempts by
politicians about the terrible realities of air warfare came in the
speech by the Conservative leader Sir Stanley Baldwin to the
House of Commons in 1932. Baldwin had been Conservative
Prime Minister from 1924–9, and traded on his reputation as a
dependable and trustworthy leader. His words had gravitas, and
he did not mince them. Highlighting the rapid improvements
in flight technology, and speedier and more powerful bomber
planes, Baldwin pointed out that no town was safe: 'The question
is: whose morale will be shattered quickest by that preliminary
bombing?'

Baldwin was content to ram home his point that rapidly evolv-
ing aircraft technology was a threat in and of itself:

> I think it is well also for the man in the street to real-
> ize that there is no power on earth that can protect him
> from being bombed, whatever people may tell him. *The*
> *bomber will always get through.* [Take] any large town
> you like on this island or on the Continent within reach
> of an aerodrome. For the defence of that town and its
> suburbs you have to split up the air into sectors for de-
> fence. Calculate that the bombing aeroplanes will be at
> least 20,000 feet high in the air, and perhaps higher, and
> it is a matter of mathematical calculation that you will
> have sectors of from 10 to hundreds of cubic miles.[28]

The famous warning that 'the bomber will always get through'
was accompanied by the latest military thinking about the need
for sectors of air defence to calibrate as far as possible the number and trajectory of incoming enemy planes, and to facilitate the

most efficient defence system, albeit within highly difficult circumstances. The point about suburbs is often ignored by historians, but it is a reminder that while the town and city centres offered higher densities of population and infrastructure to the invader, outlying areas were also vulnerable despite their more residential character. Between the wars, British cities had witnessed extensive suburbanisation. The social consequences of this were a broad segregation of the classes into mostly working-class inner-urban areas, and suburban working-class council estates. The middle classes increasingly settled in private owner-occupied suburbia.[29] The spatial consequences were visible in the much-detested sprawl of the cityscape, and the mass arrival of the semi-detached house along the new roads that spread out into the countryside from the town and city centres. When the poet John Betjeman wrote in his 1938 poem *Slough* 'come friendly bombs and fall on Slough, it isn't fit for humans now' he was only half-joking.[30] He hated the new suburban settlements around London, and had clearly understood the new realities of air power. He was air-minded.

Baldwin continued with the most chilling passage of all, warning that 'the only defence is in offence, which means that *you have got to kill more women and children more quickly than the enemy if you want to save yourselves*'.[31] This was to be the reality of the next war, he correctly predicted.[32] Like H.G. Wells before him, Baldwin emphasised the shocking scenario of killing women and children. In essence, because the bomber would always get through, the awful lesson was that the defending nation would feel compelled to violate the principles laid down in the Hague Conventions on Air Warfare. Baldwin's seemingly heartless words must, however, be viewed with the context of the disarmament debates that were taking place in Britain and across the world. Just two years later, however, Baldwin made another famous speech in which he moved toward rearmament. By then, Nazi power in Germany had been brutally entrenched, and Germany had pulled out of the Disarmament Conference in Geneva, Switzerland, as early as November 1933.[33] Baldwin pledged that the National Government would ensure that British air power 'shall no longer be in a position inferior to any country within striking distance of its shores', and he went on to issue an almost subliminal message to Germany:

> When you think of the defence of England you no longer
> think of the chalk cliffs of Dover, you think of the Rhine.
> That is where our Frontier lies.[34]

The National Government initiated an expansion of the RAF from 1934. It was opposed by the Labour and Liberal parties because it might accentuate the interwar arms race.[35] Another prominent conservative politician, Winston Churchill, was however growing increasingly fearful of air warfare. He was keenly aware of the main problems and consequences inherent in indiscriminate bombing, arguing to an American audience in 1934 that 'air bombing of the non-combatant population for the purposes of slaughter' would upset public opinion and alienate allies. He also raised what Michael Sherry has termed the 'overlooked question' of how a civilian population under heavy bombardment, who wished to surrender could make their will known to the enemy above.[36] Speaking to the House of Commons on 30 July 1934, in a debate on German rearmament, Churchill also warned that London was going to be a potential target for aerial bombing. 'With our enormous metropolis here':

the greatest target in the world, a kind of tremendous, fat, valuable cow tied up to attract the beast of prey, we are in a position in which we have never been before, and in which no other country in the world is in at the present time.[37]

Although London was the largest city in Europe during the 1930s, industrialisation and urbanisation had created large cities and towns across Western Europe, Soviet Russia and North America. Yet in another context Churchill was unwittingly correct: interwar suburbanisation was at its most extensive in England, and English cities lay prone and sprawling beneath the dangerous skies.[38]

In 1934 the League of Nations called for an international process of disarmament, a call enthusiastically supported by the various pacifist groups in interwar Britain, both religious and secular. The No More War Movement, the Quaker Friends Peace Committee, the Labour League of Youth and the Peace Pledge Union were among the leading pacifist organisations that understood the growing threat of air power, and the increased vulnerability of civilian populations to mass death and destruction. Marches and demonstrations, and signing the petition or 'pledge' to end wars were increasingly prominent during the mid-1930s, although pacifism remained a marginal cause.[39]

Such efforts were to no avail, however. In 1935 Adolf Hitler announced the Luftwaffe to the world. Despite the Treaty of Versailles, German air power would become a major element in Nazi rearmament and military production. New fighter planes were introduced. In Britain, a new Air Raids Precautions Department was created in April 1935 in a timely response to the militarisation of Nazi foreign policy. In the same year the German *Reichsluftschutzbund* (Reich Air Protection League) issued a poster of Herman Goering stating 'Air defence fighters have as much responsibility and as much honour as every soldier at the Front'. As Overy argues, civil defence under the Nazi regime was more militarised in character than British ARP. A greater pressure to participate in the collective defence of the Fatherland led to over 15 million Germans participating in the *Reichsluftschutzbund* by 1939, and 22 million by 1941. That was over a quarter of the German population.[40]

From Predictions to Realities: Air Raids in Spain and China

The second half of the 1930s witnessed a number of horrifying air raids, brutal evidence of the terrors to come. The Spanish Civil War from 1936–8 initiated the era of fascist air raids against civilian populations in Europe. German pilots were to gain their first combat experience as the Luftwaffe now put its theories of air attack into practice.[41] At the behest of the Falange leader General Franco, on 26 April 1937, the Luftwaffe bombed communist Republican forces in the Basque town of Guernica in Northern Spain. About a thousand civilians were killed. Guernica was an important moment in the growing international awareness of air warfare. During the 1930s the British public had been receiving many serious warnings about the growing importance of air warfare, alongside many novels of varying quality about the terrible nature and consequences of future air raids during war. For example, the film *Things to Come* (1936) directed by Alexander Korda and based upon the novel by H.G. Wells, depicted bleak representations of modern air warfare, as the wireless, blaring air raid sirens and barking megaphones announce the disruption and destruction of urban and suburban life. The air raids on Guernica were real, though, and marked a turning point in Britain's fear of the bomber, as the public now reluctantly accepted the certainties of air warfare.[42] This realisation was compounded by the raids conducted by the Royal Italian Air Force on Barcelona in March 1938.[43]

The threat of modern air warfare was not confined to Europe. The Japanese air raids on Chinese cities from July 1937 ran parallel to this new understanding, and were accompanied by more extreme reminders of the horrors of conflict. The Second Sino-Japanese War began when Japanese fighter planes engaged in skirmishes with the Chinese forces. The Republic of China Air Force (ROCAF) was unable to resist air penetration, and the Japanese relied heavily upon the bombing of towns and cities, attacking both military and civilian targets from September to early December. The air raids devastated many smaller towns but also larger cities, notably the then capital of China, Nanking, leading to a mass exodus of people from the city that more than halved its population. Widespread international condemnation of the bombing was reflected in the British weekly magazine *The Spectator*:

> The protests made by the British, American and other Governments had as their background far more vehement outbursts of public opinion. In this country *The Times* promptly opened its columns to a correspondence in which such various writers as Sir Francis Acland, the Bishop of Bristol and Mr. J. M. Keynes expressed the growing body of opinion in favour of bringing Britain, the United States and Holland into line, with a view to cutting off trade relations with Japan. *The News Chronicle* has followed suit by organising a national protest

meeting at the Albert Hall, with the Archbishop of Canterbury in the chair.[44]

Being killed by bombs was arguably preferable to the forms of death that were inflicted on the Chinese during the Nanking Massacre. Many thousands of men, women and children, including babies, were murdered with guns and swords, and many sadistic forms of execution were deployed. Rape, looting, arson and torture were commonplace atrocities. Biological warfare was also used against the Chinese.[45] In total, about 15 million Chinese people lost their lives during the Japanese occupation, which finally ended with the entry into China of Soviet Russia in the late summer of 1945, and with the devastation caused by the bomb.[46]

The American President Franklin D. Roosevelt was shocked and angered by the air raids in the latter 1930s, denouncing the bombing in words which have been returned to since by critics of American post-war bombing campaigns:

> The ruthless bombing from the air of civilians in unfortified centres of population during the course of hostilities which have raged in various quarters of the earth during the past few years, which has resulted in the maiming and in the deaths of thousands of defenceless men women and children has sickened the hearts of every civilised man and woman, and has profoundly shocked the consciousness of humanity.[47]

In Britain, the enigmatic J.B.S. Haldane, the Anglo-Indian geneticist, and an avowed communist, warned a crowd at Trafalgar Square that 'half a dozen aeroplanes could pulp them in a few minutes'.[48] He also argued that the sinister alignment of Germany, Italy and Japan was leading to the sharing of ill-gotten intelligence from their air raids. Haldane was by no means alone in such fears. Politicians of the Left and Right, national newspaper leader columnists and many other writers called for practical anti-aircraft and civil defence measures, and citizen awareness and training schemes, to be put into place in London and across the country.[49]

In 1937 the Air Raid Precautions Act received royal assent, creating the civil defence apparatus that would be reinforced by the Civil Defence Act 1939, and mobilised on the eve of war in September 1939.[50] The air attacks on Spain and China occurred during the gathering crisis between Czechoslovakia and Germany, and the Munich debacle in September 1938. British Prime Minister Neville Chamberlain and Adolf Hitler repeatedly negotiated over German plans to annex the Sudetenland, leading to heightened fears across Europe and in Britain that the Nazis might land a knock out blow. Over 150,000 Londoners left the capital in the autumn of 1938 in a kind of historical dress rehearsal of wartime evacuation. Thirty eight million gas masks were distributed, and trenches were dug in the Royal Parks of London. As Chamberlain argued in a BBC broadcast on 27 September 1938:

> How horrible, fantastic, incredible it is that we should be digging trenches and trying on gas masks here because of a quarrel in a far-away country between people of whom we know nothing.[51]

For reasons which were not crystal clear to them, the British people were increasingly compelled to engage in air raid precautions. The final years of the 1930s witnessed an intensification of ARP in Britain that mirrored preparations in other European countries. As Lucy Noakes argues, the ARP Act of 1937 'marked a significant shift in the relationship of the civilian citizen to the wartime state' as people were encouraged to take up defensive responsibilities, which of course reflected contemporary gendered ideas of masculinity and femininity.[52] The government issued posters and advertisements calling for both male and female volunteers to join up as ARP wardens, men to sign up as volunteer fire fighters and women as auxiliary nurses. The blackout was enforced in 1939, so that homes had to hide their interior lights to the outside world, and cars had to drive with dipped or no headlights, lest the enemy above sighted the city below. The years leading up to the war also witnessed a significant increase in social capital, in the commitment of individuals to volunteer their time and effort for the good of community and country. Yet although the British public were increasingly being prepped for total warfare and air raids, many commentators remarked upon the apathy of large swathes of the British public towards Air Raids Precautions, an indifference that continued to a degree even into the war itself.[53]

Evacuation: A Case Study in London

The declaration of war on Germany by Chamberlain on 3 September 1939 was preceded by a mass evacuation of children from London and other large cities. Over four thousand children went overseas, but most were moved elsewhere in Britain to so-called 'reception towns' in safe areas away from bombing routes. In all over 3.5 million people, most of them children, were dispersed from the largest cities.[54] From 1–2 September already rehearsed plans for evacuation were put into place across the country. Local authorities were responsible for organising this mass movement, coordinated from schools and other places of education.[55]

The experiences of young men and women at the Regent Street Polytechnic (now the University of Westminster) in the heart of London provide a fascinating case study of evacuation, and glimpses into the everyday perceptions of evacuees. The auxiliary Secondary School and Craft Schools at the Poly, located in other sites close to the base at Regent Street, provided occupational training and apprenticeships for children and teenagers. A breezy report in the *Polytechnic Magazine* for September 1940 on the evacuation of the Craft Schools was both proud and relieved at the safe removal of children, but it was clear the process was not as straightforward as it could have been:

> From various sources, chiefly the wireless, the staff and pupils of the Craft Schools heard that at last it had happened, and that the once hypothetical evacuation was to be carried out. We duly assembled at the Great Portland Street Extension on Friday, September 1st, completely equipped with luggage and gas masks, the boys having been previously well informed as to the amount of luggage, etc., required. The boys were very cheerful and there were obvious signs of disappointment when we learnt from the LCC Evacuation Officer that it would be impossible to move us on that day. We were therefore told to go back home and return on the morrow at the same hour—8.30 a.m. The next day, Saturday, the numbers in our ranks had increased, and we moved off in earnest by bus from Oxford Circus to the Holborn Underground entrance. There were a few mothers to see the boys off, but the partings seemed quite cheerful, and in spite of the serious international situation quite a holiday spirit prevailed. At Holborn we were compelled to wait for some time, and in order to avoid congestion at the railway station we spent this time at the Central School of Arts and Crafts in Southampton Row. We eventually entrained for Ealing Broadway, and on arrival, were speedily transferred to the train for 'somewhere

in England.' We had a comfortable journey with plenty of room and you can imagine our delight when we learned that we were going in the vicinity of the famous Cheddar Gorge and right into the 'Heart of Mendip'. We got out of the train at Cheddar Station, and after waiting some considerable time were conveyed by buses to our destination—Winscombe, a beautiful village nestling at the foot of the Mendip Hills.[56]

A later report on the experiences of the boys and girls coming to terms with life a long way from London, while generally upbeat, admitted that some schooling time was being lost. Young people in country towns or urban areas had more to stimulate them in common with the types of lives they had led in London, while those in small villages or hamlets had to make their own fun, and become more self-reliant, something viewed as a positive consequence of evacuation. The report then made a claim about social class mixing that became a key theme in the so-called 'myth of the Blitz' discussed in the following chapter:

Some of the boys are billeted in palatial homes, whilst others may be living in homes not quite up to the standard of their own, but all are fortunate in having comfortable dwellings with fairly modern conveniences. *This will have the effect of showing how different classes of people live*, and should be invaluable to them in later life, whether or not they become leaders in industry, professional men, or members of the working classes.[57]

Denied a normal full-time education, this was a kind of 'Polytechnic of Life' experience, increasing sensitivities across class divisions, while preparing the young for their future occupational roles in the British class system.

The nationwide evacuation scheme was voluntary, and working-class parents such as those of the young students at the Poly took advantage of the local authority educational schemes and the arrangements offered by the Poly itself. Middle-class parents, by contrast, sent their offspring to live with friends and relatives elsewhere in the country. The lack of compulsion in the evacuation process was symptomatic of the strength of democracy but also an internal weakness. By December 1939 many young people from all across Britain, not only from the Poly, had returned home for Christmas, often to the annoyance and frustration of the authorities who wished to keep them in the relative safety of the reception areas. The so-called 'Phoney War', a distinct lack of military action on the Home Front, explained why many people wanted to go back home.[58] So too, of course, did homesickness and a longing to be with family and friends in the old neighbourhood. During the early months of 1940 many evacuees trickled back home. It would take the sea-borne heroics at Dunkirk in May, and the Battle of Britain in the spring and summer of 1940, to shake them out of their complacency.

Conclusion

Whatever the context – prediction, preparation or reality – the onset of air warfare cast a dark shadow over the interwar years. As Overy argues, the 'voyage of the death ship' captivated and exercised elite writers, brought images of carnage and destruction into popular culture, and caused politicians, both local and national, to assemble air raid precautions as war loomed. The bombing of Spain in 1937, notably, was a lightning rod of realisation. Left-wing activists denounced the atrocity in demonstrations and writings, pacifists were re-energised in their hatred of warfare, while thousands of Basque children were evacuated to Britain, and elsewhere.[59] This was the compelling harshness of air raids: a local catastrophe would inevitably have significant international consequences. Those young boys and girls from northern Spain or at the Regent Street Polytechnic threw into relief the disturbances and distortions that would affect everybody, in Britain and across the world, once war broke out in 1939.

CHAPTER 3

Air Raids in Britain, 1940–45

Introduction

During August 1940, as the Battle of Britain drew towards its conclusion, the Luftwaffe began sporadic attacks on London and the
City of London. Following a reprisal attack on Berlin by the RAF
which did little serious damage, angered that the capital of the
Reich had been breached, Hitler declared that 'If they threaten
our cities, then we shall erase theirs'.[60] With the blessing of Winston Churchill, the RAF continued its air raids on Berlin, causing Hitler to operationalize his threat. Sporadic bombing raids on

How to cite this book chapter:
Clapson, M. 2019. *The Blitz Companion.* Pp. 37–75. London: University of
    Westminster Press. DOI: https://doi.org/10.16997/book26.c. License:
    CC-BY-NC-ND 4.0

London and other British cities occurred through late August and early September but on 7 September the Nazis shifted tactics to the continuous heavy bombing of London.

The London Blitz continued, with only a few respites, until May 1945. It remains, for the British at least, the most significant and emotive aerial bombardment in modern history. During the longest air campaign on a major urban centre in Europe during the twentieth century, heavy explosives and incendiary devices rained down on London night after night. Yet London did not suffer alone. Most urban-industrial centres were attacked during the Blitz. Many smaller industrial cities and towns and maritime cities were also heavily bombed, and in the case of Coventry in the West Midlands, the centre was almost completely destroyed.

Although the ferocity of the Blitz faded into recent memory as the war progressed, later raids served to remind the British they were still prey to Nazi hatred. During the spring and early summer of 1942, the so-called 'Baedeker Blitz' targeted the most beautiful cities in England. In 1944 the V1 flying bomb was launched against Britain, and the V2 flying rocket attacks, mostly on London, lent a fearful new dimension to aerial warfare in 1944–5. Hence in this chapter the Blitz refers specifically to the air raids of September 1940 to May 1941, but later bombing campaigns against British towns and cities during the war are also covered.

Nazi Intentions

In their 1940 *Invasion Plans for the British Isles*, codenamed Operation Sea Lion, Nazi Military High Command outlined the invasion strategy for Britain in general and of what Churchill had called the 'fat, valuable cow' of London in particular. They had certainly done their research, although dependence on British materials in German libraries meant that some maps and demographic data were probably out of date. The British capital was the largest city in Europe by 1940, with a population of over 8 million (much the same as it is today). This swelled to over 10 million, however, when the hinterlands beyond suburban London were included in the German calculation:

> *London*, with its suburban settlements and dependent towns: approximately 10 million (i.e. a quarter of the entire population of England and Wales).[61]
>
> *The London Basin*: the London Basin is bound by the Chiltern Hills to the north, Reading to the west, and the North Downs or the High Weald to the south. Its population has everywhere, to some extent or another, merged with that of London itself. The more heavily built-up area displays a strong industrial presence in its northern, eastern and southern parts; they are generally distinct from the commercial and administrative centre of the City, and the purely residential districts of the western sector.[62]

The rationale for the aerial bombardment of London was quite straightforward. Having lost the Battle of Britain during the summer of 1940, and with Berlin breached, the Germans served the dish of revenge hot, attacking the British capital to disrupt its infrastructure, to reduce iconic buildings to rubble, and undermine civilian morale. This would in theory render the population unable to defend itself from the invasion forces poised to sail over from occupied France and the Low Countries.

The River Thames was a significant point of reference for the Germans, because it flowed into London from the west and snaked through the centre of the capital to the east where it widened out into the Thames Estuary in the county of Essex. Along with the River Medway in Kent, the waterways were convenient guides to the capital for in-flying enemy pilots, who were also well aware of the residential and industrial zones that sat alongside the riverbanks. A moonlit night was a strong navigation aid, as the rivers were silver far below.[63] When the moon was low or little more than a nail paring, the *knickebein*, a beam transmitted from a ground station in occupied Europe, guided the bombers to their destinations. As Max Hastings shows, however, Winston Churchill was contemptuous of the *knickebein* in 1940, and later Sir Arthur Harris dismissed the beam as of little assistance to the Germans in their raids on Britain.[64]

A little over a year after war was declared, the Anti-Aircraft and Civil Defence apparatuses would be subjected to a prolonged and severe testing. An official wartime publication entitled *Front Line: 1940–1941* assessed how the Home Front in Britain weathered the Blitz. It divided the air raids into 'the onslaught on London' and 'the ordeal of the provinces.'[65] Published in 1942, *Front Line* provided the first historical summary of the Blitz, and while by no means uncritical of the anti-aircraft measures and civil defence machinery, it pictured the wardens, fire fighters, medical service personnel and others in uniform as the heroes and heroines in a dramatic battle.

'The Onslaught on London'

During the late afternoon of the 7 September 1940 a young man, cycling through suburban south-east London, was among the first to see the awe-inspiring sight of the German bombers massing over London. His oral testimony is a good example of how memory and words can evoke the atmosphere and sense of trepidation on that first day of the Blitz:

It was the most amazing, impressive, riveting sight. Directly above me were literally hundreds of planes, Germans! The sky was full of them. Bombers hemmed in with fighters, like bees around their queen, like destroyers round the battleship. So came Jerry.[66]

The first area of London to come under sustained attack was the East End, a historic mostly working-class district of the capital city, only a few miles from the wealthy and powerful West End yet many miles from it, figuratively, in social and economic conditions. Just as they had been in the First World War, the docks were an obvious initial target because of their importance to the import and export trade. On 'Black Saturday' the Woolwich Arsenal and the Silvertown Docks were hit, and as they went up in flames, millions of pounds of foodstuffs and other goods were destroyed.[67] On the first night of the Blitz 1,800 lost their lives or were seriously injured.[68]

One of the many tragedies of war from the air is that poorest people suffer the most, and the bombing of one of the poorest districts of London which initiated the eight-month Blitz is a stark reminder of that fact. The working-class districts around the extensive docklands were crammed with high-density, often poor-quality, housing. Wharves and warehouses populated the muddy waterside of the River Thames from Tower Bridge via Wapping to Canary Wharf on the North Bank, and from Tower Bridge via Rotherhithe to Greenwich along the South Bank. This urban warren was a legacy of unplanned urbanisation during the Victorian years.

The ARP and the emergency services were overwhelmed. Fire crews were brought in from Nottingham in the East Midlands and elsewhere to help fight the raging infernos.[69] Transport access to fires and victims was impeded by the amount of rubble lying across roads and streets. During the first weeks of the Blitz the physical destruction and the accumulation of debris was so extensive that about 1,800 roads were blocked, while over 3 million tons of rubble and detritus had built up, requiring an extensive clearing-up and repair operation to the infrastructure of the capital city.[70] Barrage balloons had done little to stem the tide of German attacks, and the air raid warning siren was no longer sounding for practice or to indicate a few lone bombers. To make matters worse, during the first two nights the anti-aircraft guns were largely impotent, unable to bring down large numbers of German aircraft, and even failing to fire properly in some installations. As Winston Churchill noted in his history of the Second World War, first published in 1959, when the anti-aircraft artillery finally launched its salvoes into the London night, many hud-

Figure 3: Bomb damage to Hallam Street, London. Photograph by kind permission of the City of Westminster Archives, London.

dling in their shelters or on voluntary duties felt a sense of relief.[71] Yet few were convinced the AA guns offered a robust and reliable defence to the Luftwaffe, whether along the coast or at fixed points in the major urban centres. The American reporter Ed Murrow was living in Hallam Street in London during the Blitz, and his compelling live broadcasts of the Blitz with the sound of bombs in the distance were relayed back to an American audience. His broadcasts showed that civil defence was under strain.[72]

Three weeks into the raids the cover story of the *Picture Post* was 'The East End at War.' Captioned 'two of Hitler's enemies' a mother was pictured comforting her crying little boy: 'In a street in Stepney, the crowded heart of East London', began the report:

> there stood a small boy, just old enough to write. He had a piece of chalk and with it, very carefully, almost painfully, he wrote in huge capital letters on the wall of a bomb-shattered warehouse. Gradually he formed his sentence, and with it he summed up the feeling of London about the aerial hell into which it had been pitched. The message was – HITLER IS MAD.[73]

The derangement of the enemy was secondary to the narrative that, despite the war coming to the East End, the bravery of Londoners was winning through against Nazi barbarism. In a cartoon for the *Evening News* David Low depicted the so-called 'Cockney Heart' as battered but unbowed by German bombs while the leering face of Joseph Goebbels, the Nazi Minister of Propaganda, looked down from on high.[74] The 'cockney' was the historic personification of the East End, a cheerful yet defiant working-class character despite the deprivations and poverty of living in East London.[75]

That the *Picture Post* article was published three weeks into the Blitz possibly reflected an official awareness that morale had not collapsed, so the piece could be allowed through the filters of the Ministry of Information. By late September, the nightly bombing had also transitioned far beyond East London to include Central and West London, large tracts of inner South London, and incursions into the further-flung suburbs of the capital city. Containing some of the most iconic buildings in Britain, Central London offered invaluable targets for the Nazis. Politically the Houses of Parliament and Whitehall represented not only democracy and stability, but imperial might. London was the capital not only of Britain, but of the British Empire, and the Nazis knew the propaganda value of destroying iconic buildings and institutions. Few of these were spared. On 8 September, the night following the beginning of the Blitz, the grounds of Buckingham Palace were struck by a 50kg delayed-action HE bomb, doing little damage. The Palace was hit sixteen times however, causing the much-related story of how Queen Elizabeth the Queen Mother and King George VI could feel on equal terms with those poor East Enders who had been bombed out of their home.[76] There was no equivalence, of course, but the narrative of shared suffering irrespective of class, status and income was seen as essential to national unity during the Blitz. Cinematic propaganda such as the Movietone newsreel *The Realm Remains Resolute* (1940) is one of many wartime broadcasts keen to show the monarchy moving among the people.

The Palace of Westminster, the historic heart of British government, and a powerful symbolic site of democracy confronting the fascist onslaught against Britain, was bombed fourteen times during the Blitz of 1940–1. The House of Commons and the House of Lords were removed to nearby Church House in Westminster to avoid casualties, but on 26 September the Old Palace Yard was hit, while on the 8 December the cloisters of St Stephens were badly damaged. Worse was to come on 10 and 11 May 1941 when incendiary bombs caused fires in the Commons Chamber, and the roof of the Palace of Westminster. This was a particularly heavy raid, a final spiteful flourish over London before the Nazis turned their attention to invading the Soviet Union. Other important parts of the complex were damaged, and outside, facing Parliament Square, the statue of Richard the Lionheart was hit, his sword bent but still gripped firmly in hand. Symbolically, parliamentary sovereignty was buckled but unbroken.[77]

Disruption to everyday life was another key intention of the Luftwaffe. The most famous shopping district in West London – comprised of Oxford Street, Regent Street and Bond Street – sustained considerable destruction during the Blitz. The John Lewis Department Store, for example, an iconic Victorian department store was one of a number of large retail outlets badly damaged or totally destroyed between Marble Arch and Oxford Circus. There was less to buy in the shops anyway, due to rationing, but familiar outlets on the British high street were changed forever. The visitor to Oxford Street today, walking westwards from Oxford Circus, will notice how the north side of Oxford Street was almost completely rebuilt after the war.[78]

Between the wars radio had emerged as the new modern means of mass communication. The BBC enjoyed a near monopoly over broadcasting in Britain, so destroying the BBC would have been a massive propaganda victory for the Nazis. On 15 October 1940 BBC Broadcasting House on Langham Place was hit by a 277kg delayed action HE bomb which damaged a number of offices and floors of this famous Art Deco building. A number of staff tried to remove the bomb by hand but it went off, killing seven BBC employees. A parachute mine struck Broadcasting House on the 8 December 1940, killing a police constable, wounding several passers-by, and creating a deep crater in Portland Place which was filled with water due to damage to the sewers. During the same raid, the beautiful All Souls Church on Langham Place, a masterpiece of Georgian religious architecture, was also badly damaged. Across the capital well-known buildings were damaged or destroyed leading to great satisfaction for the Nazis. Yet one of the worst air raids of 1940, the so-called 'Christmas Blitz' in late December, caused a significant if nuanced propaganda victory for Britain.

It is difficult to grasp now how dark those nights of the December Blitz were. Britain stood alone in 1940 as the sole surviving non-neutral democracy in Western Europe. London had been battered almost every night since early September, and many well-known and much-loved buildings and neighbourhoods lay in ruins. Then on the 28–9 December 1940 the capital city endured a particularly brutal raid which hit the City of London, and the area of East-Central London around St. Paul's Cathedral, particularly hard. Yet the cathedral itself, with its distinctive and beautiful dome, survived with almost miraculous endurance while much of the vicinity around it was incinerated. It was also protected by the St Paul's Watch.

In Sarah Waters' novel *The Night Watch* (2006), the experiences of three women are interwoven with the air raids on London. A particularly evocative scene around St Paul's Cathedral creates the atmosphere in the streets of the darkest nights in the Blitz, but also provides the context for reflection on the nature and purpose of the war. As one woman questions whether St Paul's should have been bombed in lieu of poor homes in Bethnal Green, another

Figure 4: Memorial to the people of wartime London at St Paul's Cathedral (photograph by author, 2017).

counters that the survival of the cathedral means something, despite the desolation all around it:

> while we've still got this and all it stands for, I mean, elegance, and reason, and – and great beauty – then the war is still worth fighting. Isn't it?[79]

In London, along with other local authorities required by the government to undertake a 'bomb census' of damage and destruction, the London County Council (LCC) commissioned bomb damage maps. These itemized and spatially represented destruction according to a colour scale from black meaning 'total destruction' through to yellow, namely 'blast damage; minor in nature.' The maps also represented the exact spots hit by the V1 and V2 reprisal weapons in 1944–5.[80] They were also a useful tool for assessing the type and level of rebuilding required for a particular bombsite. The bomb map depicting the extensive damage around St. Paul's cathedral suggests something of a miracle of survival.

So much has been written about St Paul's it can be difficult to say anything original, but the episode does reveal in relief many key themes of this book. The cathedral, designed by Sir Christopher Wren, represented the rebirth of London after the Great Fire of 1666, a symbolism that was not lost on many commentators at the time, nor since. A famous photograph by Herbert Mason for the *Daily Mail*, showing the dome standing tall and undamaged despite the smoking ruins around it, introduced a motif that was to be found in many other media, notably newsreels, documentary and fiction feature films, about the Blitz.[81] The photograph, however, was also presented to the German public on 23 January 1941, in the magazine *Berliner Illustrierte Zeitung*. Under the headline 'Die City von London brennt' ('The City of London on Fire') it depicted how the Luftwaffe were destroying London. Yet few in Britain would have seen that interpretation.

St. Paul's had also been portrayed a few months earlier in the documentary film *London Can Take It* (1940). Directed by Humphrey Jennings, an eminent British documentary filmmaker, and narrated by the American journalist Quentin Reynolds, *London Can Take It* was made just a few weeks into the London Blitz. Directed primarily at American audiences to demonstrate the bravery of the British under fire, the Germans inadvertently offered propaganda opportunities to the government, a theme repeated in later bombing campaigns during the twentieth century. The heaviness of the Christmas Blitz also exposed the limitations of saturation bombing. Over an image of the cathedral, the calmly spoken words of Quentin Reynolds were reassuring:

> A bomb has its limitations. It can only destroy buildings and kill people. It cannot kill the unconquerable spirit and courage of the people of London. *London* can take it.[82]

And London continued to take it until May 1941. As one middle-class woman noted 'In the badly bombed places, mostly working-class districts':

> the courage of these people has been marvellous. These same people in my opinion have always shown courage, courage to face unemployment, courage to face bad conditions, sickness, and all the other evils it has been their lot to bear.[83]

She was writing in November 1940, the month the air raids transitioned across the British Isles as the Nazis sought to degrade and destroy the entire industrial and military capacity of their enemy. Poor people in the provincial cities would also bear the brunt of the bombing most heavily.

'The Ordeal of the Provinces'

The German *Invasion Plans* for the British Isles gave brief but mostly accurate descriptions of the major industrial cities and port cities in Britain and of their location. As the plans also stated, however, 'mining operations' were also sewn into the landscape of the major industrial conurbations, extending in coal belts out over nearby countryside, into valleys and nearby hills.

Coal mining was one of the staple industries of the industrial revolution, and creating, like the great industrial cities, tightly-knit working-class communities often packed into poor quality, high-density terraced homes. The Nazi planners of the air raids on British cities were fully versed in these realities, terming the slums and poorest housing areas 'homes of misery'.[84] The Nazis were impressed by the generally 'excellent road system, however, arguing that troop movements would be 'helped by the density of the road network, but partly hindered by the many factory buildings and settlements'.[85]

The civil defence apparatus was far from uniform across the country, however. Many local authorities had done their best to instigate the provisions of the ARP and Civil Defence legislation, while others had been more dilatory. Levels of expenditure on public and household air raid shelters varied widely between different towns and cities. In the poorest areas where many terraced houses had at best a backyard or no outside space at all, it proved impossible to erect air-raid shelters, leaving many feeling defenceless. Londoners had been able to use some of the Underground tube stations as deep public shelters, but no other major city in Britain was possessed of an underground system so almost all shelters were built on the surface or just below it. Across Britain, the Luftwaffe often found it easy to fly above barrage balloons, anti-aircraft guns and searchlights, and many bombs often fell onto flimsy Anderson shelters, both communal and private.[86]

Local authorities were forced to re-learn the lessons of the London Blitz. Yet the government appeared to some contemporary critics as remote from the operational difficulties facing local councils. Using the weekly Home Intelligence reports compiled for the Home Intelligence Division of the Ministry of Information,

Malcolm Smith shows how many people worried about the short-comings in air raid preparations. There was often too much reliance on charities in the immediate aftermath of the raids, particularly the Women's Voluntary Service (WVS) and complaints about overcrowded rest centres and food supplies. The Blitz had contradictory effects, for example exposing comparative strengths and weaknesses in local authority preparations for bombings, while strengthening a sense of both local and nationwide defiance. Despite that, civic pride was often ramped up by the strong belief that, despite the death and destruction, and the inade-quacies in ARP and emergency provision, a particular town or city had 'taken it' and triumphed over adversity. Overall, Smith con-cludes that a sense of collective confidence during the provincial Blitz remained mostly intact but was sometimes unduly under-mined by inadequate coordination and provision of resources.[87]

A common misconception of the Blitz in the United Kingdom is that London was the only city under attack from September 1940 until the Nazis also turned their fire on other cities and towns in mid-November. Yet even before the Blitz on London began, other urban areas in the UK had been attacked from the air. As the Battle of Britain drew towards a defeat for Germany, the first significant raid on a major British city took place in Car-diff and Newport on 10 July when over seventy German planes attacked the South Wales docks. In July and August, Birming-ham, Coventry, Hastings, Liverpool, Newcastle and Southampton were all subject to air raids, signifying that when the main Blitz on the provinces began, industrial and coastal towns and cities were going to be key targets for the Luftwaffe. From the middle of November, the bombing of the major cities intensified as the Nazi campaign grew heavier and more frequent spreading beyond the capital city.[88] Initial success during the early extension of the Luft-waffe campaign to the provinces was brutally encapsulated in the heavy air raid on the West Midlands city of Coventry.

The Bombing of Coventry

Of all the provincial cities bombed by the Nazis, Coventry was the first to suffer the almost complete annihilation of its city centre. As Tony Mason shows, the first raid on Coventry had been on 18 August 1940, when both industry and housing were bombed. There were twenty-four further raids on the West Midlands city, but by far the heaviest attack on Coventry came on the night of 14–15 November. About 450 bombers attacked the West Midlands city for over eleven hours. In the wake of that terrible raid, over two-thirds of the historic city centre was smashed to pieces, over 560 people lay dead, and at least 860 people were seriously injured.[89] Further death and destruction followed. The city's beautiful mediaeval cathedral lay in ruins, and remains so today, an iconic reminder of the sacrilegious destruction of places of worship during air raids.

Tony Mason was writing in 1986, some four years before the fiftieth anniversary of the Blitz. He was ahead of the many academic histories of the Blitz and of wartime Britain written since. Although much of Coventry was devastated, he showed that the factories and workplaces were soon repaired and producing essential munitions and other supplies. He also emphasised that the saturation bombing of Coventry gave rise to popular and media myths that disintegrated under scrutiny, from the alleged collapse of civilian morale to the notion, shared by many citizens of the city, that Coventry was deliberately sacrificed by Churchill to fool the Germans into thinking British air defences were weak.[90] As Frederick Taylor notes, the BBC and the print media, under the watchful eye of the Ministry of Information, usually referred obliquely to the air raids on 'a southern town' or 'a Midlands town' in order to play down the damage and as far as possible deny the Nazis any attempt to audit the true extent of destruction. After the air raids on Coventry, however, the city was named so that the British government and media could demonstrate the heinous depths to which the Germans sank when gloating about the destruction of Coventry. This may have encouraged many in people to feel their city was a sacrificial lamb, but that was untrue.[91]

The government was almost always reading the thermometer of morale and when the phenomenon of 'trekking' occurred, alarm bells rang. Trekking was the voluntary flight of people from the city to the relative safety of the countryside prior to nightfall. Viewed officially as potentially symptomatic of a mass adverse reaction to air raids, the Labour Home Secretary Herbert Morrison was fearful that ostensible manifestations of mass demoralisation might be exploited by the enemy. Along with Lord Beaverbrook, the Minister of Aircraft Production, he visited Coventry to inspect munitions and aircraft parts manufacture. King George VI visited Coventry to express solidarity and reassure the local population they were in his thoughts.[92] Yet a recent study of the Blitz has argued that trekking was less a symptom of declining morale and mostly a rational response to the bombings.[93] People were removing themselves and their families away from danger, and also relieving the pressure on the ARP and emergency service workers.

After all that, Coventry remained resilient. During the raids and in their immediate aftermath, the city lived on throughout the

war, only to be rebuilt to a comprehensive and ultimately unsuccessful modernist city plan that replaced bombsites with cold precincts and uninspiring public buildings. This is discussed further
in chapter seven.

Coventry was one of the smaller urban-industrial centres in
Britain, but the almost complete destruction of its city centre led
to its special place in the history of air raids in the Second World
War. It was also one of the so-called 'arms towns', along with Birmingham, Bristol (and Avonmouth) and Sheffield producing
munitions in the factories. During the course of the Blitz from
November 1940 to May 1941 citizens in the industrial heartlands
of the United Kingdom endured the Nazi onslaught.

Front Line also focused on the experience of the port cities of
Cardiff and Swansea in South Wales, Liverpool in the North West
of England, Portsmouth, Plymouth and Southampton on the
South Coast, Hull in North East England, Glasgow (Clydeside) in
Central Scotland and Belfast in Northern Ireland. All were subject
to heavy bombardment, at different times. Liverpool and Merseyside on the north-west coast of England was the second most-
bombed conurbation after London. The city had taken small air
raids during August 1940 but on the night of 28–9 November over
350 tons of HE bombs smashed into the city. In common with
East London the docks were a primary target, and the warren
of small, often dilapidated terraced streets was heavily bombed.
Liverpool was attacked for three nights at the end of August 1940,
and many other raids followed. During December 1940 and May
1941 further raids took a terrible toll on Liverpool. The May raids
alone killed 1,900 people and injured or seriously wounded 1,450
others.[94] Extensive damage to the housing stock resulted in widespread homelessness in a city that already possessed large tracts
of impoverished housing and some of the worst slums in Britain.

Literary memoirs provide vivid information on living through the air raids. The writer Helen Forrester, a young woman in wartime Liverpool, recalled how as London was blitzed 'we became more and more apprehensive that our turn would be next.' Forrester describes in vivid detail her experiences of running home through the centre of Liverpool during the days of violence targeted on the Merseyside city. She dipped in and out of air raid shelters where some people were simply taking cover, others were singing, and others praying as they worked their rosary beads. ARP wardens would order her to stay put but like so many people she had other ideas as she headed for home. Forrester experienced feelings of rage as she witnessed German planes, spiteful and murderous in the night sky, and saw and heard explosions and flares as the bombs fell near to where she was running:

> The city was in turmoil, with service vehicles zipping recklessly through the battered streets. There seemed to be a very big fire at the beginning of Dale Street, and behind the buildings past which I ran up to the far end of Lime Street, there was obviously another very heavy conflagration, which I afterwards was told was St. John's market burning. Roasted in it were most of the turkeys which Liverpudlians had dreamed of eating on Christmas day, and to hear the talk in the shopping queues after the holiday, one would imagine that the loss of the turkeys was more deeply mourned than the loss of three hundred and sixty five men, women and children who died during the three days of the Blitz.[95]

Forrester experienced the full gamut of emotions during air raids, from hatred toward the enemy, relief at respites from the bombing, fatigue from the efforts of running and walking through the dangers of an attack, sorrow at the loss of much-loved and familiar buildings and landmarks, to the dark sense of humour reflected in her wry observations on the loss of a turkey dinner as opposed to living people.

England's 'second city' Birmingham was near to Coventry in the West Midlands. Larger than its neighbour, it shared a modern industrial manufacturing base, much of it given over to munitions production. Birmingham was bombed in August and suffered many raids between August of 1940 and April 1941. The world famous Birmingham Small Arms factory was badly damaged, along with many other industrial premises. Thousands of homes were destroyed, but as Adams and Larkham note, while extensive, the damage was spread across the second city, rather than being heavily concentrated in a few areas.[96]

In Scotland, Glasgow and Clydebank were historically associated with traditional manufacturing industries, alongside the docks and military installations along the River Clyde, providing an extensive strategic target for the Luftwaffe. Clydebank, to the west of Glasgow, 'was hit by two nights of devastating raids' on 13–14 March 1941. The destruction and mortality rates were horribly high, due to the extensive domestic architectural form of the high-density and often overcrowded tenement blocks in the Glasgow region. In common with London and other cities during their first air raids, ARP services found it very difficult to cope. About 35,000 out of a population of 50,000 in Clydebank were made homeless. The Scottish Regional Commissioner 'described the Clydebank Blitz as a "major disaster".'[97]

Bristol in south-west England had been bombed since August 1940 but suffered its heaviest raids on 24 November, when attacks on the docks and on the aircraft factories, obvious strategic targets for the Nazis, killed 207 people and left over 180 seriously injured. Heavy explosives and incendiaries laid waste to large tracts of the city. Further west in South Wales, another important port city, Swansea, suffered a ferocious 100-bomber raid in mid-January

1941. In addition to severely damaging the Prince Albert Dry Dock, thousands of incendiaries fell upon the city. And the following February Swansea suffered heavy bombardment on three successive nights.[98] As John Ray notes, Swansea developed its own heroic story of 'blood, sweat and tears' during that bitter winter, and the January raid enabled the ARP and fire services to learn and perform more effectively in the subsequent attacks.[99]

Other port and naval cities also suffered extensive bombing, notably Plymouth, Portsmouth and Southampton on the south coast, and the larger urban areas of Hull, and the Newcastle-Upon-Tyne conurbation in north-east England. Their fate was finally visited upon Belfast, on the banks of the River Lagan in Northern Ireland. The Lagan in East Belfast was home to the great Harland and Wolff shipyards, and other shipyards, docks and factories. In what was the penultimate month of the Blitz, Belfast was attacked on 7–8 April and again a week later. The pattern of death and destruction was strongly similar to other port cities: the docks and nearby factories were badly hit, while the surrounding streets of terraced houses suffered extensive bomb and fire damage. Both Catholic and Protestant districts came under attack The fire services of both Britain and the Irish Republic were required to supplement the city's auxiliary and official fire brigades.[100] Initial official estimates of casualties were 'too low':

> and possibly 800 to 900 people were killed, and a further 1,500 injured. About 1,600 houses were destroyed, 28,000 were damaged, and some 20,000 civilians were rendered homeless.[101]

Many lodged with friends and relatives; some took refuge in rest centres; others did what so many others had done before them and voluntarily evacuated the city as 'ditchers', known on the British mainland as 'trekkers'.[102]

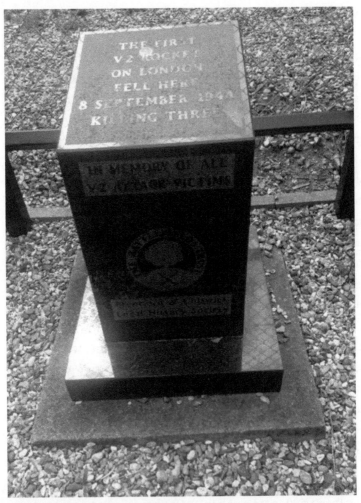

Figure 5: V2 Memorial, Chiswick, West London (photograph by author, 2017).

Morale: Impact and Aftermath

Morale refers to the confidence and discipline of an individual or group. Any major collapse of civilian morale was held by the government and local authority officials to potentially undermine the social life of cities, possibly cause anarchy and chaos, threaten industrial production, and destroy the ability to fight the enemy. How did the people of London and the great provincial cities of Britain respond to the air raids in 1940–1? The answer lies in the experience of the working-class East End of London as the first district to be heavily bombed from 7 September. Mass Observation (MO), the eyes and ears of the government was on the scene, because the East End was a testing ground, in a sense, for all of those pessimistic predictions about civilian behaviour and morale discussed in the previous chapter. As head of MO, Tom Harrisson, was also a member of the Morale Committee of the Ministry of Information. A social anthropological organisation, MO consisted of volunteers, mostly middle class, who moved among the people, writing down what they saw and heard, in notebooks. Conscripted by government, MO and its volunteers contributed to the intelligence received by the Ministry of Information.

In *Living Through the Blitz* (1976) Harrisson was clear that propaganda about national unity ignored continuing class divisions and snobberies. He was critical of inadequate provision of air raid shelters and other weaknesses of civil defence, and his reports on Birmingham and Coventry, among other cities, never shied from highlighting panic, and the despair and anger of many caught up in the raids.[103] Using one of many excerpts from MO materials, Harrisson vividly described the shock of people huddled together in an air raid shelter in East London following the end of heavy bombing:

> When the all-clear goes, about 4.30 a.m., there is a groan of relief. But as soon as the first people get outside the shelter, there are screams of horror at the sight of the damage…smashed windows and roofs everywhere…

> smoke streaming across the sky from the direction of
> the docks. People rush and scramble out of the shelter
> doorway, and there is a wild clamour of shouting, weep-
> ing and calling for absent relatives.

Harrisson went on to describe the general loss of everyday order,
the 'turmoil of comings and goings', the fearful evening rush out
to the relative safety of the suburbs and the nearby countryside.[104]

Across Britain, Mass Observation materials and other contemporary reports provide historians with a mixed picture. Drawing extensively on MO materials, Beavan and Griffiths focused
upon the working-class communities most heavily affected by
air raids. MO was the intellectual and methodological creation
of left-leaning wing middle-class academics who often resorted
to regional and class-based stereotypes in their readings of the
popular mood. So East London cockneys and 'northerners' in
the heartlands of the industrial revolution would endure the
raids with cheerful fortitude, born of their lifelong experience of
a community of poverty. Similarly, sailors' wives in the port cities were used to enduring loneliness and hardship. In Coventry,
by contrast, where new industries such as engineering and motor
car manufacturing lay alongside new suburban housing estates,
locals lacked the fortitude of the older industrial working class.[105]

There was certainly evidence that many people were traumatised by the violent interruption into their lives and their homes.
Historical trauma studies is a growing field, and in relation to air
raids, historian have made some important points about the hidden history of psychological damage caused to civilians, which sits
uneasily with triumphalist tropes about the 'Blitz spirit'. Furthermore, as Hazel Croft argues, unlike military personnel returning
from the battle front, whose claims to psychiatric disorders could

be verified, it was more difficult for civilians on the Home Front to make a special case for themselves as suffering from what would now be incorporated within the umbrella term of 'post-traumatic stress disorders'.[106] It is possible to infer from Croft's that work untold numbers of people carried psychiatric disorders into their post-war lives. As Noakes has argued, in a similar vein, the social taboo on expressing fear during wartime has tended to marginalise narratives of fear in post-war testimonies of the Blitz and other air raids.[107]

Nonetheless, by May 1941 the collective will had held. Harrisson summed it all up thus: 'the predicted crack in nerves did not send a large slice of Londoners gibbering in 1940. The hospital beds and poised psychiatrists waited, unemployed.'[108] In broad terms, and with local variations, this pattern was replicated nationwide, leading to a mostly heroic official interpretation of the Blitz and of the Home Front more widely. Wartime propaganda insisting upon national unity and shared resistance to the enemy was the origin of this heroic interpretation. Put another way, a narrative of brave popular resistance to aerial bombardment was at the heart of the 'Peoples War'. Wartime social unity, the argument goes, created a new national mood for a better society: from the 'People's War' to the New Jerusalem. The reality was very different, as Selina Todd argues, but many looked beyond sectional, regional and class divisions in the hope of a more egalitarian future.[109]

The Blitz and Social Change

One of the earliest interpretations of the Blitz as a catalyst for social change was by Richard Titmuss, a social scientist and civil servant. His *Problems of Social Policy*, published in 1950, amounts to the first notable history of the Home Front.[110] The mass participation of civilians in wartime employment, higher levels of voluntarism than in peacetime, shared suffering and the contribution of ostensibly all classes and groups in society engendered an atmosphere of heightened egalitarianism that encouraged the transition from the warfare state to the welfare state. The widespread support for the Beveridge Report in 1942, with its call for greater levels of social policy, appears to support this perspective. Politically, the Labour Party had the most to gain from an alleged new sense of egalitarianism forged between people of different classes who huddled together in air raid shelters, served alongside each other fighting fires or tending to the wounded, or ostensibly brought closer together by the experience of evacuation. For the first time, provincial middle-class households were up close and personal with the poverty and illiteracy of the poor urban children billeted within their home. The Labour Party Manifesto for the general election of 1945 explicitly linked its post-war agenda to the collective efforts initiated by the events of 1940:

> The problems and pressures of the post-war world threaten our security and progress as surely as - though less dramatically than - the Germans threatened them in 1940. We need the spirit of Dunkirk and of the Blitz sustained over a period of years.
>
> The Labour Party's programme is a practical expression of that spirit applied to the tasks of peace. It calls for hard work, energy and sound sense.[111]

This neat relationship between the Blitz and subsequent social policy was challenged by the Scottish Marxist historian Angus Calder. His *The Myth of the Blitz* is highly-regarded as revisionist history by many. His position is summed up on its back cover:

The Myth of the Blitz was nurtured at every level of society. It rested upon the assumed invincibility of an island race distinguished by good humour, understatement, and the ability to pluck victory from the jaws of defeat by team work, improvisation and muddling through.

In fact, in many ways, the Blitz was not like that. Sixty thousand people were conscientious objectors; a quarter of London's population fled to the country; Churchill and the Royal Family were booed while touring the aftermath of air raids. Britain was not bombed into classless democracy.

Calder has been hugely influential in bursting the myth bubble, but his own approach was not without problems. He mostly ignored *Front Line, 1940-41: The Official Story of Civil Defence in Britain* which was by no means an upbeat whitewash of the official preparations for and responses to the German air raids. Conceding that that the strategy of air attacks on civilians was neither new nor unforeseen, the government admitted that 'Some things were not anticipated; some guesses were wrong.'[112] British military and political planners also initially underestimated the extent of the damage that would be caused, and therefore the consequent level of homelessness and reparations required.[113] Calder underestimated this measure of official self-criticism in his discussion of *Front Line*, merely pointing out that some people who had lived through the Blitz in Bristol and Croydon felt their story had been under-represented.[114]

It would be unfair to criticise Calder for ignoring the heroism of the emergency services, or the stoicism of the British under the bomb. He gives some recognition to both while creating a more nuanced picture of the Home Front which focuses upon division and discordance. Throughout the war, Calder argues, Britain remained a society cleaved by class inequalities and status divisions. Within the sphere of politics he highlights fear and loathing in Whitehall of the strength of communism and pro-Soviet sentiment during the Nazi-Soviet Pact. He fastens upon the propensity of some trades unionists to go on strike despite the need to meet essential production targets, a responsibility which most trades unionists and almost all Labour leaders agreed with throughout the war. Calder also exaggerates the appeal of pacifism in Wales and Scotland to question the myth of national unity.[115]

The relationship of the Blitz to the qualities of 'Englishness' and the predominance of English national identity is also explored by Calder. He anticipates later revisionist work by historians such as Susan Grayzel, Lucy Noakes, Sonya O. Rose, and H.L. Smith whose gendered analysis reflected upon the very different and unequal experiences of women as opposed to men on the Home Front.[116] Rose and Smith also explore the problematic relationship of the language of unity and of 'national identity' across different ethnic groups in wartime Britain. For Rose, 'identity politics' was a commonplace in 1940s Britain, hence no single or universally accepted promotion of 'Britishness' was possible.[117]

Certain views that Calder espoused, however, allow us to ask questions about the overall integrity of his position, and thus to reclaim a more positive version of mass behaviour during the Blitz that by no means denies a complex understanding of civilian morale. Calder claims he was angered by the way the Labour Party promulgated the myth of the Blitz for its political agenda. At the very beginning of the *Myth of the Blitz* he notes that the book was commissioned 'in the early eighties soon after the war for the Malvinas'.[118] He railed against Margaret Thatcher's evocation of 'Churchillism' in 1981, while his use of the Argentinian name for the Falklands suggested support for the highly contestable claim that the islands were historically Argentinian territory.[119] That Argentina was ruled by a neo-fascist dictatorship which invaded British sovereign territory goes ignored. Yet both Argentina and Nazi Germany were aggressive right-wing dictatorships exploiting foreign policy to stir-up domestic support through the intended oppression of foreign populations.

Calder's interpretation of the film *Hope and Glory* (1987) furthermore, an autobiographical movie written and directed by John Boorman about the Blitz in suburbia, draws a dubious distinction between the experience of air raids over outer London compared with the suffering in the more heavily-bombed inner-city areas. Boorman was raised in Carshalton in Surrey, and *Hope and Glory* depicts family life in the classic suburban semi-detached home during the Blitz. He hated the suburbia of his childhood, and later decried it as the birthplace of Thatcherism, a reactionary lower-middle-class culture of limited horizons and petty privatism thriving among the tidy houses and trim lawns.[120] A socialist, Calder was also offended by the perceived politics of suburbia. He admired Boorman and made the perfectly ridiculous statement that like Boorman he was 'ashamed of his suburban origins'. He goes on to provide a reductionist view of suburbia during the war and afterwards, dismissing the notion of suburban voluntarism and linking forward to the era of reconstruction discussed in chapter six:

> 'Suburban values' and the suburban lifestyle, created in the new housing estates of the inter-war period, did have in 1940 a flourishing future ahead of them. Ravaged by the Luftwaffe or not, the working-class areas of British cities were due to be devastated by town planners; while in the Sixties, poor people were shifted from 'communities' into tower blocks, the suburbanites who despised

> them continued to mow the lawn every Saturday, make
> tea in trim little kitchens, and keep up with the ever-
> more-affluent Joneses.[121]

Such stereotypical and static images of suburbia jar with the often
nuanced approach in *The Myth of the Blitz*. Worse, his anti-sub-
urbanism marks Calder out as an elite historian surveying 'the
masses' with a particularly critical eye on the lower middle classes
who populated suburbia. In fact, thousands of suburban clerks,
uniformed workers, self-employed business people and 'house-
wives' who were living in semi-detached homes joined up to
become ARP wardens, fire fighters, emergency medical service
volunteers, and munitions workers. Social capital in the suburbs,
both in peace and wartime, has been proven to be just as high if
not higher than in other areas of the city or in rural villages. And
that was true for working-class suburban council estates, too.[122]

Overall, Calder does not give due attention to the suburban
Home Front. As two eminent historians of London have argued,
however, by the end of the war the impact of air raids on the
capital city was as wide as the metropolis itself. During the Blitz
bombs and incendiaries by no means spared the suburbs, while
later air raids and V-weapons attacks hit outer London hard. As
White argues, the bombs respected no notion of the 'two Lon-
dons', inner and outer.[123] Furthermore, despite attacking suburbs
more than a few times in *The Myth of the Blitz*, Calder ignores
them in his index.

Drawing upon MO reports and other official readings of morale,
however, the fluctuations in popular mood and sentiments during
and after air raids are cleverly portrayed, as are the petty tensions
and class-based resentments engendered by evacuation. Overall,
however, Calder accentuated the negative while acknowledging

the positive. His analysis may be compared with that of Juliet Gardiner, who places voluntarism and humanitarian impulses at the centre of her approach, while accepting that pre-war social divisions continued during and after the conflict. Unlike Calder, however, and in common with Titmuss, Gardiner emphasises the glue of morale, the huge contribution of voluntarism despite differences and division, the 'unity of resolution and purpose' during the Blitz and the socio-political dividend:

> A social contract, no matter how informal and unspoken, had been forged during those months of attack. People who 'took it' should be entitled to 'get it', if 'it' meant better housing, a fairer education system, more job opportunities. It was partly for this reason that when the Beveridge Report was published in December 1942, a year and a half after the Blitz, what was essentially a tidying-up operation of welfare provision assumed iconic status, appearing to offer a new beginning, a safety net from the cradle to the grave, an attack on the five 'giant evils' in society: squalor, ignorance, want, idleness and disease.[124]

Robert MacKay and Andrew Thorpe come to similar conclusions. During the early days of the Blitz, while people were evacuating or grubbing around in the ruins to salvage what they could, a sense of despair was mostly absent. MacKay's emphasis upon 'the enhanced sense of being part of a group' did not rule out difference and even division, but as he argued such cohesion was strengthened by government propaganda on posters, newspapers, radio and film. It was also boosted by participation in such hands-on organisations as the ARP, AFS (Auxiliary Fire Service), the Home Guard and the WVS.[125] The events of 1940, namely the evacuation of Dunkirk, the Battle of Britain, and the Blitz from

September, instilled in the British people a sense of 'moral authority' and of national community. With the first and arguably worst
phase of the Blitz over, due to the terrible novelty of the experience, the British were able to bear the later months with resigna-
tion or fortitude, or both.[126] And for Malcolm Smith, that spirit
and sense of unity lasted long into the post-war years.[127]

Targeting Heritage: The Baedeker Blitz

On 28 March 1942 over 230 RAF planes attacked the medieval
city of Lubeck in Germany, using the 'double blow' technique by
following the first bombing raid with a second equally destructive one. Although Lubeck was of negligible military value due
to its peripherally located industries, much of its manufacturing
remained untouched or only partly damaged. But its wooden-
beamed housing and chocolate-box architecture was razed to
the ground. Over 300 local residents were killed, while 16,000
were rendered homeless.[128] The assault on Lubeck prompted the
so-called Baedeker Raids on beautiful English cities. And when
planning their raids, and seeking to maximise destruction to English heritage sites, the Germans had an easy-to-use guidebook at
hand.[129]

The Karl Baedeker Company of Leipzig had begun publishing their travel guides during the 1830s, but few budding tour-
ists could have grasped the irony that aids to cultural tourism
would become tools to assist in the destruction of much-loved
and much-visited centres of heritage. By the beginning of the
Second World War, the Baedeker *Great Britain* was in its ninth
edition, having been updated and republished in 1937, the year
that Germany, Italy and Japan completed their pact, Guernica was

bombed by German airplanes, and France extended its defensive Maginot Line to the German border.

Baedeker's Handbook for Great Britain was written by H.A. Piehler, a British-born travel writer who motored extensively around the country recording his impressions. 'Bath', wrote Piehler, 'is a handsome city'. Its beautiful location in the Avon Valley was noted alongside its 'unrivalled' status 'among English provincial towns for its combination of archaeological, historic, scenic and social interest'. Its Georgian streets and town houses were praised while Bath Abbey was awarded an asterisk, the Baedeker 'mark of commendation'.[130] Exeter, the county town of Devon, was described as an attractive ancient city on the banks of the River Exe. Its quaint public buildings, attractive streets, city walls and beautiful cathedral were foremost among its considerable range of attractions.[131] Further East, Canterbury in Kent was given extensive treatment. Described as nothing less than 'the ecclesiastical metropolis' of England and 'an ancient city, with numerous quaint old houses', it was historically significant as the seat of the Archbishop of Canterbury. The cathedral was awarded two asterisks. Other ancient religious buildings and notable features in Canterbury were also starred with an asterisk.[132]

Norwich in Norfolk was noteworthy for its irregular building, and its beautiful cathedral was awarded a number of single asterisks for some of its most significant features. Norwich was also home to thirty old East Anglian churches which nestled alongside many other ancient and interesting buildings defined by unique architectural 'flushwork'.[133] And in the heart of the North, the picturesque ancient city of York was praised for the conservation of its city walls (one asterisk) and its network of quaint mediaeval streets and variety of old buildings. York Minster, standing proud above the surrounding streets, earned two asterisks, signifying high levels of approval from the Baedeker guide.[134]

In his introduction, the editor of the 1937 *Baedeker Handbook to Great Britain* thanked the Deans of the Cathedrals visited, and the officials of the cities and towns for the information they had offered to the author. He noted the importance of 'fair dealing and courtesy' from the traveller to England.[135] From April to June 1942, over 1,000 people were killed by the Baedeker Raids, and hundreds were seriously injured. Significant losses were sustained to the country's heritage. Exeter was bombed in April and May. The shopping centre was destroyed by high explosives, incendiaries and parachute mines. At Bath over two nights in late April the railway station was demolished, and many historic buildings including churches were burned down or smashed by HE bombs. Norwich was bombed on 12 April and at the end of June, losing the historic St. Julian's Church and many attractive old buildings. At York, raids on 28–9 of April destroyed the mediaeval Guild Hall, and damaged many houses and buildings in the city centre. And in the final raids on Canterbury on 31 May and 1 June, although the loss of life was mercifully small, the 'ecclesiastical metropolis' lost a number of churches, two schools, the Corn Exchange, the City Market and many houses and shops.[136]

Architecture embodies memories, and familiar buildings shape and reinforce how people feel about their built environment. When something as ostensibly permanent as a church, cathedral, town hall or any ancient public building is obliterated, not only the environment but the memory of the environment is disrupted.[137] Beyond the bereavement of those who had lost loved ones, and the pain and suffering endured by injured people living in these beautiful cities, many survivors grieved for the buildings they had known and loved, and the streets they had grown up in. As Michael Hebbert argues, the street is a locus of collective memory, a hub of social life, where personal identity and urban identity fused. Hebbert points to other contexts of destruction such as slum clearance, urban renewal and highway building, where residents attempted to defend their communities from the developer or the local authority.[138] But citizens under the bomb were powerless. Beautiful streets and buildings had lain at the heart of the historical identity of the cities, and now they lay in ruins. These had also been spaces of sociability where people worked, enjoyed leisure, or worshipped. So the legacy of destruction went deep: loss was felt immediately and brought about feelings akin to grief for something that could not be brought back.

Of course, such emotions were not just confined to those who lived in the cities attacked during the Baedeker Raids, but were common to anyone who saw their little corner of the world left in ruins by bombs and fires. Prior to the war the *British Medical Journal* published an article in July 1939 on 'demolition melancholia'. The term, coined by a Medical Officer in Sheffield, was applied to those who, mostly elderly and mostly women, had experienced profound feelings of loss on 'the sudden dispossession of a lifelong home to which the patients have probably developed a strong emotional attachment'.[139] The state of mind referred to here was caused by removal from an old home to a new house in the suburbs or beyond. But the complex of feelings induced by the brutal overnight destruction of known and familiar worlds must have included displacement, mild depression, loneliness and an inability to adapt to new circumstances. Such emotions, of course, are felt by many people in similar circumstances of destruction. Hence the historical study of air raids and their consequences possesses a powerful relevance to the growing academic fields of Disaster Studies and Trauma Studies.[140]

The Revenge Weapons, 1944–5

In January 1944 German bombers returned to London for a relatively small-scale re-run of the conventional HE and fire-bombing raids they had visited upon London some four years earlier. An unwelcome reminder of the earlier campaign, the air raids of early 1944 were dubbed the 'little Blitz', and killed over a thousand people.[141] Yet during the summer of 1944 worse was to come, and it would manifest itself in a frightening new weapon. For some months rumours had been circulating in Britain about a flying bomb that had no pilot and which could be guided almost mysteriously through the air at great speed to attack the capital city.[142] This was the V1, the 'V' standing for vengeance. The Allied bombing campaign against German cities and industrial towns had intensified during 1943 and into 1944. Hitler, outraged by these damaging intrusions into the Fatherland, was keen to see the development of the flying bomb expedited to its deadliest effect.

The inventor of the vengeance weapons was the rocket scientist Wernher von Braun. His conceptual expertise was converted into deadly hardware by slave labour at the research base in Peen-emünde, on the Baltic Coast of Germany.[143] The first V1 launched against Britain fell not on London but on Gravesend in Kent. But on the 13 June, however, a warm summer day in London was cruelly interrupted by the first V1 rockets to hit the capital city, smashing into a railway bridge in Bow, East London, cutting the railway line.[144]

Launched on Britain from bases in Northern France between June and September 1944, the flying bomb possessed a distinctive sonic signature, a rattling and chugging sound, a little like an intermittent moped somewhere on high. Then the noise would suddenly cease, as the fuel was cut off, and the bomb fell to the ground. This was not a highly accurate technology, and many fell harmlessly into the sea or onto open countryside. Those that did get through however brought a new phase of death and destruction. Many Londoners became weary and fearful at the incessant threat and irregular strikes of the doodlebug. Home Intelligence reports described exaggerated and fabricated stories about deaths and destruction circulating among the public, and identified a significant lowering of morale in June and July, 1944.[145] Increasing numbers of voluntary evacuees left London, and there were more complaints about the inadequacy of shelter provision, and symptoms of 'strain' and 'weariness'. Herbert Morrison was booed while in East London.[146] More Anderson shelters were produced, along with the indoor home shelters or Morrison shelters, originally introduced by the government towards the end of the Blitz in 1941.[147] These would prove to be of little use against the next fearsome weapon to hit London.

The V2 flying rocket was much more difficult to defend against than the doodlebug. Its faster, higher searing power made it almost impossible to deter. The final version of the flying rocket was test launched in Germany in August 1944, and on 18 September 1944 the first V2 to hit England smashed into the west London suburb of Chiswick, destroying a pair of interwar semi-detached homes in Staveley Road. Croydon and other south London boroughs were hit by many V2 attacks, but two were particularly tragic. In New Cross in Deptford, 168 people were killed while Christmas shopping in Woolworth's department store, while soon afterwards Smithfield Meat Market in Farringdon 115 people lost their lives. V2s also hit central London; the upscale department store of Selfridge's was also damaged during the pre-Christmas rush to buy presents.[148] The fiction feature film *Operation Crossbow* (1965), a British spy thriller about wartime attempts to sabotage the V2 programme, contains some vivid scenes of flying rockets smashing into the streets of London, killing anyone at the point of impact. (See Fig. 5).

The V1 and V2 attacks brought the suburbs back into the war, again exposing the failure of Angus Calder to view the suburban experiences of air raids in a serious and detailed manner:

> V1s alone damaged to some degree 54,000 houses in Croydon and 18,000 out of 22,000 in Sutton and Cheam. Twice as many V2s fell on outer London as on inner, and the frontline status of London's Essex suburbs later in the war was sufficient to win it the nickname 'Doodle-bug Alley'.[149]

By the end of the war V-weapon craters pockmarked the metropolis. The V1s killed over 5,000 people and injured 15,000, while the V2s that smashed into London from September 1944 to March 1945 caused over 2,700 fatalities.[150] These losses were perceived as particularly tragic and futile as the war drew towards its close. London did not suffer the V2 alone, moreover. They were fired on Paris as the Germans were defeated during August 1944. The port city of Antwerp in Belgium was liberated in September 1944, but the retreating and resentful Germans took revenge with a hail of flying rocket attacks which smashed into the city during the months of November and December 1944, killing both civilians and military personnel. After London, Antwerp was the most heavily attacked city by the V2. A tragedy reminiscent of some of those visited upon London occurred at the Rex Cinema in central Antwerp in mid-December when a flying rocket killed 567 people, nearly 300 of them American, British and Canadian soldiers.[151]

Conclusion

The Nazi Blitz on London, the Baedeker Blitz, sporadic air raids and the V-weapons only partly succeeded in their intention to destroy the built environment of British cities. More importantly, they failed to destroy the morale of the British people. Although many citizens felt fear, trepidation and sometimes panic, the overriding patterns of behaviour were defined by bravery, heroism and stoicism, with a dose of cheerful humour thrown in for good measure. A key word here is 'resilience', the ability of a city and its people to survive and renew after a devastating event.[152]

London had suffered sustained aerial bombardment first, and 'took it' more than most cities, but even those urban areas that suffered relatively higher levels of environmental destruction when their size is considered, notably Coventry and some of the port cities, demonstrated resistance and resilience. The Blitz on Britain revealed that those dire pre-war prognostications of anarchy and chaos, and the anticipated collapse of civil society, simply did not materialise. The British had proved the pre-war experts, both military and political, wrong. Even during the V-weapon raids from 1944–5 the increasing fragility of spirit among many Londoners refused to break down. Hence Londoners and British people more generally were establishing an important pattern that can be traced in almost all subsequent air raids. The Blitz, and the British wartime experience of air raids, were indeed paradigmatic events.

CHAPTER 4

European Cities Under the Bomb: Nazi and Allied Bombing Campaigns, 1939–45

Introduction

During the Second World War the Germans bombed most of their neighbouring countries to the east, north and west. In 1941 the relatively forgotten air raids on Soviet cities began following the collapse of the Nazi-Soviet Pact, and the failure of the Blitz on Britain. For their part, the USSR also engaged in attacks on the allies of Nazi Germany at various times during the war. The British began bombing German cities in August 1940 and stepped up the Allied bombing campaigns from 1942, assisted by the United States Army

How to cite this book chapter:
Clapson, M. 2019. *The Blitz Companion*. Pp. 77–95. London: University of Westminster Press. DOI: https://doi.org/10.16997/book26.d. License: CC-BY-NC-ND 4.0

Air Force (USAAF). Significant bombing raids were also mounted by British and American air forces on Nazi-occupied European countries, notably France, Belgium and the Netherlands. Italy was also bombed both by the Allies and the Nazis.

Much of this has been covered by Overy in his peerless histories of the bombing war in Europe. Furthermore, a convenient short cut into his and others' work on the effects of bombing on cities and civilians can be found on the webpages of the Centre for the Study of War, State and Society at Exeter University, where Overy is based. Drawing upon these materials and other sources, this chapter focuses upon the experiences of European urban populations as the bombs rained down. While it would be impossible in a book of this scope to provide a completely representative picture of all air raids and their victims, the chapter does focus upon the most significant or infamous bombing raids and their consequences for civilians. Key themes and similarities with the experience and behaviour of civilian populations are identified across counties.

Blitzkrieg over Europe

The German attacks on Barcelona and Guernica during the Spanish Civil War provided minor dress rehearsals for the massive suffering inflicted by Nazis upon European cities from September 1939. On the first day of that month, Operation Wasserkante was launched against the Polish capital city, Warsaw. Blitzkrieg had begun, and with it, the Second World War. The Luftwaffe entered the war with over 4,300 combat aircraft, and deployed over 1.5 million military personnel during the invasion of Poland. Although the Nazis had carefully studied Polish strengths and weaknesses, and possessed overwhelmingly favourable resources, the Poles resisted bravely. But heavy air raids on the people and urban fabric of Warsaw during the early days of September 1939 led to a bloody and hugely destructive victory for the Germans.[153] Anyone searching online for images of the Warsaw Blitz can find many photographs of environmental destruction, and harrowing images of the people killed, maimed or left homeless by the bombings. The air raids were significant not only for their indiscriminate targeting of the urban population, but for the barbaric manner in which German fighter pilots wilfully selected individual civilians in the open spaces of Warsaw, and strafed them with machine gun fire.

In April 1940, Denmark and Norway were targeted for invasion by the Nazis. Sweden remained neutral throughout the war, while Finland was an ally of Germany. On 10 May 1940, however, Nazi Germany simultaneously invaded Belgium, the Netherlands and Luxembourg. Four days later the Luftwaffe mounted a further infamous bombing raid on the historic Dutch port city of Rotterdam. Dive bombers attacked mostly military and commercial targets, and communications. Although no incendiary bombs were deployed, the resultant fires killed almost one thousand people, mostly civilians. Over twenty thousand buildings were burned down and 78,000 people rendered homeless. Rotterdam yielded quickly to the invasion forces, but even historians who have been sometimes sympathetic to Nazi war narratives have viewed the bombing of Rotterdam as excessive: the Germans had 'sewn the wind' and would reap a terrible harvest later in the war.[154]

Polish cities would again be bombed in late June 1941 as Hitler launched Operation Barbarossa, the abortive attempt to invade the USSR in pursuit of *Lebensraum* (German living space). The Nazis followed a strategy of interdiction, an attempt to disrupt and destroy Soviet materiel, personnel and supply lines. Many civilians were killed in Poland, Latvia, Lithuania, Estonia, the

Ukraine and Soviet Russia. The initial air war instigated a terrible period of German war crimes and atrocities in Eastern Europe in 1941, including the mass starvation of over 3 million people and thousands of summary executions. The Nazis deported, executed and tortured about a million Jewish people during Operation Barbarossa, which came to an end as the Red Army prevailed in the winter months of 1941, during the five-month Battle of Stalingrad. The Luftwaffe initially enjoyed air superiority during the early phase of the campaign, and Soviet cities were heavily bombed. Minsk suffered twenty-one air raids in June and July 1941, and Moscow was attacked from 21 July to 22 August. Neither of these urban campaigns were very successful in military terms, argues Overy. Loss of civilian life was slight, but on 22 September Hitler called for Leningrad 'to be erased from the earth.'[155] The city was bombed during the autumn and winter of 1941, and again in April 1942. Despite Hitler's apocalyptic claim, bombing and destruction was on a relatively small scale. High casualty rates in the Battle of Stalingrad, and a significant lengthy bombing of Moscow and Leningrad, failed to lead to the capitulation of Soviet citizens. The Soviet Civil Defence Programme and the Self Defence Groups that mobilised against the Germans were certainly operating within a totalitarian system, but they played a significant role in defeating the expansionist plans of the Nazis.[156]

The failure of Operation Barbarossa is widely viewed by military historians as a turning point in the Second World War. Nazi Germany suffered heavy losses of men and materiel in an ignominious defeat, which now presaged a more coordinated response by the Allies, particularly after the USA entered the European arena in the aftermath of the Japanese attack on Pearl Harbor in December 1941. And those nations that had supported the Nazi

invasion – Hungary, Romania and the Slovaks – suffered retalia-
tory air raids from the Russians towards the end of the war, as did
Finland, used as a launching pad for Nazi air raids. Helsinki was
subject to three heavy air raids in 1944, but according to Overy
they had little impact on the city and its people, nor on the outcome of the war.[157]

The Ordeal of France

France was subjected to over a quarter of the Allied bombing in
wartime Europe.[158] From the Blitzkrieg and the Fall of France in
1940, through campaigns to target Nazi V-weapon launch sites
during 1944, and the heavy bombing during the fight to liberate the French from Nazi occupation, many towns and cities
suffered extensive levels of destruction. Almost 60,000 French
civilians were killed, and twenty of the largest industrial cities
were declared 'bombed out' during the Second World War.[159]
Most were in north-eastern France. In Alsace-Lorraine for example industrial and mining areas were bombed the urban centres
of Metz, Mulhouse, St. Dié and Strasbourg suffered extensive
destruction.[160]

Lyndsey Dodd extends the notion of the 'Blitz', traditionally
associated with Britain, to the French civilian experience of bombing, arguing that the 'Blitz' was a transnational phenomenon.[161]
Using oral history, she provides an often emotional account of the
devastation to homes, streets, communities and families in the
industrial region around Lille in north-eastern France. She also
portrays the effect on the individual. Since the later twentieth century social history has witnessed an increasing focus on the body
as the locus of historical change, and Dodd shows how the fragile

bodies of children were affected by the invasive and cruel nature of bombing, and provides vivid images of distorted corpses being extricated from bombsites. Her oral history focuses upon subjectivity: the way her oral respondents experienced, remembered and processed what they went through.

While the 'Blitz spirit' was alive amongst those who lived in the ruins of French urban communities, the theme of the ferocious disruption to people and places is powerfully evident in oral testimonies. 'Finding home intact was a relief,'

> After that life continued in the monotonous bombscape. Walking through once familiar streets, Cécile saw 'ruined houses, ruined houses, ruined houses. All down the street – another one, and another.' Lucien too illustrated such stunned disbelief: 'Now it was just a field of ruins. The whole district destroyed. We walked for months and months in ruins. There was nothing to repair it with.[162]

Overy details the wider social impact of the bombing of French cities during 1943–4, and the outrage and resentment that many French people felt. In Lorient and Nantes for example, the ferocity and destruction of Allied air raids in the autumn of 1943 led the Germans and French to combine forces to put out fires, patch up buildings and repair infrastructure. The area bombings of Nantes also exposed weaknesses in the evacuation scheme organised by the French government. Many perished unnecessarily.[163] Large tracts of the urban-industrial sprawl of north-eastern France lay in ruins by the time liberation was secured in the summer of 1944.

The Bombing of Italian Cities

Over 60,000 people were killed by air raids in wartime Italy. This tragedy was triggered on 10 June 1940 when the Italian leader

Benito Mussolini declared war on Britain and France. Now that Britain had its metaphorical back to the wall, and the Nazis had occupied Paris, Mussolini felt he was on the winning side. In Britain, Italians were swiftly interned, and the RAF began its bombing campaign firstly upon Italian military positions, but soon afterwards against cities. The day after Italy took up arms against the Allies, Turin was bombed, and other Italian cities came under attack, notably Milan, Genoa, Taranto and Naples. As the University of Exeter's Centre for the Study of War, State and Society webpage notes, the historic heart of Venice was spared. But during the campaign to oust the Italian fascist dictatorship, heavy bombing was inflicted on the historic capital of Rome. In northern Italy, Genoa, Milan and Turin were among the leading urban centres to come under attack, while in southern Italy Naples and Taranto, and Palermo and other Sicilian cities were bombed by the Allies, particularly the USAAF. The Germans also bombed Italy following the Allied landings, but in vain, as the Italians surrendered to the Allies on 8 September 1943.[164]

The historic period between the surrender and the final defeat of fascism in the summer of 1945 witnessed further Allied and German air raids on Italian cities. As in all other air campaigns over cities, the death and destruction visited upon urban populations profoundly distorted the environment, and tragically disrupted people's lives. The fusion of personal experience with the degraded cityscape is expressed beautifully on website of the Centre for the Study of War, State and Society:

> Cities became symbolic and emotional spaces which had to be defended by their inhabitants when their 'soul' was wounded by bombs: for many civilians, an outrage to their home town was an outrage to the motherland. Grazia Alfieri Tarentino, a young woman in Milan from

1941, for example, expressed a painful resentment of the
enemy when she saw La Scala theatre burning: it was
'all that had remained of the heart of the city'. In October 1944, when a bomb killed 200 school children in
the Gorla working class district of Milan, she witnessed
the pain and the tragedy of innocent children. The whole
city was in mourning on the day of the funerals, the
women in black beside the small white graves:

*On the church square, among the silent crowd, some-
one dared to say: 'these are the Anglo-Americans, assas-
sins of children'. Among the sincere pain, propaganda was
insinuating; on the walls posters appeared with images of
death to remind those who persisted in refusing to believe
it, that the so-called 'liberators' were the enemies …. Ideas
were confused.*[165]

The resentment felt towards the forces that were effectively liber-
ating Italy from fascist occupation and Nazi aggression is palpable, while the reference to the wounded 'soul' of the city implicitly
references the spiritual desolation many Italians felt as practis-
ing Roman Catholics who held their country to be sacred territory. Ultimately, however, ill-feeling towards the liberators cannot
ignore the fact that Mussolini brought the bombs upon Italy.

The RAF Bombing Campaigns Against German Cities, 1942–5

The British bombing of Berlin in August 1940 and the smaller
raids of 1940–1 can be viewed as an early and particular stage in
the RAF campaign against Germany. British propaganda boasted
that the RAF was inflicting serious damage on the Nazi war
effort, but while reassuring, that was far from the truth. The RAF
engaged in relatively minor attacks on industry, infrastructure

and military targets, with limited success. The attacks on Lubeck and Rostock were small if highly destructive strikes. In the summer of 1942, however, the RAF changed tactics.[166]

When Bomber Command installed Air Marshall Arthur 'Bomber' Harris in February, 1942, the area bombing campaign against Germany was significantly ramped up. Concerned that the reputation of Bomber Command was waning in Whitehall, Harris wanted his air fleet to be much more effective, more deadly and destructive, than in previous raids. His famous statement that the British had to kill as many 'Boche' as possible in order to win the war echoed the point made by Baldwin some ten years earlier, that victory meant killing more men, women and children of the enemy.[167] This was expressed in the bluntly described policy of 'de-housing', of rendering the civilian population homeless and helpless.[168] His justification was that Nazi Germany had started the war and mass aerial bombardment, known as area bombing, would help to end it. Under the proactive leadership of Harris, Bomber Command initiated a programme of massive air raids to destroy industrial capacity, infrastructure and housing, and to create chaos and submission, the very conditions that Hitler had unsuccessfully attempted to create during the Blitz.

With elite officials in the RAF, Harris planned his first signature bombing event, the Thousand Bomber Raid on Cologne on the 30–1 May 1942, which continued until 17 August. The RAF website notes that the exact number of bombers used on the first two nights of the raid is unclear, but the figure was most likely up to one thousand. Over 3,300 buildings were destroyed, most of them by fires. Large-scale firms were put out of action, roads and railway lines were incapacitated, and the power supply was destroyed in many areas of the city. Hospitals, churches, schools and university buildings, and many shops and places of leisure were razed to the ground. Over 13,000 homes were completely destroyed, 6,360 were seriously damaged and 22,270 less badly damaged. These statistics are from an RAF source that notes 'These details of physical damage in Cologne are a good example of the results of area bombing':

> Similar results can be expected in those of Bomber Command's raids, which were successful during fol-lowing years. The estimates of casualties in Cologne are, unusually, quite precise. Figures quoted for deaths vary only between 469 and 486. The 469 figure comprises 411 civilians and 58 military casualties, mostly members of Flak units. 5,027 people were listed as injured and 45,132 as bombed out. It was estimated that from 135,000 to 150,000 of Cologne's population of nearly 700,000 peo-ple fled the city after the raid.[169]

German cities thus witnessed the phenomenon of 'trekking' in common with British cities under the bomb. The experiences of female and child evacuees also demonstrated strong similarities with their British counterparts, including feelings of separation from family members; rationing and squabbles over food; petty or more significant tensions between hosts and evacuees; and worries over the loss of the home. A high number of evacuees in a city also greatly increased overcrowding and exacerbated the struggle to find safe and suitable accommodation. For these rea-sons, many German evacuees unwittingly emulated their British counterparts during the Phoney War: they went back to whence they had left, despite official warnings to the contrary.[170]

When the USAAF began operating from British bases later in 1942, the capacity for combined bombing offensives between the Americans and the British was mobilised to devastating effect. By

1943 the British had developed more sophisticated aids to their bombing operations, for example a scanning device known as the H2S apparatus, which allowed for a more accurate bombing of German urban areas by providing 'an outline of the city and its buildings.'[171] The device was first deployed against Hamburg in January 1943, initiating a phase of bombing from March to July of that year aimed at Aachen, Krefield, Duisburg, Dortmund, Essen, Wuppertal, Dusseldorf, Cologne, Munster, Berlin, Nuremberg, Frankfurt, Stuttgart and Munich. During the Battle of the Ruhr a number of these cities were attacked more than once, and some over many nights.[172] On the 16–17 May 1943 the RAF instigated one of its most famous raids, the attack on the dams of the Mohne and Eder Reservoirs, subject of *The Dam Busters* (1955), a popular British war film about the 'bouncing bombs' that skimmed across the reservoirs. While historians have argued that the military value and the industrial damage of the Dam Busters raids can be overstated, there was some impact upon morale. Germans were shocked and saddened at the intrusion and at the tales of an 'incredible deluge.'[173]

The raids on Dortmund on 23–4 May 1943 saw 2,000 tons of bombs dropped, and a death toll of about 15,000 people. Visiting Dortmund after the bombing, the German Minister of Propaganda Joseph Goebbels found the destruction 'virtually total' and was only cheered by the 'respectable' number of planes brought down.[174] As Stargardt argues, the noise of the raids on Dortmund was audible in Cologne, and casualties were rendered higher than they might have been by the flooding of air raid shelters caused by the bombing of the Mohne dam.[175] Contemporary estimates put mortalities at 17,000 in Dusseldorf and 27,000 in Wuppertal.[176]

John Betjeman expressed sentiments that many British men and certainly airmen would have agreed with as the Allied bombing campaign began. In his poem *Westminster Abbey* he exhorted

God to 'bomb the Germans' but to 'Spare their women for Thy Sake'.[177] Betjeman was also railing against the destruction of beautiful English churches by air raids. Many churches in Cologne were smashed to pieces, while the cathedral mostly survived. The attack on Cologne was hailed by Bomber Command and the British government as proof positive that the RAF were now successfully fighting back against the Germans. Yet despite such propaganda value the philosopher A.C. Grayling has shown how well-prepared the German authorities and German people were for the heavy raids on Cologne. While he does not explore the degree to which such efficiency was superimposed on the German population by the Nazi regime, it could be countered that the extensive consent to the regime by millions of Germans did not require much coercion.[178] German preparations for the attack on Cologne greatly ameliorated the death and destruction meted out by the raid. As Grayling notes, the city had prepared 'public shelters for 75,000 people':

> with twenty-five deep special bunkers for a further 7,500 (and twenty-nine additional such bunkers in the process of being built). A total of 42,000 small air raid shelters had been provided under or next to houses for apartment buildings or residents. Fourteen auxiliary hospitals had been constructed, giving an extra 1,760 emergency beds. The total cost of air-raid defences in Cologne prior to the 1,000 bomber raid was thirty-nine million marks. It was money well spent. The 1,000 bombers dropped 2,500 tons of high explosives and incendiaries, and destroyed centuries of history; the German dead numbered 469.[179]

The raid on Hamburg in the summer of 1943 was the largest following Cologne. The Allies were increasingly deploying phosphorous incendiary devices to start fires that spread rapidly, and Hamburg was to suffer hugely from them. The specific intentions for Hamburg revealed the wider rationale of, and perceived justification for, the area bombing of German cities. On 27 May 1943 Bomber Command's Operations Order No. 173 made it clear that the importance of Hamburg as the second city of Germany with a population of over 1.5 million 'needs no further emphasis':

> The total destruction of this city would achieve immeasurable results in reducing the industrial capacity of the enemy's war machine. This, together with the effect on German morale, which would be felt throughout the country, would play a very important part in shortening and winning the war.
>
> The 'Battle of Hamburg' cannot be won in a single night. It is estimated that at least 10,000 tons of bombs will have to be dropped to complete the process of elimination. To achieve the maximum effect of air bombardment this city should be subjected to sustained attack.
>
> *Intention*: To destroy Hamburg.[180]

Bomber Command and the RAF were to operate under cover of darkness, while the strategy called for the USAAF to follow through with 'heavy daylight attacks.'[181] Given the strength of German air defences, and the vagaries of the weather, meticulous planning preceded the sustained bombing of Hamburg. Lancaster, Halifax and Stirling bombers carried sizeable loads of powerful HE bombs but 'a large number of incendiaries are to be carried in order to saturate the Fire Service. The proportion of high explosive bombs to be carried may be increased after widespread fire damage has been achieved.'[182]

The tragic and defining consequence of the raids on Hamburg was the terrible overnight firestorm that consumed the city and

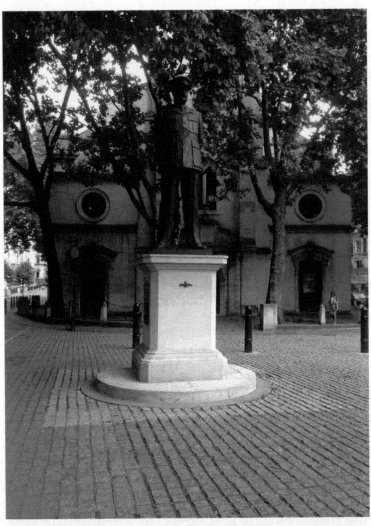

Figure 6: Statue to Sir Arthur Harris, St. Clement's Danes, Aldwych, London. The inscription reads: 'In memory of a great commander and of the brave crews of Bomber Command, more than 55,000 of whom lost their lives in the cause of freedom. The nation owes them all an immense debt' (photograph by author, 2017).

its population. As Musgrove argues, Harris was delighted with the scale of the devastation wrought by the RAF, quoting from the Bible that the Germans 'had sewn the wind, and now they reaped the whirlwind'.[183] The Hamburg raids lasted for a week and resulted in about 40,000 civilian deaths. Much of Hamburg was razed to the ground by the terrible firestorms which raged through the city.[184] People were burnt to ashes, suffocated by the lack of oxygen, or died from heat exposure which raised their body temperature to intolerable levels. The city was strewn with corpses, and the authorities faced a monumental task in clearing them away while dealing with practical problems such as gaining clean water for the survivors, and rendering buildings safe.[185]

Many German cities were badly damaged and others bombed close to complete destruction by the Allies. Yet the destruction of Dresden in eastern Germany, the seventh largest city in the country, has been the subject of intense historical attention. The 'Florence of the Elbe' was subjected to bombing raids on 13–14 February 1945, just a few months before the war in Europe came to an end. 'Operation Thunderclap' had been planned since July 1944 as a late knockout blow to the German city, further evidence of Harris's unwavering belief that air power was a key force in winning wars.[186] In the novel *Slaughterhouse 5* by Kurt Vonnegut, the narrator Billy Pilgrim is an American ex-prisoner of war who was in Dresden when the bombs fell. Years later Pilgrim flicks through a copy of the *Gideon Bible* he finds in his motel room, to look for 'tales of great destruction' reading 'Then the Lord rained upon Sodom and upon Gomorrah brimstone and fire from the Lord out of Heaven; and He overthrew those cities, and all the plain, and all the inhabitants of the cities, and that which grew upon the ground'.[187]

Vonnegut must have been aware that the raid on Hamburg in 1943 was code-named Operation Gomorrah. Dresden was to suffer a similar cataclysm. From their bases in Britain nearly 800 RAF Lancaster Bombers delivered over 2,646 tons of bombs tons of bombs over Dresden, including 1,180 tons of incendiaries, while USAAF B-17 Flying Fortresses unloaded over 460 tons of bombs the following day. The resulting firestorm devastated its cultural treasures as over 15 square miles of the city were devoured by flames. Over 75,000 out of 220,000 homes were destroyed.[188] The German military was forced to use fire in mass cremations of the dead, in order to avoid the spread of disease, and to quell the stench of putrefying burnt flesh.

One of the earliest historians to interpret the bombing of Dresden as an unnecessary atrocity by the Allies was the now-discredited British writer David Irving. *The Destruction of Dresden* (1963) claimed that the firestorms in Dresden were the culmination of the allied war on Germany's cities and civilians. Irving estimated that 135,000 people were killed in the February air raids, an unscientific estimate that he later revised, and that other historians have also questioned. Exact mortality rates are impossible to verify due to the unaccounted number of refugees and the number of almost completely incinerated corpses that did, or did not, receive mass burials. In *Slaughterhouse 5* Vonnegut references Irving, and as Billy Pilgrim emerges from the underground abattoir, where he had heard the bombing overnight, he observes that '135,000 Hansels and Gretels' had been 'baked like gingerbread men'.[189] As Overy argues, however, the original estimate by the President of Police for Dresden of about 25,000 mortalities is probably the most accurate estimate, although a further 1,858 skeletons were dug up during the reconstruction of the city after 1945.[190]

Dresden was so comprehensively wrecked that little of the city was left standing at the end of the war. Thousands of refugees had also made their way there from the Eastern Front, and this influx amplified the death toll. Leading politicians in Britain, including the Prime Minister, now questioned the validity of blanket bombing. Cynics may view the following assessment by Churchill as one based upon public relations and utilitarian consideration, rather than any humane sense of remorse:

> It seems to me that the moment has come when the question of bombing of German cities simply for the sake of increasing the terror, though under other pretexts, should be reviewed. Otherwise we shall come into control of an utterly ruined land. We shall not, for example, be able to get housing materials out of Germany for our own needs because some temporary provision would have to be made for the Germans themselves. The destruction of Dresden remains a serious query against the conduct of allied bombing.[191]

But it also asked a serious question of the corruption and selfishness of local Nazi officials whom, as Kevin Wilson argues, were lax when setting up air and civil defence facilities for Dresden: 'The city authorities had woefully neglected the building of shelters except for themselves'.[192] This failing should be accounted for when assessing the mortality rate after the February raids, and the devastation to the built environment. The bombing of German cities represented an intensive campaign of conventional air raids deploying HE bombs of varying payloads, parachute mines, and incendiary devices. For Bomber Command, as for Churchill, Eisenhower and Truman, aerial warfare hastened the end of the German war, degrading the urban infrastructure and demoralising its citizens. The Blitz on Britain had demonstrated the failure of intentions by Nazi military planners, and there was little hard evidence to support the Allied interpretation of German capitulation. As Beck argues, 'it seems clear that the bombings tended to draw people together in a community of striving against adversity.'[193] Nicholas Stargardt presents a more nuanced picture of German morale and responses to air raids, showing how many used the language of 'taking it' as did the British during the Blitz. Some tried to sleep through the raids, others immediately set about clearing away rubble or broken glass from their homes, some demonstrated 'strong hearts' and 'even developed a kind of pride in what they endured'. Others displayed their 'nerves' more readily.[194] Moreover, many Germans manifested anti-Jewish feeling during the air raids, blaming the responsibility for them on 'World Jewry', unsurprising given the anti-Semitic ideology of the Nazi regime. Yet many ordinary Germans simply did not believe the raids on the dams were a consequence of 'Jewish terror' despite what the Nazi Party told them, and blamed the English instead.[195]

Conclusion

Writing during the early post-war years, the esteemed military historian Michael Howard argued that air raids, if anything, initially strengthened morale by increasing a sense of defiance and hatred of the enemy. He admitted, however, that bombing in the later stages of war created apathy and war-weariness, but rarely the ultimate defeat of civilian fortitude.[196] The air raids and their consequences discussed in this chapter appear to confirm this judgement, even for heavily-bombed Germany.

So whither the reputation of 'Bomber Harris'? Max Hastings views him as sometimes vulgar and narrow-minded, but also as a driven and shrewd Commander in Chief, whose indifference to

German suffering during the area bombing campaigns contrasted with his passionate commitment to his aircrew. He was deeply saddened at the losses incurred by the often terrifying raids, and often given to bouts of emotional anger.[197] For Henry Messenger, Harris may have been 'blinkered, boorish and stubborn' but he inspired his crews to take enormous risks.[198] In similar vein to Hastings, Messenger argues that the strategy of continuous area bombing has been subsequently proven to have been a mistake, 'but during much of the war there was no way of knowing this.'[199] Henry Probert, in his study of Harris, even includes an evaluation made in 1959 by the Nazi architect and confidante of Hitler, Albert Speer, that the unpredictability and sustained heaviness of the raids caused Germany enormous problems, possibly more so than defeat on the Russian Front.[200] Whether the comparison stands or not, within the context of a bitter, continuing and un-won war, tactics and tragedy were united in the unwavering belief of Harris that area bombing was a successful strategy.

Despite the complexity of morale and its ultimately resilient nature, some lessons learned or at least believed to have been learned from the air raids on Germany were applied by the Americans to the bombing of Japan from late 1944. Incendiaries had a huge and destructive potential in a land known for its traditional use of lightweight building materials, and its high concentrations of buildings and populations in mountainous country where settlements were only possible on a large scale on the coastal plains and some inland areas. The campaigns in Japan were to prove that air power could assist the winning of wars.

CHAPTER 5

The Conventional and Atomic Bombing of Japan

Introduction

The remarkable history of modern Japan began with the arrival of
Admiral Perry from the United States during the 1850s.[201] Centuries of self-imposed isolation came to an end. During the following decades and long into the twentieth century Japan underwent
a torturous modernisation process. Industrialisation and urbanisation swept through the country. Large multi-faceted corpora-
tions came into existence, many supported by modernisers in the
Japanese government who looked to Germany and the United

How to cite this book chapter:
Clapson, M. 2019. *The Blitz Companion*. Pp. 97–118. London: University of
    Westminster Press. DOI: https://doi.org/10.16997/book26.e. License:
    CC-BY-NC-ND 4.0

States as exemplars of commercial and manufacturing econo-mies. Liberals in Japan were impressed by British parliamentary democracy and the social reforms of the Victorian and Edward-ian years, and pushed for Japan to become more democratic, less hide-bound by religious and patriarchal traditions. Against these ambitious projects traditionalists in Japan invoked isolationism, the samurai military code, and the religious culture of a patriar-chal Shintoism to prevent westernisation and the perceived pol-lution of moral values. A powerful reactionary, militaristic and conservative coalition of politicians versus a smaller clique of lib-eral reformers cleaved Japanese society and politics prior to, and during, the Second World War.[202]

Presided over by Emperor Hirohito, 1930s Japan aligned itself with the fascist dictatorships of Germany and Italy, creating the Axis Powers. This triangulation between Europe and the North Pacific led to catastrophe for the Japanese that few in the coun-try envisaged prior to the air raids on Pearl Harbor in December 1941. This incursion brought the USA into the war and marked a huge step on the road to the devastation and defeat of Japan.

The Pacific War and the Conventional Bombing of Japanese Cities

A foretaste of the conventional air campaigns over Japan came during the 'Doolittle Raid' in April 1942, named after their mis-sion leader Lieutenant Colonel Jimmy Doolittle. Also known as the first Tokyo Raid, sixteen US bombers attacked military and industrial targets in and around the Japanese capital as payback for the attack on Pearl Harbor. A number of civilians were killed, and a small number of American pilots were captured and exe-cuted. While returning from the raid, however, some members of the air crews made it to China where they bailed out or crash landed due to inadequate fuel supplies.[203]

With help from many friendly Chinese people, most of the pilots made it home following 'America's first World War Two victory'. Yet Doolittle and his crew had inadvertently and tragically sowed the seeds of a vicious revenge taken by the Japanese against the Chinese who had assisted the American airmen. In his study of the Doolittle Raid and their aftermath, James M. Scott argues that the Japanese began their terrible revenge from June 1942. Subsequently, the Japanese Air Force mounted raids on the Chinese city of Chaozhou, killing over 10,000 people, leaving 27,000 destitute, and devastating the urban infrastructure and agriculture of the surrounding region. Many suffered from the appalling treatment that the Japanese had meted out to the Chinese since the 'Rape of Nanking' in 1937.[204] The ferocity of Japanese behaviour in China was symptomatic of the wider course of Japanese history. The historic nature of Japanese military culture was a legacy of hundreds of years of atavistic isolationism that explained the conservatism and intransigence of hyper-nationalist Japanese leaders until the very end of the War in the Pacific.

In his famous address to the US Congress in May 1943, Churchill summed up Allied war aims for Japanese cities in stark terms. 'It is the duty of those who are charged with the direction of the war':

> to begin the process, so necessary and desirable, of laying
> the cities and other munitions centres of Japan in ashes,
> for in ashes they must surely lie before peace comes back
> to the world.

It was an apocalyptic vision of urban destruction in the cause of global democracy. Churchill was well aware of the power of bombing to turn cities to ashes. The firestorms caused by the area bombing in Germany had also convinced the USAAF that incendiary devices would be particularly effective in Japan, where light construction materials and wooden houses would go up in flames relatively quickly.[205]

Tokyo was attacked from the air many times from November 1944. American air raids on Japan were celebrated in *Target Tokyo*, an official military documentary film dedicated to all personnel on the mission. Narrated by the actor who would become President, Ronald Reagan, the film begins with preparations for the bombing campaigns in American air bases. Unashamedly patriotic, visuals and voiceover play to the fact that young American men from all walks of life and states of the country are serving their nation. This was an American trope of wartime unity and national effort, wherein a vast teeming continent could come together in the singular aim of defeating Japan. The iconic B-29, or Superfortress, is also celebrated in the film: 'designed to carry more destruction, to carry it higher, faster, farther than any bomber built before'.

Taking off from Saipan, the bombers fly high and away, reaching Tokyo as Reagan states 'Within a radius of fifteen miles of the Imperial Palace live seven million Japanese':

> people we used to think of as small, dainty, polite, concerning themselves only with floral arrangements and rock gardens, and the cultivation of silk worms. But it isn't silk worms, and it isn't imperial palaces these men are looking for. In the suburbs of Tokyo is the huge Nakajima aircraft plant. Well bud, *what are you waiting for*?[206]

The bomb doors open to expose the expansive city below. Martial music accompanies the sight of B-29s raining HE bombs on Tokyo. No destruction is pictured but the Battle for Japan is declared underway.

Yet from March 1945 the bombing of Japan was intensified. Authorisation for the firebombing of Japanese cities was given by General Curtis LeMay. In charge of the Eighth Air Force, he led bombing missions over Germany from late 1942 until he was transferred into the Pacific War operations, taking charge of 21st Bomber Command in July 1944. Having witnessed the firestorms in Germany, LeMay felt that firebombing would shorten the war in Japan. During the final year of the war the USAAF engaged in a huge and coordinated firebombing of Japanese cities. In addition to HE bombs, incendiary devices now rained down upon hundreds of thousands of commercial and municipal buildings and on homes made of wooden frames and interior paper walls.

The Great Tokyo Air Raid on 9–10 March 1945 threw into relief the nature and consequences of the new campaign. Nearly three hundred B-29 bombers unloaded over 1,665 tons (1,510,463 kilograms) of incendiaries. Over 100,000 people were killed, mostly by the conflagration that engulfed the Shitamachi district of Tokyo and its environs. Thousands were burned alive, others suffocated as the oxygen was consumed by fire. A million were rendered homeless and almost 16 square miles (41.4 square kilometres) of Tokyo were, as Churchill had wished, in ashes.[207]

An oral history of the Japanese people at war provides vivid memories of the effect on those below the bomb doors. With faint but discernible echoes of the 'Phoney War' in Britain, one woman recalled being sent home with her friends from their evacuation area in a nearby town just days before the raid because of the relative infrequency of attacks. Then the incendiaries began hitting the school and other public buildings as people rushed to the air raid shelters. Flames soared from factory windows, people rushed into the nearby park, while others threw themselves into the river to escape the searing heat. Many were drowned. Others burned to death in streets and shelters. And many also rushed to the safety of the nearby countryside, a common form of escape from air raids.[208]

Japan is a mountainous and wooded country whose lowlands host the vast majority of the population in towns and cities of varying sizes. Across the length and breadth of the main island of Honshu, the smaller northern island Hokkaido, and the southern island of Kyushu, American area bombing did enormous damage. The architectural historian Neil Jackson points to important differences between the Japanese and European experiences of urban bombing. European cities were bombed to almost complete destruction over relatively long periods but their ruins remained partly inhabitable. The urban bombing experience in Japan, however, saw large swathes of cities razed to the ground in just a few hours by incendiary bombing.[209] Homelessness became an immediate and pressing issue.

Even swifter devastation was visited on Hiroshima and Nagasaki in August 1945: both of these southern Japanese cities were wiped out in less than three minutes by the atomic bomb.[210] The atomic bombings held within their impact and the devastating aftermath a question mark for the future survival of humanity. Three important questions can be asked here, which historians profoundly disagree upon. First, why did the USA knowingly kill so many innocent civilians in the final phase of the war? Second, did the devastating raids on Hiroshima and Nagasaki actually terminate the Pacific War, or was this caused by other factors, thus rendering the bombings of Hiroshima and Nagasaki unnecessary tragedies? Third, were the atomic bombings of Japan ethically and morally worse than the conventional air raids that killed greater numbers of people?

The Manhattan Project

In order to understand the widespread deadly and destructive consequences of the atom bomb, and the reasons why it was deployed, some knowledge of its provenance is necessary. The atomic bomb was developed in the USA during the course of the Second World War. While forever associated with American technological prowess and power, the Manhattan Project drew upon weapons research in Europe. As Paul Ham argues, the 'Paris Group' of scientists for example first discovered the power of nuclear fission in 1939, while the wartime Maud Committee in Britain initiated the Tube Alloys programme to develop a British atomic weapon. While German bombs were raining down on London and other British cities the Maud Committee was, in effect, unwittingly preparing the ground for the instantaneous destruction to be visited upon Japan. The British atomic weapons programme and some key personnel were subsumed into the Manhattan Project once the USA entered the Second World War.[211]

Fear that Nazi Germany might reach the terrible achievement of atomic weaponry before the Allies drove research and development into the controlled destructive potential of uranium and plutonium. A further justification for the Manhattan Project in the USA and the development of the atomic bomb was the great strides that Nazi Germany made in guided missile and rocket technology during the Second World War, technology that had visited death and destruction on British and European cities in 1944. Supposing the Germans been a few steps ahead of the Allies, and particularly the Americans, the terrible counterfactual scenario could have seen the Nazis dropping atomic bombs on London and New York. As President Truman noted privately at the Potsdam Summit in July 1945, 'It is certainly a good thing for the world that Hitler's crowd or Stalin's did not discover this atomic bomb.'[212]

The USSR, although an ally against the Germans following the collapse of the Nazi-Soviet Pact in 1941, was also deemed to be a post-war threat, lending further urgency to the Manhattan Project. Chief among the foreign experts heading up the research was Julius Robert Oppenheimer, a Jewish physicist investigating the formula at which uranium would reach the critical mass that led to a ferocious chain reaction. He calculated the critical mass of uranium-235 to make the atomic bomb effective, and together with his team of brilliant expat physicists developed the construction of graphite blocks embedded with uranium that formed the atomic bomb.[213]

The first nuclear bomb in history was not dropped from the air but was detonated in the New Mexico desert on 16 July 1945. As an American scientific advisor to the government wrote:

> in a remote section of the Alamogordo Air Base, New Mexico, the first full-scale test was made of the implosion type atomic fission bomb. For the first time in history there was an explosion. And what an explosion![214]

Following the death of Roosevelt in 1945, Harry S. Truman was sworn in as the US President. According to the Truman Library website, the favourite poem of the president was *Locksley Hall* by Tennyson, with its prognostications of celestial warfare.[215]

Truman informed Churchill and Stalin of the momentous event
in New Mexico at the Potsdam Summit which began on 17 July.
Truman and his Secretary of State for War Henry Stimson were
persuaded by US scientific advisors that dropping the atom bomb
on significant Japanese targets would hasten the end of the war
and save American lives. As Robert Griffith has argued, however,
in a paragraph worth quoting at length, the decision to use atomic
weapons raises 'chilling moral questions':

> To what extent was the decision influenced by racial
> prejudice and by the institutionalised wartime depiction
> of the Japanese as evil and inhuman? Before using the
> bomb should the United States have demonstrated its
> terrible destructiveness – perhaps in Tokyo harbour, as
> some scientists suggested at the time – or at least have
> provided an explicit warning? Was the use of atomic
> bombs, weapons that in a blinding instant killed tens of
> thousands of men, women and children, immoral? Was
> the bombing any more immoral than the reliance on
> weapons that produced the millions of other deaths dur-
> ing World War 2, than the aerial assaults on London or
> Dresden, or than the awful firebombing of Tokyo? What
> is one to say of a weapon that not only kills, but through
> radiation and the resulting genetic damage, continues to
> kill long after the debris settles?[216]

'Even if the Japs are savages, ruthless, merciless and fanatic',
argued Truman:

> we as the leader of the world, for the common welfare
> of humanity, cannot drop this terrible bomb on the old
> capital [Kyoto] or the new [Tokyo]. [The] target will be
> a purely military one and we will issue a warning state-
> ment asking the Japs to surrender and save lives.[217]

Accusations of racism sometimes form too quickly on the lips and keypads of many left and liberal academics today, but it is not unreasonable to highlight the brutal behaviour that led to the stereotypes.[218] Truman would have been fully aware of the terrible atrocities committed by the Japanese against the Chinese during the later 1930s and the Second World War, while in the arenas of combat between Japan and the Allies, American and British prisoners of war were tortured, starved, kicked, doused in petrol and set on firm, beaten, or beheaded. Over 150 Australian soldiers were bayoneted to death after being tied to trees. And in one unconscionable episode, an American crew were dissected by Japanese doctors who extracted vital organs and performed invasive brain surgery while their victims were alive and conscious.[219]

Truman was writing on 25 July. The Japanese government was issued with the Potsdam Declaration the following day, in which Britain, China and the US called for unconditional surrender from Japan. The Japanese government rejected the declaration. And while some Japanese politicians were softening their stance on surrender, fearful of the consequences, others were not so inclined. This culture of defiance persisted despite the fact that much of the Japanese economy was unable to function. The Soviet Union was by then fighting back Japanese forces in China, bringing further humiliation, but no declarations of surrender.[220] Hence to hasten victory, the Americans decided to target the port cities of Hiroshima in Honshu, the largest of the Japanese islands, and Nagasaki, in the island of Kyushu. Both contained industry and military facilities, and were not associated with large numbers of prisoners of war.

On the early morning of 6 August 1945 a Boeing B-29 Superfortress infamously named 'Enola Gay' flew from the American Pacific Base on the island of Tinian toward the city of Hiroshima, a large industrial, commercial and maritime centre with a population of 350,000 people. Piloted by Colonel Paul W. Tibbets, the B-29 was carrying *Little Boy*, a 9,000-pound uranium-235 device attached to a parachute. It detonated some 200 metres above the hypocentre marked by the domed Industrial Promotional Hall. Apart from a few steel-framed and reinforced concrete buildings almost everything within a two-kilometre radius of the hypocentre, including some 50,000 buildings and homes, was obliterated. Estimates vary, but at least 70,000 people died almost instantaneously, and at least 40,000 more subsequently perished from cancer and other terminal illnesses related to the radiation that seared through the city and its suburbs.[221]

The death and destruction caused by *Little Boy* might have been the context for a Japanese surrender. Griffith points to the judgement of the United States Strategic Bombing Survey in 1946 that Japan was about to surrender even if no atomic bombs had been dropped. This has been a keystone of the anti-war position toward Hiroshima and Nagasaki ever since, and also of those who view the atomic bombings as a 'crime against humanity'. The philosopher A. C. Grayling, for example, also appears to accept uncritically the view that the Japanese were 'suing for peace' months before the atomic bombs were detonated.[222] As Robert Maddox argues, however, while the Japanese were certainly on the verge of defeat, the real problem was 'how long Japanese militarists were willing to go on fighting in hope of gaining a negotiated peace through Soviet intercession'. In that hiatus, many thousands of American lives could have been lost.[223] The distinguished Japanese historian Mikiso Hane argues that the influential militarists and many right-wing nationalist politicians were prepared to fight not only to the death, but even to call for 'one hundred million' to commit the glorious sacrifice of death or suicide to defeat the enemy.[224]

In other words, Japanese leaders were prepared for the collective suicide of a nation. Hastings agrees, pointing out that many Japanese generals preferred death to humiliation, while the war party in the Japanese government remained intransigent to the last, even following the Nagasaki bombing.[225] As a former President of the Japanese Medical Association stated bluntly but honestly:

> When one considers the possibility that the Japanese military would have sacrificed the entire nation if it were not for the atomic bomb attack, then this bomb might be described as having saved Japan.[226]

That was a brave statement to make in the face of strong nationalist currents of opinion in Japan that refuse to this day to say sorry for the Japanese war record. A toxic combination of Japanese intransigence and American determination led to the devastation of Nagasaki just three days after the incineration of Hiroshima. Smaller than Hiroshima, Nagasaki was a maritime city with shipyards and a sizable naval presence. A B-29 Superfortress, *Bockscar*, piloted by Major General Charles W. Sweeney and Tibbets, flew from Tinian, detonating a 10,000-pound plutonium bomb nicknamed *Fat Man*. Within seconds the blast from the bomb killed over 30,000 people, causing injuries and suffering to many thousands more. Because Nagasaki was partly surrounded by a hinterland of ravines and hills the spread of the radiation blast was less extensive than Hiroshima, but the devastation was still considerable.[227]

Having steadfastly refused to surrender, the Japanese now did so. In his speech declaring the end of Japanese hostilities, Emperor Hirohito showed himself to be a master of understatement. He was also something of an existentialist, grasping the terrible realities that came with total war and now atomic weaponry. The sacrifice of dignity would save not only Japanese lives, but the existence of humanity:

> But now the war has lasted for nearly four years. Despite the best that has been done by everyone – the gallant fighting of the military and naval forces, the diligence and assiduity of Our servants of the State, and the devoted service of Our one hundred million people – *the war situation has developed not necessarily to Japan's advantage*, while the general trends of the world have all turned against her interest.
>
> Moreover, the enemy has begun to employ a new and most cruel bomb, the power of which to do damage is, indeed, incalculable, taking the toll of many innocent lives. Should we continue to fight, not only would it result in an ultimate collapse and obliteration of the Japanese nation, but also it would lead to the total extinction of human civilization.[228]

It is no exaggeration to argue that the blinding light of the atomic bombs put an end to what many Japanese refer to as *kurai tanima*, the 'dark valley' of the 1930s and the Second World War.[229] Yet the bomb alone did not end the war. It was the most spectacular manifestation of the air campaign over Japan, operating in synthesis with the advances made by the American navy, and the USSR attack on Japanese forces in China in the summer of 1945.[230]

Yet the fallout from those blasts has reverberated throughout post-war history, polarising public and professional opinions, and creating a powerful pacifist sentiment in Japan which gained considerable sympathy worldwide. More than that, as Oppenheimer and many experts in the summer of 1945 realised, the history of the future had now changed irrevocably from what it had been before the bomb detonated in the New Mexico desert. Atomic weaponry could not be un-invented, and the shadow of nuclear catastrophe became a background insecurity for everyone on the planet who was aware of the bomb as the Cold War evolved from the late 1940s.[231]

The Effect on Civilians and the City

The environmental devastation to Hiroshima and Nagasaki has been widely depicted and described. Contemporary photographs and films by the United States Strategic Bombing Survey evidence an obliterated landscape, with only a few reinforced concrete buildings standing in ruins above the incinerated remains of the buildings and natural landscape. In Hiroshima, the skeletal frame of the dome of the Industrial Promotional Hall in the heart of the city marked the spot where the detonation of *Little Boy* occurred some metres above it. Like St Paul's Cathedral, it is crowned by a dome. Yet all around the charred trees, flattened shops, offices and houses, and the twisted tram lines, reflected the common-place devastation wrought by aerial bombing and the accompanying firestorm.

Over 100,000 people had been killed instantly by the atomic bombs, a shocking statistic yet representing a lower death toll than the mortality rate caused by conventional air raids on Japan. The nature of the mass injuries and deaths at Hiroshima and Nagasaki was entirely new, however, creating 'injuries never before seen on mortal creatures':

> the cavalry horse standing pink, stripped of its hide; people with clothing patterns imprinted upon their flesh; the lines of schoolgirls with ribbons of flesh dangling from

their faces; doomed survivors, hideously burned, without hope of effective medical relief; the host of charred and shrivelled corpses.[232]

Testimony from a survivor from Hiroshima vividly describes the impact on the bodies of civilians:

I was a 14-year old high school boy at the time of the atomic bombing. Students at that time were mobilized to tear down certain houses to make firebreaks in the city. I was 1.7 kilometres (1 mile) from ground zero on the morning of August 6, 1945, so I suffered many serious burns on my face and hands, which left large scars known as keloids. On the same day, my mother was killed by the bomb as were many of my friends and teachers. All these sorrows came to me all at once. I was suffering and ashamed of my keloid burns all the time, and I did not know how to make a living. I felt like shouting at the top of my voice in despair. But I could only murmur, 'If only the A-bomb had not been dropped!' I was completely overwhelmed with grief, which resulted in the autism from which I suffered for a long time after the war.[233]

My father has a special ID which is called *The Certification of Victims of the Atomic Bomb*. It guarantees he can receive free medical care until he dies.[234]

In the immediate aftermath of the bombing, survivors sought shelter as well as medical treatment and water to relieve their burns. Many were traumatised by the violent loss of loved ones, and the horribly disfigured human casualties dying in front of them. Hundreds of others trekked into the nearby countryside out of Hiroshima and Nagasaki, away from homes, streets and neighbourhoods that had been extinguished forever. Others kept walking as far as the next bomb-torn town. In the graphic novel series *Barefoot Gen*, among many testimonies of a survivor of the atomic bombings, the terrible disruption and death wrought by the bomb is sketched in gory detail from the perspective of a young boy whose family home was obliterated by the blast.[235]

Those who survived the atomic bombings in August 1945 possess a uniquely Japanese noun to describe them: they are the *hibakusha*, or 'bomb-affected people.'[236] Beyond the survivors of the concentration camps of the Second World War, theirs are among the most harrowing accounts of how war disrupts, degrades and destroys lives. In his moving account of the *hibakusha*, Ham interviewed many whose lives had been changed for ever, yet who were enormously brave: a woman whose face and body bore terrible scars but who refused to accept a date with a man she did not like because she would not let her appearance affect her self-esteem; a young girl, whose body was burnt, infected, crawling with maggots, and unrecognisable to her father who picked her up from the hospital, yet who lived while her pretty friend who appeared to have been unblemished by the bomb died in terrible pain from radiation sickness a few days after the detonation. Age was no barrier to succumbing to terminal illness.[237] Yet the stories of survival, of the endurance of pain and suffering, represent the fact that even the most appalling bombing did not ultimately break the will of the people on the ground.[238] This lesson had not been learned by the Nazis who attacked London again in 1944–5, despite the Blitz of 1940–1, nor was it absorbed by the Allies whose ambition to bomb the German people into submission was mostly unfulfilled.

Towards the end of the 1940s the American psychologist Irving L. Janis argued in *Air War and Emotional Stress* that 'chronic psychological disorders were rarely produced by heavy bombing attacks'. He concluded that while enhanced levels of anxiety, apathy, depression, pessimism and stress were observed in the population under the bomb, these were temporary.[239] Tom Harrisson of Mass Observation drew upon these conclusions as proof that even the worst episodes of heavy aerial bombardment, be they on British, German and Japanese cities, would not definitively destroy the resilience of their citizens.[240]

More than that, however, the sense of defeat felt in the immediate aftermath of the bomb was transformed into powerful sentiment of opposition to nuclear weaponry, a process of commemoration and memorialisation that, whilst unique to those Japanese civilians who overcame the atomic bombs, shared key similarities with memorialisation in other countries. The important historical legacy of the *hibakusha* is discussed further in chapter eight.

Verdict

A documentary film by the US War Department in 1946, sharing the title of Charles Dickens' *A Tale of Two Cities*, emphasised the justifications for the attacks on the 'arsenal cities' of Hiroshima and Nagasaki. The film was made for members of the American armed forces. That the bombs helped to shorten the war is a key theme, and the US War Department did not hold back when depicting the devastation to the two cities. It also drew upon the testimony of a Roman Catholic Priest to detail the death and injuries to the bodies of the Japanese.[241] Yet the American interpretation was not one of uncritical triumphalism, and the film ends by asking whether the future has to be one of destruction.

One of the pilots who dropped the bomb on Nagasaki, Charles Sweeney, returned to the city soon after the war. His feelings were fairly straightforward, as far as this testimony allows, although more complex emotions may be hidden beneath his words:

'I took no pride or pleasure then, nor do I take any now, in the brutality of war, whether suffered by my people or those of another nation,' he wrote. 'Every life is precious. But I felt no remorse or guilt that I had bombed the city where I stood.'

'The true vessel of remorse and guilt belonged to the Japanese nation, which could and should call to account the warlords who so willingly offered up their own people to achieve their visions of greatness', he said.[242]

The American feature film *Above and Beyond* (1952) tells the story of Colonel Paul W. Tibbets, the B-29 pilot who was trained to release the atomic bomb on Hiroshima. Tibbets was played by the American actor Robert Taylor, who had served in the US Naval Air Corps during the Second World War, and was better-known for his starring roles in Westerns. A key scene depicts *Enola Gay* banking as it turns away from the blinding flash below, and the realisation of Tibbets of the magnitude of his task, now completed.

In his autobiography, Tibbets recalls how he felt about flying over Hiroshima to drop the bomb. 'In the buildings and on the streets there were people, of course':

but from 6 miles up they were invisible. To the men who fly the bombers, targets are inanimate, consisting of build-ings, bridges, docks, factories, railroad yards. The tragic consequences for humanity are erased from one's thoughts in wartime because war itself is a human tragedy.[243]

Such sensitivities raise questions about simplistic views of war-fare as the product of testosterone-driven machismo. In his play

Happy Birthday, Wanda June (1970), made into a film of the same name, Kurt Vonnegut introduces the fictional character of Colonel Looseleaf Harper, a pilot of the B-29 that bombed Nagasaki. Alongside the dark humour there are insights into war, connections with the macho hunter of wild animals, and hints of post-traumatic stress disorder. This is another trope about war in general and bombing in particular: it is an extension of competitive masculinity, a powerful sexual tendency to humiliate, dominate, destroy or control. As the writer Oliver Kamm argues, sometimes a lack of sophistication and negativity runs through Vonnegut's writings.[244] Men were peacemakers too. And those who facilitated the development of the atom bomb held nuanced views of it. During the Falklands War, moreover, Prime Minister Margaret Thatcher was gung-ho for military intervention compared with some male Conservative politicians whose objections to war were viewed as a 'deficiency in the spirit of machismo.'[245] Ultimately, the decision to drop the bomb was not taken lightly.

Paul Boyer argues that the atomic bomb became a powerful motif in post-war American culture. But any notion that the USA or the West in general was universally triumphant about the cataclysmic events in August 1945 is misleading.[246] Many who visited the country soon after the war were aghast at what they witnessed. In 1946, the journalist Martin Halliwell wrote a report for *The Spectator* magazine entitled 'December in Hiroshima', which asked a series of significant questions about the dropping of the atom bomb that are still discussed today:

> Would a bomb of such known destructive capacity, if ready say 6 months earlier, have been dropped without warning on a town in Europe? It is difficult to escape the feeling that the Japanese, by their remoteness from the

Western scene, have been regarded as teeming guinea-pigs for whom no particular pity need be felt. This is not of course a Christian conception.

Was a strategy worked out for the use of the atomic weapon, and who conceived the plan for dropping only two bombs, the second of which, at Nagasaki, was actually on a secondary target? It is again difficult to picture a responsible commander authorising the release of so novel an engine of destruction. Anywhere but on its primary target, or in the sea on the way home. (The Nagasaki bomb burst over the centre of the town and left the docks intact.)

Is there ultimately anything to choose between the Japanese massacre of 60,000 civilians in Manila, and the Allied massacre of 70,000 to 120,000 civilians in Hiroshima? The Japanese worked by hand, in cold blood, and were responsible for countless outrages against individuals, too horrible to describe; the Allies worked from the air, also in cold blood, and do not even care to know what suffering they caused.[247]

Halliwell was observing a landscape of devastation that would have moved most visitors to an emotional reaction. Less than eighteen months ago, Hiroshima had been a living noisy coastal city. Now its gutted terrain was slowly being repopulated and rebuilt, a haunted radioactive shadow of its former self. But his judgment was distorted. The comparison between Manila and Hiroshima was specious, given the wider geography of atrocities inflicted by Japan on its enemies. And there was certainly a lot 'to choose' between atomic bombing from a distance and the face-to-face slaughter of many millions of innocent civilians. The annihilation of Hiroshima was the product of what Hastings calls a total bomb for a total war.[248] The architects of the bomb knew that swift incineration of large numbers of people was inevitable, but preferable to the outcomes outlined above.

Conclusion

Cultural echoes of the Japanese military code still exist in contemporary Japan. In December 2016 during his visit to Pearl Harbor, the Japanese Prime Minister offered condolences but no apology for the attack in December 1941.[249] This is partly because he was pressured to show no remorse by many Japanese conservatives who accepted expressions of honour to the war dead, but felt it shameful to demonstrate contrition for acts of murder committed in combat. That US President Barack Obama did not apologise for the atomic bombing when he visited Hiroshima, including the Peace Park, in 2016 also lent the American-Japanese interactions an air of tit-for-tat.[250]

The absence of an apology offends the *hibakusha*, and challenges the pacifist view that mass casualties from area bombings can only have negative consequences. The atomic bombing seared into the Japanese national consciousness, providing an enduring and catastrophic reminder of their martial stubbornness. The American 'occupation' of defeated Japan, moreover, from 1945 to 1952 has been viewed by a number of revisionist historians as an essential, if sometimes complex, phase in the democratisation and modernisation of the land of the rising sun.[251]

In total, the Americans bombed 215 Japanese cities of varying size, killing over 330,000 people and destroying 2.3 million homes. Entire neighbourhoods were levelled to ashes while many cities had over half of their urban fabric swept away by fire and ruinous bombings.[252] The atomic bombings can be construed figuratively as two almighty exclamation marks at the conclusion of the air raids that Japan endured before its ignominious defeat. National identity was profoundly wounded by the attacks on Hiroshima and Nagasaki.[253] Across the urban lowlands of this mountainous and heavily forested country, furthermore, the immensity of the environmental destruction required extensive reconstruction. The next chapter focuses upon the three countries where bombing and its consequences was heaviest: Britain, Germany and Japan.

CHAPTER 6

The Global Phoenix: From Destruction to Reconstruction, 1945–60

'You have to give this much to the Luftwaffe: when it knocked down our buildings it didn't replace them with anything more offensive than rubble. We did that.' (Prince Charles, Mansion House speech attacking modern architecture and post-war town planning, 1987.)[254]

Introduction

Airborne destruction left large areas of towns and cities in heaps of rubble. Bombsites and ruined buildings created an almost apocalyptic landscape. All heavily-bombed urban areas faced significant housing shortages. Homelessness and overcrowding required immediate solutions. Broadly speaking, the years from 1945 to 1960 have been termed by urban and planning historians the era of post-war reconstruction. Alongside the clearing away and renewal of bombsites, government prioritised new housing

How to cite this book chapter:
Clapson, M. 2019. *The Blitz Companion*. Pp. 119–146. London: University of Westminster Press. DOI: https://doi.org/10.16997/book26.f. License: CC-BY-NC-ND 4.0

to address the accommodation crisis caused by both destruction but also the cessation of home building due to more pressing wartime priorities. New modern buildings and cityscapes were also embraced to promote visions of the future rather than remind citizens of the past. As Nick Tiratsoo argues, however, reconstruction was a *process*, involving politicians in central and local governments, architects, town planners, private interests and companies, and the wider public.[255] In a similar vein, Catherine Flinn argues that grand visions for post-war reconstruction were undermined by 'restraints and realities', a point she makes for Britain but which is relevant to all countries rebuilding themselves after 1945.[256]

In Britain, Germany and Japan the experience of reconstruction threw into relief the renewal of cities across the world. This chapter focuses upon key themes in their reconstruction, highlighting some key similarities and differences. It concludes by drawing out important global trends evident in reconstruction, and their interplay with national and local specificities in the reconstruction of bomb-damaged countries.

British Reconstruction

In May 1940, as Britain 'stood alone' against Nazi-occupied Europe, Churchill pushed through the Emergency Powers Act, empowering the state with unprecedented levels of control over both the public sphere and private lives. The extension of the state provided the broad context for growing debates about the need to plan. The government took on an enormous apparatus of powers from 1939 to 1940. There were ministries of supply, economic warfare, food, information, health, home security, labour, and works and buildings.

By 1941, as the bombs were still falling, a professional coalition of town planners, architects, politicians, civil servants, socialists, liberal reformers and left-wing journalists began to integrate the notion of a fairer society in post-war Britain with the re-planning and rebuilding of towns and cities. Following the 'People's War', nothing less than the modernisation of the built environment was promised as an essential component of the New Jerusalem, a brave new modern world that would arise from the rottenness of the blitzed and blighted city. Housing was at the heart of this reconstruction promise. A Mass Observation poll in 1945 found that homes and the need for many more of them eclipsed all other social policy issues among the British electorate. The Labour Party made the most elaborate promises for new-build homes per year, which goes a long way to explaining their election victory in 1945.[257]

A leading figure in the promotion of planning was Sir John Reith. The former director general of the BBC between the wars, Reith was an efficient administrator who became Minister of Works and Planning from 1940–2. Based in the bombed-out heart of the capital city, he famously called upon the London County Council (LCC) and other local authorities to 'plan boldly' when drawing up reconstruction schemes. Undertaken by the indubitably patrician architect-planner Sir Patrick Abercrombie, with the assistance of the architect J.H. Forshaw, the *County of London Plan* was published as early as 1943.[258] Its publication was promoted by the media and in exhibitions, signifying strongly to the public that this war would be won and a new London would be built from the ruins. Yet the *County of London Plan* was superseded by the much grander *Greater London Plan*, which also included the extensive suburban boroughs of outer London. Damage and destruction continued to be visited upon British cities towards the end of the war by the vengeance weapons. The *Greater London Plan* called for not only the reconstruction of central London and the renewal of blitzed and blighted areas, but for large new flat-filled housing estates, and an extensive new road infrastructure across the capital city to accommodate the growing demand for motor cars. Significantly it also endorsed the principle of decentralisation: of thinning out the population of London by 'decanting' mostly working-class households to large new council estates (social housing projects) built in the country-side beyond London.[259]

Abercrombie and Forshaw took centre stage in the educational film *London: The Proud City* (1946). Made for the Ministry of Information it outlined the ambitious reconstruction plans for the capital city to any members of the general public who cared to watch it. Yet despite the emphasis upon public information, which was replicated in other cities across Britain, the majority of the public were more motivated by the need for housing rather than by participation in planning. Apathy and self-interest were more common than an active interest in urban renewal. Most people had experienced the war as an interruption into normal-ity, and wanted a return to a comfortable private life as opposed to a new era of communal participation in architectural and town planning debates.[260]

Furthermore, despite the intellectual effort that informed the *Greater London Plan*, it was mostly never implemented. This can be explained to a large degree by the influence of powerful local landowners, party political differences on the LCC and continu-ing divisions between modernisers and traditionalists among the architects and towns planners of the LCC. The traditionalists wanted to rebuild in neo-classical, Victorian or Georgian styles, not the modern functional buildings that Prince Charles would later attack in his Mansion House speech. Furthermore, smaller competing local borough plans and improvement initiatives helped steer the Abercrombie Plan onto the rocks. Only the aptly named Churchill Gardens in Pimlico, an estate of modern flats near the River Thames, stands as a testament to what might have been. The reasons for the failure reflect what Adams and Larkham term 'a lack of joined-up thinking', a pragmatic planning culture rather than a clear and efficacious framework for implementation. One of the largest-scale modernisations of any western European city, to be rebuilt out of blitz and blight, never came to pass.[261]

The major conurbations of Birmingham, Glasgow and Manchester and the larger port cities of Bristol, Hull, and Liverpool, also required radical urban surgery after the war, as did the smaller port cities such as Plymouth, Portsmouth and Southampton. Medium-sized industrial cities were also re-planned as a consequence of the extensive destruction caused in 1940–1. Across Britain local authorities in blitzed towns and cities began preparations and plans for post-war rebuilding, although as Larkham and Lilley demonstrate, many local authorities did not produce plans at all.[262] A huge stimulus to post-war reconstruction planning was provided by the instigation of the Ministry of Town and Country Planning in 1943. As the Allies laid waste to German cities from 1943–5, the Ministry of Town and Country Planning was laying the foundations for British urban reconstruction.

The Labour Party, converted to interventionist Keynesian economics, and committed to the social policy reforms outlined in the Beveridge Report, became the major political vehicle for the boldest vision of reconstruction. Many leading Labour politicians also had links with the garden city movement.[263] While the

Labour Party general election manifesto in 1945 made no specific promises about the imminent apparatus of town planning, the Labour government passed two important pieces of legislation that would frame the reconstruction of post-war Britain: namely the New Towns Act of 1946 and the Town and Country Planning Act of 1947.

The New Towns Act created the first wave of fourteen British planned new towns: eight were introduced around London to relieve 'blitz and blight'. The London new towns alone housed over a million people by the end of the last century, proving that the Blitz had accelerated a longer-term trend in urban dispersal.[264] Although the conflict from 1939 to 1945 had created the opportunity for a programme of new towns, decentralisation was not a new idea born of the bomb and the need for thinner cities. The garden cities of Letchworth from 1903, and of Welwyn from 1919, were planned and built as antidotes to suburban sprawl and the chaotic industrial centres. They provided working models for the post-war new towns.[265] The interwar years also witnessed official debates about and enquiries into the urban problems of overcrowded, insanitary and polluted areas of Britain's industrial cities.[266] During the 1930s slum clearance programmes made some advances, although Nazi bombs would prove to be an effective slum remover.[267] Building new homes beyond the metropolis proved cheaper, because land was less expensive.

The new towns were planned according to zoning principles. Unlike the mixed-use town and city centres that had grown up over centuries, employment and industrial areas were zoned separately from residential districts, in order to prevent noise and pollution within safe housing areas. Again, this was a principle which had been pioneered at Letchworth and Welwyn Garden Cities, and in a number of municipal housing schemes between the wars, where housing was spatially separated from places of employment, and from the commercial activities of the town centre.[268]

Creating a sense of community in the new towns was an important element of social reconstruction. The residential areas were designed to American 'neighbourhood unit' principles, wherein facilities such as shops, schools, places of worship and recreational spaces were within walking distance from the front door. The neighbourhood unit was also viewed by socialist politicians as the right tool for recreating the 'Blitz spirit', the alleged mood of wartime unity across the class divide. As Lewis Silkin, the Minister for Town and Country Planning, argued to the House of Commons during the reading of the New Towns Act, the new towns were to be divided into neighbourhood units:

> each unit with its own shops, schools, open spaces, community halls, and other amenities. [I] am most anxious that the planning should be such that the different income groups living in the new towns will not be segregated. No doubt they may enjoy common recreational facilities, and take part in amateur theatricals, or each play their part in a health centre or a community centre. But when they leave to go home I do not want the better-off people to go to the right, and the less-well-off to go to the left. I want them to ask each other 'are you going my way?'[269]

Here in a speech to parliament was the idealised Blitz spirit of cross-class unity appropriated for a vision of egalitarian decentralisation. For Suzanne Cowan, however, politicians and planning officials often drew upon the myth of wartime unity to legitimise grand reconstruction schemes, despite little evidence of a galvanised egalitarianism within the post-war British class system.[270]

Meanwhile, what of the blitzed city centres? In the short term, even before the end of the war, prefabricated housing was introduced to whittle away at the edges of the housing shortage. Yet the wartime promise by Winston Churchill of half a million new 'prefabs' after the war was not met – only 157,623 had been built by 1949.[271] Even in towns which suffered relatively little bomb damage the moratorium on housing construction during the war led to the provision of prefabs as a temporary solution to the housing crisis.[272] But grander more permanent schemes were required. Many wartime and early post-war plans were drawn up for the bomb-damaged cities. Some were brave new urban worlds, grand visions for a modern townscape, which included the comprehensive redevelopment of bombsites. Others were significantly more modest in ambition, and across the country plans were implemented to varying degrees of success.

Classic examples of large-scale comprehensive redevelopment include Coventry City Centre, the Plan for Plymouth, the massive road-centred rebuilding of Birmingham, and the Barbican scheme in the City of London. The Barbican has been widely praised as a modernist vision for urban living. Drawn up by the architect-planners Chamberlin, Powell and Bon, it was a confident vision for city living to replace a massive bomb site. Completed during the late 1960s, hence later than most reconstruction projects, the Barbican may be viewed as a prototypical 'urban village' intended for 7,000 residents living and working in close proximity to the City of London. Its brutalist architecture and pioneering high-rise towers, however, have not been popular with traditionalists. Yet the quality of the buildings, and the success of the 'urban village' created there proved that large-scale planning superimposed onto an extensively bomb-damaged district, could work.[273]

In Coventry, the city centre was certainly completely redesigned and rebuilt according to the modernist plan by Donald Gibson. The reconstruction of this Midlands city was the most famous British example of comprehensive redevelopment. About 7 per cent of the city's housing stock had been destroyed by the Blitz so the council was under pressure to build lots of new homes, and quickly. Many living in Coventry yearned for a new city: 'The Jerries cleaned out the core of the city, a chaotic mess, and now we can start anew.'[274] The *Plan for Coventry* was being publicly discussed as early as 1942, and was steered into place after the war by a Labour council. Yet the new cityscape that emerged from the ruins threw into sharp relief the strengths but many weaknesses of modern town planning. By the mid-1950s Coventry had gained a smart new pedestrianized shopping precinct; modern department stores; an upgraded road system that replaced the mediaeval chaos of the older city centre, and large new housing estates comprised of terraced homes, semi-detached houses and blocks of flats. The new housing areas were designed to neighbourhood unit principles, as were the new towns, to foster a sense of local community. And in a gesture of confidence in the future, and of reconciliation with former enemies, the boldly designed new Coventry Cathedral was inaugurated in 1962, and is situated alongside the ruins of the older place of worship.[275]

Yet for many the city centre looked unimaginative and soulless, and by the 1970s it had a run-down appearance. As Tiratsoo has argued, the reconstruction of Coventry was influenced by a cautious socialist council during the early post-war years, by differences between the political parties on the council and their consequences for public expenditure, by financial constraints imposed from central government, and by conflict between the different ministries in government. During the 1950s the Conservative government rejected some of the proposals in the plan because they were considered too expensive.[276] A new city centre was constructed in Coventry, but it was hardly an expression of the gleaming New Jerusalem promised by the Labour Party in its general election campaign in 1945.

The only other city of comparable size to be comprehensively redeveloped on such a scale was the port city of Plymouth, where the architect-planner Sir Patrick Abercrombie was given sway. Plymouth had experienced over 600 air raid alerts; over 4,000 people were killed or injured. Over 22,000 properties were hit, 4,000 of them completely destroyed.[277] The city appears to have avoided many of the difficulties and problems facing planners elsewhere. The powerful political dynasty of Lord and Lady Astor explains much of this success, as they supported the scheme. The plan was robustly modern, containing provision for new housing neighbourhoods, a rationalised road system for the city centre and the outskirts, and many modern public and commercial buildings. Today, Plymouth city centre is a conservation area. Conversely, in Hull, the Abercrombie scheme met the same fate as the *Greater London Plan*: it was never properly implemented.[278]

The picture was uneven across the country, but similar issues affected other significant reconstruction schemes in other towns and cities where the results were often disappointing. In Birmingham, for example, the chief planner and architect Herbert Manzoni completely re-planned the city centre according to the principles of zoning. The retail areas were pedestrianised; slums were cleared away and modern housing estates comprising both houses and flats were built. But it was the road scheme for which Manzoni's plan became famous. He was influenced by the Swiss

modernist Le Corbusier, who had called for the clutter of narrow courts and small streets designed for the packhorse to be
swept away, to be replaced by modern streamlined thoroughfares
to facilitate the ever-growing number of motor cars. The inner
ring around the city centre and the dual carriageways from the
centre to the outskirts of small streets were superimposed upon
the bombed but historic landscape of urban-industrial Birmingham.[279]

The reconstruction of Birmingham continued into the 1960s,
when the iconic new Bull Ring shopping centre was unveiled.
Using oral testimonies, Adams and Larkham found that many
living in Birmingham during reconstruction were impressed and
proud at the new city arising from the ruins. Yet some memories
were also characterised by nostalgia for pre-war Birmingham,
and concern at the loss of surviving old buildings due to the radical nature of the plan.[280]

By the 1950s contemporary cultural critics bemoaned the slow-
ness of reconstruction, but were also critical of the loss of the
utopian vision at the end of the war. Bombsites were castigated
as 'horrid empty spaces', haunted by the ghosts of the dead and
of the communities that had existed before the bombs.[281] The
bombsites around St Paul's Cathedral, for example, were flagged
by critics of the government as proof that Britain was too slow to
rebuild.[282] It also appeared to have become not a vibrant egalitarian urban public community but a shabby inward-looking suburbia, the very thing that Angus Calder and others hated so much.
This was 'subtopia', the disappointing reversal of the utopia that
many had expected in 1945.[283] Yet there were good reasons for
this. Many plans were quite humdrum. Other more ambitious
visions for a brave new urban landscape were tempered by

financial constraints, by conflicts of interest between public and private organisations, by the changing political composition of the local councils, and sometimes simply because of a shortage of construction materials. A similar story unfolded in other countries

The Reconstruction of Urban Germany, 1945–60

> For ordinary Germans, the first priority was to clear the streets, and make houses habitable where it was possible, make new ones where it was not, and repair the utilities. But how? A fifth of the nation's men were dead, many were injured, traumatised, incapable of working: who was going to embark on the Herculean task of simply clearing the rubble from the endless ruins?[284]

The answer to the question lies partly in the German nation, but also in the United States of America, and to a lesser degree the British and the Soviet Union. Each of these powers controlled zones of occupation in a defeated Germany.[285]

As Jeffry Diefendorf has argued, possibly the biggest problem facing the post-war reconstruction of Germany was the absence of any effective German state until 1949, and therefore the dearth of any national framework of reconstruction.[286] The USA was the wealthiest of the occupying powers, but any notion that the Americans footed most of the bill for urban reconstruction is false.[287] In the contexts of housing construction, and the large scale rebuilding of bombed-out urban areas, the imprint of the American Military Government on urban Germany remained surprisingly modest. German reconstruction demonstrated some compelling similarities with the British experience. An obvious one was the pressing need for a massive house-building programme. Another was the tension between modern architecture and town planning compared with widespread support for traditional and historicist urban designs (The opening quote by Prince Charles shows him to be a traditionalist with historicist leanings). A further key similarity was the role of many different agencies and organisations seeking to influence or modify town plans.

Air raids on Germany left not only the built environment but the political structures of Nazism in ruins. The Americans attempted to modernise and democratise German town planning, within the wider context of political re-education and economic re-modelling. This created a tension between American forward thinking and a more conservative culture of German aspirations for the urban future. Within the context of rising tensions between the American and the Soviet zones in early post-war Germany, the US Military Government invited the leading modernist architect and town-planning consultant Walter Gropius to Berlin in August 1947. An émigré to the USA from interwar Germany, Gropius argued perceptively that 'there is a political corpse buried in Germany's rubble, and it is the job of reconstruction planners to ensure that it isn't revived.'[288] Viewing urban modernisation as compatible with democratisation, Gropius favoured the American small town ideal, with its open meetings and apparently active levels of neighbourliness and political participation.[289]

Urban planning and development in Germany had long been dominated by powerful local elites and a bureaucratic apparatus that the USA was barely able to modify. This was partly about American priorities, as urban policy was 'never a central concern' compared with the wider rehabilitation of democracy and the German economy.[290] But the severe housing shortage required urgent attention. The failure of the Nazi regime to provide a major house-building programme, and the influx of refugees, exacerbated the shortage of homes caused by air raids. It took Marshall Aid to kick-start the much-needed housing programme in West Germany, along with deficit financing.[291] Even then, the US administration was fairly modest in its investment. West Germany received $1,472 million in economic aid, significantly less than Great Britain or France, and only some of that was allocated for physical reconstruction.[292] There were also significant cultural and material differences between the Americans and Germans over the types of homes to be built. The US favoured the exporting of many modern prefabricated homes to Germany, and the use of lighter building materials, such as wood. The Germans preferred more solid traditional masonry and stone. As Diefendorf shows, however, the American authorities did manage to promote the building of cheaper modern houses and apartments. The construction of mass housing also assisted the recovery of the shattered German economy.[293]

Germany was not the sole preserve of the US Military Government, however. While the British, bankrupted by the war, were much less able to forge the modern future of Germany through finance and global influence than the USA, they were more energetic when it came to promoting a more centralised yet democratic town planning apparatus. In Hamburg, western Germany, where over 25 per cent of housing was damaged or destroyed by the Allies, post-war plans were already being drawn up before the war ended. The modernist planner Konstanty Gutschow, who had cooperated with the Nazis in urban design, was instrumental in drawing up a plan which decentralised a significant section of the population to a new 'city' alongside the River Elbe. The road system was modernised, including an autobahn ring road around

Hamburg. More green spaces were planned, and the housing shortage was addressed through a construction programme of high-density town housing and apartment blocks. The plans were completed after the war but were not as fully implemented as Gutschow would have liked. Nonetheless, Hamburg adopted a more comprehensive modern plan when compared with other German cities.[294] All across Germany, however, tensions between traditional rebuilding with historic-looking buildings and the pre-war street pattern versus a more modernist template permeated the architectural and town planning professions in Germany. This tension was also evident in German public opinion.

Public buildings in the smaller chocolate-box cities such as Lubeck were reconstructed to re-capture their historical heritage. This is termed facsimile reconstruction, where the emphasis of rebuilding is on continuity and the reminder of the past.[295] Hence in Munster, the town hall or Rathaus was rebuilt to resemble its pre-war medieval glory. This was referencing a romantic view of the past which many modernisers and American officials were suspicious of. Hence in other larger cities what Diefendorf terms 'the reconstruction of civic authority' meant bringing legitimacy to local government administrations many of whose personnel were associated with Nazi activities and oppression before liberation at the end of the war. In Stuttgart the nineteenth-century town hall was destroyed by bombing, and following a competition among local architects for the best design, in which no clear winner emerged, during the early 1950s the Lord Mayor pushed for a more modern design to represent the new city being built from the rubble, and the post-war spirit of democracy.[296] Nazi Germany had of course been a police state, so in some cities new police headquarters were also built to represent a break with the recent past. In Cologne an austere but elegant police building was opened in 1955. Praised by leading architectural and planning experts, the design was less popular with the mainstream media. And as Diefendorf argues, a distinct lack of public engagement in the merits or otherwise of the Police HQ possibly implied a reluctance to engage with the nature of policing under the Third Reich.[297]

In many major German cities the popular desire for historical continuity reflected a preference for the known and familiar city of the pre-war years. In Cologne in central Germany, and Munich, in the Bavarian Deep South, public opinion and many leading local professionals and organisations favoured an emphasis upon re-building to the traditional cityscape. Although this did not always occur, and many unpopular modern buildings were constructed, post-war re-planning emphasised the need to resurrect the character of vernacular architecture and the symbolic local and national importance of grandiose monumental buildings. In Cologne, furthermore, the Catholic Church assumed responsibility for repairs to the many churches damaged by the Allies. As Diefendorf argues, today some central city churches are underused, 'but they do constitute dominant features in the old heart of the city.'[298]

Among the most difficult urban reconstruction processes was that of Berlin, the ancient Prussian capital and the seat of Nazi power since 1933. Alongside the need to remove the imprint of the Third Reich, Berlin faced significant problems. Environmentally, the extent of its destruction was 'staggering'. Politically and administratively, Berlin was divided between East and West by 1949.[299] Hence post-war planners viewed the extent of the destruction as a significant opportunity to liberate Berlin from its reactionary past, and to create a visionary new modern city. As in other cities across Europe, however, grand ideas were confronted by practical difficulties. The Americans injected huge sums of reconstruction capital into West Berlin during the 1950s, following partition, prioritising modern factories, offices, retail and hotels. Housing was less of a priority, and the entrenched influence of traditionalists in town planning and architecture departments often acted as a bulwark to the modernisation project of the USA.[300]

In East Berlin, by contrast, austere modern buildings, workers flats and wide boulevards, notably the Stalin Allee, were viewed by many modernists on both sides of the Iron Curtain as an impressive modernisation of the urban landscape. By the end of the 1950s, architecture and town planning had become a 'battleground' in the German Cold War, with East and West Berlin trying to outdo each other with competitions for the regeneration of city districts. And in a belated, unwitting admission that prefabrication was required in communist East Germany, the Soviet leader Nikita Khrushchev called in 1954 for less-boastful Stalinist buildings and a drive for prefabrication and modern materials to address the lingering housing shortage.[301]

In East Germany, those living within the Soviet zone of occupation developed a more centralised and straightforward if undemocratic apparatus for reconstruction even before the establishment of the GDR in 1949. Following the passing of the 'law for rebuilding the cities of the German Democratic Republic and the capital of Berlin' in September 1950, the East German state undertook something of a land-grab of private holdings and property, often without compensation. Privately-owned housing was allowed to continue, but much of the land was nationalised.[302] In 1951, key areas of cities were designated for large-scale reconstruction plans. Properties required for reconstruction purposes were requisitioned by the Ministry for Planning, Building and the Building Industry. 'Derived in part from Soviet models' the GDR principles of reconstruction adopted a very different model from West Germany:

> They called for the immediate repair of designated war-damaged urban areas, restoring certain monuments of 'national' cultural importance, such as the Zwinger in Dresden, and construction representative arteries such as the Stalin Allee (later Karl-Marx-Allee) in Berlin. The sixteen principles called for the rebuilding of compact, dense cities with monumental, representative forums in modern form, including magisterial avenues and towers to serve as cultural centres and sites for political demonstrations. Clearly defined city centres and major squares were to define cities that were technically modern and socially responsible, reflecting the aims of the new socialist society.[303]

Hence communist reconstruction emphasised the unifying and symbolic importance of shared public space to a much greater degree than the West. Planners and politicians looked forward to 'model socialist cities' defined by a public socialist urbanity rather than Western privatism or the fascism associated with pre-war German cities. Dresden, to take a key example, saw some of its older central areas rebuilt within the German baroque style. City squares were redesigned to emphasise their public function, while some key buildings were left in ruins as reminders of what the Anglo-American Allies had inflicted upon the city, notably the *Frauenkirche*. Large-scale plans for Soviet-style blocks of worker's flats around the city centre were implemented to varying degrees, partly due to a failure by the local authority to fasten upon and implement a single strong plan. Even in a country with ostensibly more powerful governance, bold schemes were not always fully realised.[304]

Ultimately, how successful were German reconstruction efforts? As Diefendorf argues, there were many disappointments after 1945, evidenced by the failure to enact visionary plans, a rash of modest or unpopular houses and commercial and public buildings, and a sense that much of the fifteen years to 1960 had been a missed opportunity. On both sides of the German border the housing problem was close to a solution by the late 1950s, however: many significant housing programmes had created large residential areas of light, airy and often spacious apartments and town houses.[305]

Reconstructing the Japanese City, 1945–60

Partly in common with Germany, Japan was an 'occupied' country under the political and military jurisdiction of America until 1952.[306] An awesome task of reconstruction was initiated, demonstrating some key similarities with house building programmes and urban repairs in other countries. But this chapter also focuses upon the unique nature of Japanese urban rebuilding in the devastated landscapes of conventional and atomic bombing.

As Tiratsoo and his co-writers have argued, over 200 towns and conurbations in Japan were bombed by the Allies in the Second World War, and 115 of them were later officially designated as 'war-damaged cities':

By the time the conflict ended in 1945, destruction was immense: approximately 2.3 million houses (or 20 percent of the stock) destroyed or seriously damaged; 63,000 hectares of land burnt out; 330,000 persons killed and a 426,000 injured. The large cities were particularly badly affected. Tokyo suffered most, with 712,000 housing units damaged, followed by Osaka (311,000), Kobe (128,000) and Yokohama (98,000).[307]

The accomplishment of reconstruction was also immense. As Carola Hein argues, 'Japan's cities have risen from the utter destruction of the Second World War with astounding speed.'[308] In the immediate aftermath of war hundreds of thousands of wooden temporary homes were constructed, but in common with the prefabs in Britain and in other countries, these were mere patches over a critical nationwide housing shortage. Most of the reconstruction projects in Japan were pragmatic and piecemeal, concerned to provide low-rise cheaply-built wooden housing, erect new public and commercial buildings, and renew roads, railways and manufacturing plants. A much larger solution was required for the longer term, hence in December 1945 the National Government had established the guidelines for the Policy for the Reconstruction of War-Damaged Areas, embracing building methods, land-use planning, modern construction materials and higher construction standards.[309] Its record would prove to be uneven.

The reconstruction plans for Tokyo and Osaka, both large conurbations, were initially ambitious but, in common with the Abercrombie Plan for London for example, went largely un-realised. The reconstruction of smaller cities in Japan demonstrated some important similarities with post-war planning projects in other countries, while highlighting some specificities of the Japanese path towards urban modernisation in the decade following the end of the Second World War. The vast majority of the millions of homes built during the reconstruction era of 1945–55 resembled much of the pre-war housing destroyed by conventional and atomic bombing: 'flimsy wooden constructions and slum-type housing dominated many areas until the 1960s.' The modern high-rises and the emergence of mass apartment-style housing now so prominent in Japan was a product of the 1960s and since, not the era of reconstruction.[310]

Under the auspices of the Americans, the Japanese Cabinet appointed the War-Damage Rehabilitation Board (WRB) in October 1945 to oversee reconstruction and in particular accelerate the drive to build much-needed homes. Local newspapers in Japan were important voices both in promoting public interest in re-planning and in calling for local needs to be addressed as quickly as possible.[311] Town planning was not only a local and national activity. International diffusion of town planning and architectural theories and concepts between the wars had influenced pioneering modern Japanese town planners. The post-war planning of Tokyo, for example, was led by Hideaki Ishikawa, a long-standing head of the Tokyo Metropolitan Government town planning department. He had been active in overseeing the enactment of the Air Defence Act (1937) for the capital city, which called for more open spaces to be given over to military use, and for the arrangement of evacuation procedures, fire-fighting and other aspects of the civil defence apparatus. After the devastation wrought by the USAAF over Tokyo, Ishikawa drew up the post-Blitz comprehensive plan, calling upon Anglo-American town planning principles that emphasised zoning, neighbourhoods, and road planning for motor traffic. A significant improvement to the badly damaged railway network was also called for. The Tokyo Local Town Planning Committee first met in March 1946 and worked with the WRB, other government ministries, and private and commercial organisations, to promote house building and the new plan. But implementation problems soon arose. Despite the efforts of newspapers, public involvement in planning was 'very limited', echoing British experience. The WRB was sometimes riven with tensions between new post-war officials suspicious of continuing pre-war civil servants associated with the militant nationalism of the 1930s. The organisation sometimes also suffered with insufficient funding from government, which affected its ability to negotiate land-readjustment schemes required for new-build, and a close relationship with local town councils and prefectures was not always forthcoming.[312] Only one third of the destroyed homes in Tokyo had been rebuilt by 1949. An Emergency Housing Plan of 1945, furthermore, to provide over 300,000 emergency prefabricated homes was largely a failure by 1949.[313] And in that year the so-called 'Dodge Line', a new financial regime imposed by the USA, also cut back on reconstruction expenditure. Tokyo had hardly advanced in the years since 1945, except for the growing sprawl of cheap housing, often in shanty towns and overcrowded residential areas, to accommodate the homeless, and the growing number of Japanese families.[314] Hence reconstruction enables us to understand why, today, 'Japan's large cities are made up of dense, vital, apparently unplanned neighbourhoods.'[315]

The re-planning of Osaka, the 'second city' of Japan, shared some key similarities with Tokyo. Osaka was the leading and industrial and commercial centre in Japan by 1939, subsequently enduring over thirty heavy bombing raids in 1945. Osaka lost over 310,000 homes and over 50 square kilometres of the built-up area were damaged or destroyed. As in Tokyo the local version of the newspaper *Asahi Shinbun* began a series on the need for reconstruction as early as August 1945, and ambitious plans for a bright new Osaka were drawn up. These were to be implemented by the City Corporation Reconstruction Section, the Osaka Local Town Planning Committee, the WRB and various government ministries. Yet conflict between the different wards, tensions between more cautious conservative politicians and the socialist mayor, and shortages of labour, material and money conspired to reduce the effectiveness of the plans by 1950.[316]

The re-planning of metropolitan Tokyo and Osaka was vastly different in scale to reconstruction in smaller provincial cities, yet bold visions for smaller urban centres in Japan were also modified by time and process. Nagoaka, an inland city with a population of less than 75,000 people in 1945, was visited by the USAAF on the first two nights of August 1945, razing most of the city centre to the ground. Almost immediately after the war's end planning became an important subject of local debate, with the original schemes calling for comprehensive land-use planning and a more modern cityscape. A Reconstruction Measures Committee for Nagoaka was established. Local newspapers enthused about the new vision. The plan was originally based upon rigid zoning between residential, 'exclusive commerce', commerce, heavy industry, light industry, railways, public buildings and new green spaces. A new commercial district in the centre, high-density dispersed residential areas towards the outskirts, and upgraded roads and railways were at the heart of the plan, which was approved by the WRB in July 1946. Divisions between the planners, however, a sometimes dilatory attitude by local authorities, and obstinate landowners objecting to land-use changes, all led to modifications in land-readjustment, street layouts, and a reduction in the original scale and scope of the plan. Nagaoka was declared the first Japanese city to be reconstructed by 1953, but in reality the process was by no means ended.[317]

Difficulties in implementation affected other medium-sized Japanese cities. At Maebashi, for example, an original plan was drawn up by Kenzo Tange, who would go on to design the Hiroshima Memorial Peace Park, and become one of the most influential modern architects in Japan. Yet public distrust and even opposition to his plans, financial concerns, anger at compensation payments for land-use changes, and also the 'folly' of wide new roads which evidenced a possible cultural affection for the older pre-war street pattern, encapsulated public suspicions, many of which were aired in open meetings. It took a more united front between the city council, the WRB and the Ministry of Construction, based in Tokyo, to get a less illustrious plan implemented by the mid-1950s.[318] And in Sendai, early post-war planning for the width and route of a major stretch of road revealed sharp differences in public opinion, the power of vested interests of local landowners, and local scandals over funding and bribery.[319]

In common with Germany, the renewal of cities and the construction of public buildings to promote a newer more democratic urban society was often a delicate matter. Japanese national pride had been severely wounded by the defeat, and grand symbolic reconstruction projects symbolising modernity, or an 'out-with-the-old, in-with-the-new' mentality were not deemed appropriate. As Hein argues, this was in contradistinction with some of the bolder urban renewal schemes in heavily-bombed European cities in the Netherlands and Poland.[320]

Reconstruction: Some Wider Conclusions

The built environments of Britain, Germany and Japan were ostensibly 'reconstructed' by the end of the 1950s. In each country, despite the difficulties outlined above, the housing shortage had been addressed, but by no means completely solved. In Britain, the Labour governments of 1945–51 failed to build enough houses, a reason why Labour lost the general election in 1951. Conservative governments of the 1950s prioritised home building, with some success.[321] In East and West Germany, an impressive number of homes were built by 1960, and in Japan piecemeal urban extensions and myriad planned new suburban settlements mostly accommodated a rapidly growing post-war population.

In post-war Europe, urban reconstruction also played a significant role in the modernisation of urban landscapes, and in stimulating economic growth through the multiplier effect of large-scale construction industries demanding primary and secondary goods and a massive labour supply. In Germany, however, as in Japan, the rebuilding of the bombed-out towns and cities possessed other layers of significance. A new urban environment was part of an American project to remodel former reactionary systems of rule, and the citizenries under them, into democracy, modernity and prosperity. This powerful synthesis of post-war imperatives was intended to negate atavistic politics and more immediately to act as a bulwark to communist influence during the early Cold War.

Key themes and issues in reconstruction identified in Britain, Germany and Japan also moulded the character of reconstruction in two countries with political traditions of strong state intervention, namely Soviet Russia in Eastern Europe, and France in the west. In France, the state took a more consistent centralist and managerial position towards reconstruction project areas. In the heavily-bombed north-east, the French Minister for Reconstruction deemed the Alsace-Lorraine region to 'have suffered most of all'.[322] Yet even in the country of the *grand projet*, a combination of practical and political problems mediated the outcomes. As Hugh Clout argues, 'before definitive reconstruction might begin':

> a vast array of emergency tasks had to be accomplished, which included investigating the extent of the damage, organising labour, clearing rubble and ruins, making urgent repairs, installing temporary accommodation, employing architects and planners to prepare master plans [and] finding accountants to verify claims for compensation.[323]

A cultural preference for vernacular architecture in the Alsace region also undermined a much-vaunted plan for Saint-Dié, drawn up by Le Corbusier, but in the Lorraine by contrast reconstruction eventuated in a 'mundane functionalism' characterising much of the built environment by 1960.[324]

In the Soviet Union, following the 'Great Patriotic War' huge areas of urban-industrial regions lay in ruins. Stalin placed great emphasis upon social unity to act as the glue for what would be a vast reconstruction project across the war-damaged regions. In common with Britain, to a degree, victory became part of the 'foundational myth' for Soviet society, a celebration of triumph that was to transcend sectional differences and accompany modernisation. Yet the myth of national unity as a foundation for post-war reconstruction in Soviet Russia has been critically interrogated, with propaganda far in excess of popular enthusiasm for the wartime re-planning and reconstruction programmes.[325]

Soviet cities were planned to be standardised, but to include inspiring and rational spaces for a productive, engaged but never challenging proletariat. Across the communist world, post-conflict cities were reconstructed according to Soviet-style planning principles. In Poland, for example, Warsaw had suffered terribly during the war. Its renewal was adopted by the Soviet authorities as a potent symbolic of communist renewal from the ashes of barbaric fascism, and as an egalitarian alternative to western capitalism.[326]

But socialist planning was also beset by internal divisions and practical problems across the eastern bloc. The plan for Warsaw 'was focused on the value of bringing back what was to be erased', namely the historical pre-war image of the city destroyed by the German and Soviet air raids.[327] In the port-city of Gdansk, by contrast, as with bombed-out maritime cities in other countries, reconstruction became a more nuanced process of balancing the pre-war heritage with 'the new urban thinking of Modernism' in its overall urban design.[328] Soviet town planning was exported without any meaningful public consultation across the USSR and later to other communist countries. As the following chapter shows, post-war North Korea and Vietnam were also influenced by Soviet-style urban reconstruction.

Ultimately, the global phoenix was an international manifestation of urban resilience. As Vale and Campanella have argued, no matter what might be thrown at them from the air, 'cities are among humankind's most durable artefacts':

> Whether they are reconstructed to accommodate and restore ongoing urban life or rebuilt to serve as sites for periodic visitation and commemoration, it has become exceedingly rare for a major city to be truly or permanently lost.[329]

Lessons from the reconstruction of post-blitzed cities have wider relevance to other major disasters visited upon urban areas, whether by earthquakes, hurricanes or tsunamis. Most of all, they have thrown up key themes in the reconstruction of cities destroyed in conflicts since the Second World War. Those themes are clear. Destruction creates new opportunities for urban renewal. Planning for the post-war era becomes a policy imperative even while the conflict is raging. Plans are implemented to varying degrees of success due to social, economic, political and practical pressures. Housing is always a priority in reconstruction due to the loss of homes during conflict. Cities and their surviving citizens become experiments for new directions in architecture and urban design, experiments often mediated by a desire to rebuild the pre-war cityscape. This last point reminds us that cities are also sites of a violent disruption to the urban fabric and to people's experience and memories of their city. These themes deserve to be continually emphasised by historians lest their significance become neglected in urban development born of trauma.

CHAPTER 7

American Bombing of
Civilians since 1945

Introduction

This chapter assesses the nature and consequences of American
air campaigns since 1945, and their impact upon people and
urban places. The Korean War from 1950 to 1953 and American
involvement in the Vietnamese War from the mid-1960s until
1973 witnessed extensive air raids whose efficacy and legitimacy
has been interrogated by historians since. The broader contexts of
these conflicts were the legacy of European and Japanese imperialism, and the polarisation between communism and capitalism

How to cite this book chapter:
Clapson, M. 2019. *The Blitz Companion*. Pp. 147–172. London: University of
    Westminster Press. DOI: https://doi.org/10.16997/book26.g. License:
    CC-BY-NC-ND 4.0

that defined the Cold War. Following the collapse of Soviet Communism in Eastern and Central Europe, however, the Americans also participated in the NATO air raids during the Balkan Wars (sometimes referred to as the Yugoslavian Wars during the 1990s). So did the British and other member countries of NATO but the USA has been the target of most of the criticism of the bombings since. In the Middle East following the terrorist attacks on New York in September 2001, the USA also took the lead in UN actions to defeat the dictatorship in Iraq, and later in Libya and Syria. The USA has also been active in attacking the Taliban in Afghanistan and Pakistan, sometimes with tragic consequences for the local populations.

The Korean War

The causes of the Korean War are complex. As the world was divided between capitalist and communist blocs, Korea became a site of brutal conflict in the war for hegemony between western and communist expansionism. The Korean Peninsula had been fought over by both the Chinese and the Japanese, and Korea became a Japanese 'protectorate' during the early years of the twentieth century. From the Korean perspective the Second World War was effectively a war of liberation from Japanese occupation, but following the defeat of Japan, Soviet Russia installed the North Korean guerrilla leader Kim Il-sung as the new head of state. He had fought the Japanese both before and during the Second World War, an unlikely ally of the Americans who from 1945 supported South Korea. In other words, a former ally became the new enemy.[330]

Some five years after the horrors of the Second World War came to an end, the Korean peninsula was thrown into a terrible conflict that cost millions of lives, caused hundreds of thousands of casualties and created an eastern version of the Iron Curtain between North and South Korea. The crossing of the thirty-eighth parallel into North Korea, by UN forces led by the American General Douglas MacArthur, was rebutted by a Chinese invasion across the Yalu River, forcing the Americans south.[331] Subsequently, the USA successfully helped to defend South Korea from the communist invasion during the summer of 1950, but from the winter of 1950–1 the situation deteriorated, leading the USA and their allies to engage in an aggressive and prolonged air campaign over the Korean peninsula. A Movietone newsreel in 1950 was titled *Korea: Air Blitz Checks Reds* is further evidence of transnational application of the word during the early Cold War.[332]

'What hardly any Americans know or remember', argues the American historian Bruce Cumings:

> is that we carpet bombed the North for three years with next to no concern for civilian casualties. [The] air assaults ranged from the widespread and continual use of fire-bombing (mainly with napalm) to threats to use nuclear and chemical weapon, finally to the destruction of huge North Korean dams in the last stages of the war.[333]

Cumings goes on to argue that the air war on Korean civilians was an extension of the air campaigns against Germany and Japan during the Second World War, but in contrast to those urban-industrial societies, North Korea was an agrarian third world country.[334] One such example was the attack on the German dams by the RAF and the USAF destruction of dams in North Korea toward the end of the war. In May 1953 the Americans bombed five large dams, causing major flooding, wiping away roads and railways, saturating rice fields and drowning many people.[335]

A further criticism points to American hypocrisy, and the US condemnation of German and Japanese atrocities against civilians while claiming justification for Allied bombing raids in the Second World War. Now from 1950 it applied a conventional bombing strategy to North Korean cities. American military leaders, including General MacArthur, expressed reservations about civilian casualties and the resultant negative propaganda, calling for precision bombing of military targets. Despite a strategic distinction between legitimate military objectives and the need to avoid civilians, 'a dynamic of escalation' led to the mass bombing and burning of key cities such as Sinuiju, Kanggye, Manpojin and the later capital of North Korea, Pyongyang.[336]

In his magisterial history of the Korean War, Hastings comes to similar but less condemnatory conclusions. He agrees that airborne destruction of almost all towns and cities of any size in the Korean peninsula, the bombing of industry and infrastructure, and the terrible losses of civilian population caused by air raids, failed in the most important sense, because there was no victory of the UN in North Korea. Hastings concludes that the lessons from the Second World War were being unlearned as 'intensive strategic bombing could kill large numbers of civilians':

> without decisive impact upon the battlefield or even upon the war-making capacity of an industrial power. Bombing could inflict a catastrophe upon a nation without defeating it. North Korea was a relatively primitive society which contained only a fraction of the identifiable or worthwhile targets of Germany or Japan.[337]

The inevitability of mass civilian deaths in the context of mass bombing led to a parallel propaganda war between communists and western governments. Communists in Britain, for example, tried to persuade public opinion that the aggression was the sole preserve of the USA and their British allies. The *Daily Worker*, the newspaper of the Communist Party of Great Britain (CPGB), ran many articles on the barbarity of American and British military actions in North Korea. One of its contributors, Monica Felton, an outspoken critic of American and British bombing. A civil serv-ant and town planner, in 1951 Felton famously walked off the job as 'Chairman' of Stevenage New Town Development Corporation to travel to North Korea with the Soviet-backed Women's Inter-national Democratic Federation. In her self-published pamphlet *What I Saw in Korea* (1951), she countered what she saw as the cynical reluctance of British newspapers to 'tell the truth' about the Korean War. She elaborated in merciless detail on the destruc-tion of towns and villages, the slaughter of women and children, the wrecking of Christian churches, the bombardment of hospi-tals, schools, public buildings and shops, the institutions of eve-ryday life that were vulnerable against the might of American air power, claiming 'we did not see one place that that had not been completely and utterly destroyed'. She described the deaths and devastation in the city of Sinuiju, 'about as large as Wolver-hampton', which was in complete ruin.[338] The comparison with Wolverhampton, a sizeable industrial city in the Midlands, was to indicate the scale of the destruction to her British readers through a familiar reference. 'Korea today is a ruin so absolute' she wrote, 'that no one can see it without getting the most clear and terrible warning of what a third world war would inevitably mean.'[339] In linking the American bombings in Korea to the spectre of nuclear catastrophe, just six years following the atomic bombings of Hiro-shima and Nagasaki, Felton strengthened her position a leading woman peace campaigner, with a growing following in Japan.[340]

How did the North Koreans respond to this sustained assault from the air? The American historian Bradley K. Martin shows that just as North Korean and Chinese soldiers built a network of military tunnels, 'civilians likewise dug into mountainsides to construct underground factories that could withstand bombing raids. Children, according to official accounts, kept going to school during the war "while their pencil cases rattled"'. As Martin also argues, however, according to the testimony of defectors from the subsequent regime, most North Koreans were so war-weary they just wanted the conflict to end, no matter which side prevailed.[341]

For some US historians the terrible death toll resulting from the Korean War amounted to nothing less than an 'American holocaust'.[342] Over 40,000 Americans were killed, a figure that includes over eight thousand missing in action. South Korea endured over 1.3 million casualties including 415,000 deaths, while North Korean casualties numbered about 2 million, including 1 million civilians and over 520,000 soldiers. About 900,000 Chinese soldiers perished in the conflict.[343] Many of the civilians in the North were killed by bombing, but many were also killed by soldiers, illness and starvation.

As with previous modern wars, widespread destruction presaged renewal. North Korean urban areas became the context for a massive programme of reconstruction, financed partly and with some practical assistance from communist allies. Pyongyang and other cities were planned according to the Soviet theory of the 'microdistrict' which emerged in Russian town planning during the mid-1950s. This resulted in model housing estates based around 'an integrated model' that emphasised standardised modern housing, and the social control of everyday life based on the arrangement of urban public space. Built from the mid-1950s until the mid-1970s, North Korean residential dwellings took the form of row-housing or large Soviet-style blocks of medium-rise flats organised around open spaces and communal facilities.[344] Beyond these modern developments, however, much of small-town North Korea and the rural areas remained mired in inadequate housing, while the elite enjoyed superior residential conditions.[345]

The American bombing left other legacies, one being a lasting hatred of the USA in North Korea, which has since been continuously exploited and stimulated by the regimes of Kim Il Sung, Kim Jong Il, and now Kim Jong Un. As a number of writers, including Christopher Hitchens have observed, North Korea is the closest approximation to the totalitarian hell that George Orwell described in his novel 1984, where the television is a propagandist tool of the state, constantly mobilising its people to hate and to prepare for war with the USA.[346] This oppressive totalitarian society is also overlaid by hideous levels of poverty.[347]

It is pause for thought that had the United Nations successfully destroyed the communist forces in Korea by 1953 – the counterfactual scenario – the entire peninsula might have followed the path of South Korea. While the North placed itself on permanent war footing, repeatedly reminding its citizens of the threat of American nuclear or conventional attack from the air, the South became a strong ally of the USA. Since the end of the Korean War, it transitioned through authoritarian regimes to the greater levels of social and political freedoms enjoyed since the 1980s, the decade when the South Korean economy became one of the fastest growing in Asia. These achievements helped to explain the International Olympic Committee's decision to award the

Olympic Games to the South Korean capital, Seoul, in 1988, despite the background threat of North Korean air strikes. Such threats have lasted to this day.

From Korea to Vietnam

The Korean War was a relatively short-lived conflict compared with the history of military intervention in Vietnam. The origins of the Vietnam War predated the Korean War and lasted long after the DPRK and South Korea ceased direct hostilities. The Vietnam War was in no small part a legacy of French colonial rule, which was followed by the occupation of Vietnam by the Japanese during the Second World War. The French collaborated with the Japanese in a colonialist echo of Vichy betrayal. During that conflict the communist Ho Chi Minh had assisted the Allies in fighting the Japanese in Vietnam but as with Korea, those who fought for liberation now turned against Western imperialism. In the years after the Second World War, Vietnam was divided into two countries, the communist North and the American-backed South.

In 1946, less than year following the end of the Second World War, the First Indochina War began. Despite collaborating with the Japanese occupation, following the Potsdam Conference France was reinstated as the colonial ruler with the assistance of Britain and the USA. The Viet Minh, led by Ho Chi Minh and supported by Soviet Russia, resisted. So too did the People's Army of Vietnam (PAV), led by Vo Nguyen Giap. The Viet Minh had been fighting during the Second World War against the Japanese occupation of the French colony of Vietnam, and on VJ Day even initiated a short-lived government in Hanoi, the Democratic

Republic of Vietnam. This was routed by the French, leading to a guerrilla war which the Viet Minh fought from their strongholds in the villages of rural North Vietnam while French forces occupied the cities. A decisive turn came in 1949 when Communist China also began to support the Viet Minh against perceived French imperialism. Despite support from the Americans, the French lost the war to the communist forces in 1954 following the ignominious defeat at the Battle of Dien Bien Phu. A lack of air support from the USA for French forces helps to explain this defeat, as did significant Chinese support for the Viet Minh.[348] In 1955, the Vietnam War began. It would last for nineteen and a half years, and cost 3.8 million lives.[349]

The Geneva Accords signed between France and Vietnam established a communist government in North Vietnam on one side of the demilitarised zone, and transitional arrangements for the South on the other. French forces withdrew completely from Vietnam. From 1956 South Vietnam came under the authoritarian government of Ngo Dinh Diem, causing Vietnamese communists in the South, the Viet Cong, to fight a clandestine war for unity with the North. In 1960 North Vietnam set up the National Liberation Front, mostly made up of Viet Cong combatants. The United States, which had been assisting the Diem government, became increasingly drawn into the war on communism in the North, and increasingly frustrated with the Diem government. The USA was party to the assassination of Diem in 1963, and when Vietnamese torpedo boats attacked the USS *Maddox* in the Gulf of Tonkin in August 1964, the subsequent Gulf of Tonkin Resolution escalated the American military campaign in Vietnam.[350] Further civilian catastrophes lay ahead.

The Bombing of Vietnamese Military and Civilian Targets

Air power was crucial to the escalation of the US war in Vietnam. Given its superior economic and military might the USA appeared to have a significant advantage over the Vietcong. American soldiers were better equipped, trained and fed than their enemies, but more importantly, the USA waged a hi-tech war: its B-52 bombers were superior to the B-29, and supplemented by fleets of combat helicopters. During its major air campaigns in Vietnam the USA deployed an aerial arsenal comprising dumb bombs, guided bombs and missiles, air explosive devices, napalm and the defoliant 'Agent Orange'. The first significant American bombing campaign in Vietnam began in March 1965 and terminated in October 1968, Code-named 'Operation Rolling Thunder', it was dubbed 'The Vietnam Blitz' by Movietone.[351]

Operation Rolling Thunder

President Lyndon B. Johnson had been sworn into office following the assassination of John F. Kennedy in November 1963. His Secretary of Defence was Robert J. McNamara, an advocate of air power. During his time at the White House he presided, sometimes reluctantly, over Operation Rolling Thunder, the longest bombing campaign in the history of the United States Air Force (USAF). Its key intention was to disrupt and degrade supplies to the enemy by targeting fuel storage facilities, power plants, warehouses, steel works, military installations and army barracks, and infrastructure.[352] From 1965, Operation Rolling Thunder was accompanied by the first boots-on-the-ground deployment of

American troops, who fought simultaneously against communist forces in South Vietnam.

With assistance from the USSR, the North Vietnamese managed to construct an air-defence system and a civil defence apparatus. Using surface-to-air missiles, and with the support of Russian MIG fighters, the North Vietnamese brought down hundreds of American B-52s. Civilians and active combatants created an improvised network of tunnels and shelters, a continuation of the defensive strategy witnessed in earlier total wars. Civilian workers also assisted emergency workers to repair infrastructure damaged by bombs, a further manifestation of the 'people's army' trope used in 1939–45. This demonstrated a degree of resilience in the face of heavy odds.[353]

American peace activists were keen to report the tragic consequences of air raids on the very people the bombs were intended to liberate. In October 1966 David Dellinger visited Phy Ly, a city with a population of over 10,000 people, described as a 'Vietnamese Guernica'. That Guernica was bombed by the airplanes of a fascist dictatorship at the behest of a fascist leader, while the USA was a democracy raises many moral questions, but the main point Dellinger wished to transmit was that when women and children were killed and horribly maimed, when straw huts, temples and churches were destroyed by the USAF, the Viet Cong gained in support, as did anti-American sentiment.[354]

Dellinger was not the only peace activist in Vietnam during Operation Rolling Thunder. The American folk singer and peace activist Joan Baez was in Hanoi during a major air raid. Her attempt to sing the Lord's Prayer at a Christmas Service in 1966 was interrupted by the wail of an air raid siren. It was the first of twelve days of air raids that the Vietnamese were subjected to, with Baez as their sympathetic witness. In her interview with *Rolling Stone*, magazine Baez recalled her recent experiences of debris, bomb craters, of dead and dismembered people. She painted a picture of Vietnamese citizens carrying bicycles to negotiate the rubble; an old man hobbling with difficulty through the wreckage; of women crying but defiant: 'Nearby there was a bomb shelter that had taken a direct hit. Everyone was dead.'[355]

Rolling Thunder has been mostly adjudged a failure by military historians when measured against its intentions to destroy the military, industrial and communications capacities of communist forces in Vietnam.[356] The USAF suffered significant losses of air crew and aircraft, and many Americans were captured to endure the hell of becoming prisoners of war. In 1968 President Johnson called for a termination of the campaign, as its lack of success became cruelly apparent in harrowing spectre of American servicemen returning in body bags from the conflict. Despite this very recent and humbling lesson, however, his successor in the White House viewed bombing, and lots of it, as an essential strategy to winning the war.[357]

Operation Menu

President Richard M. Nixon took office in November 1968. Robert McNamara was replaced by Henry Kissinger as Defence Secretary. Nixon had promised to end the war within months, but as 1969 progressed he became deeply frustrated at the failure of the American military to end the ongoing North Vietnamese offensive. Taking advice from Kissinger, Nixon considered that the neighbouring countries of Cambodia and Laos were aiding the People's Army of North Vietnam and the Viet Cong, Nixon authorised Operation Menu, a prolonged and supposedly secret air campaign that lasted from March 1969 to May 1970. Targeting Laos and mostly eastern Cambodia, the campaign extended the sphere of conflict beyond Vietnam. The operation partly ran alongside an unsuccessful US-South Vietnamese invasion of Cambodia to capture or destroy North Vietnamese positions.[358]

Operation Menu was subdivided into smaller raids aimed at specific bases code-named as 'Lunch' 'Snack', 'Dinner', 'Supper' and 'Dessert'. Historians disagree on the military achievements or otherwise of Operation Menu, but some firm conclusions have been drawn by social historians: the Cambodian bombing led to terrible consequences for the people of Cambodia in the subsequent regime of Pol Pot; reinvigorated the anti-war protests in the USA, and gravely damaged the American image across the world.[359]

Operation Linebacker

By 1971 Nixon was increasingly frustrated with the lack of success and the growing unpopularity of the war in the United States. A policy of 'Vietnamization', of increasingly allowing the Vietnamese to take control of the conflict as the USA pulled back, was also undermined by the weaknesses of the South Vietnamese army. As Nixon shouted during a taped Oval Office conversation between himself and Kissinger on 2 June 1971, 'we're not gonna go out whimpering ... we're gonna take out the power plants, we're gonna take out Haiphong, we're gonna level that goddam country.'[360]

The almost impotent rage of the world's most powerful man became tragi-comically apparent as the North Vietnamese launched the Spring Offensive of 1972 against American ground forces. Nixon opted for an intensification of the bombing campaigns on the capital Hanoi, its chief port city of Haiphong and other key cities and battlefields where the North Vietnamese were holding sway. B-52 bombers fighter bombers attacked Haiphong Harbour and petroleum storage facilities near Hanoi.[361] In a recorded Oval Office conversation between the president and Kissinger on 25 April 1972, the potential consequences of bombing the docks and key oil and petroleum plants had been laid bare:

> Kissinger: That will drown about 200,000 people [unclear]… [The volume of Kissinger's voice perceptibly drops at this point].
>
> Nixon: Well, no, no, no, no, no. I'd rather use a nuclear bomb. Have you got that ready?
>
> Kissinger: Now that, I think, would just be, uh, too much, uh…
>
> Nixon: A nuclear bomb, does that bother you? [I] just want you to think big Henry, for Christ's sake [said in an animated, angry-sounding tone of voice].[362]

The Linebacker campaign was in two phases, culminating in the Christmas bombings from 18 December to 22 December 1972. Nixon was angry that the ongoing pattern of hostilities and negotiations had achieved little, arguing that 'only the strongest action would have any effect in convincing Hanoi that negotiating a fair settlement with us was a better option for them than continuing the war.'[363] The Christmas bombings, a term with distant echoes of the Luftwaffe strikes on London some thirty-two years earlier, was made up of over 700 sorties by the B-52s, targeting railways stations, storage depots, rail lines, and the electricity supply. According to both Mark Clodfelter and Tucker, over 15,000 tons of bombs were dropped in a fairly accurate campaign that hit military targets while leaving adjacent residential areas mostly intact. Nonetheless, civilian mortalities still numbered 1,138 in Hanoi and 305 in Haiphong. Witnesses said that many buses evacuated the citizens of Hanoi into the nearby countryside, an echo of the trekking seen in so many air raids.[364]

Linebacker II 'did unsettle the North's urban populace.' Many North Vietnamese people were disorientated and suffering from sleep problems, 'their nerves strained by the continual attacks.'[365] Clodfelter was writing during the 1980s. Some years later a revisionist teaching text argued that the Christmas bombings saw 36,000 tons of explosives, more bombs than were dropped during the fourteen months of Operation Menu. According to this revisionist estimate, about 1,600 civilians were killed in Hanoi and Haiphong, and many were injured. Whatever the exact figures, the Christmas attacks contributed to a resuscitation of peace talks, but also led to a sharp fall in the popularity of Nixon, who was increasingly seen by many critics of the war as a madman.[366]

Such was the view of the actress Jane Fonda who visited Hanoi in August 1972 during the Linebacker bombings. In common with Joan Baez some years before her, Fonda sheltered with the Vietnamese. Her testimony also reveals patterns of civilian behaviour under the bomb witnessed by many previous visitors to war zones. Yet Fonda possibly had more in common with Monica Felton during the Korean War than Baez, speaking out against American imperialism at a time when many captured US soldiers were enduring suffering and torture, and drawing upon a more explicitly politicised language than the folk singer. She wrote of the defiant militia girls who kept singing as US imperialists bombed their country; of an evacuee from Hanoi who offered her the safety of a bomb shelter while all around she witnessed 'the systematic destruction of civilian targets- schools, hospitals, pagodas, the factories, houses, and the dike system'. And in words partly echoing those of another American expounding his impressions of a civilian population under the bomb, namely Quentin Reynolds during the London Blitz, Fonda stated:

> [One] thing that I have learned beyond a shadow of a doubt since I've been in this country is that Nixon will never be able to break the spirit of these people; he'll never be able to turn Vietnam, north and south, into a neo-colony of the United States by bombing, by invading, by attacking in any way.[367]

Fonda has since regretted some of her antics in Vietnam.[368] Yet while her use of the language of imperialism to describe American bombings reflected the other side in the Cold War, her prognosis of the consequences of mass bombardment was broadly correct, certainly more so than that of the American president. As noted in previous chapters and above in this one, heavy and continuous bombing wrecked buildings, infrastructure, and killed and maimed many fragile human bodies. But it did not crush the collective morale of the Vietnamese people, whether they lived in cities or villages.

Despite their impressive arsenal, the United States lost the air war in Vietnam. Clodfelter argues that American air commanders mistakenly believed that strategic bombing campaigns during the Second World War had been essential to ultimate victory.[369] Unlike the defeated German and Japanese, whose urban centres had been soundly reduced to ruins, the rural Vietcong had ultimately triumphed over the USA, while the urban populations of Vietnam remained mostly unbowed by American air raids.

American Movies and Vietnam

The American bombing war in Vietnam has featured in a number of compelling scenes in Hollywood representations of the conflict since 1975. As the B-52s flew on and away, they left behind a legacy that was both immediate and longer term. Images of mothers carrying the twisted bodies of their infants or of little children running from their destroyed villages, their skin burning with napalm, their faces contorted with fear and pain, were common in transatlantic and European news reports of the Vietnam War during the 1960s. Such images influenced not only public opinion and media criticism against the USA; they shaped a post-1975 discourse that saw America not as a defender of Western values against communist belligerence, but as an imperialist, even demotic country whose guiding principle of manifest destiny had tragically become globalised. The same contempt for Native American cultures during the westwards spread of the Frontier in the nineteenth century, was now writ into American foreign policy. Older films about General Custer had depicted him as a hero defeated by treachery and inhuman Native Americans. In the film *Little Big Man* (1970), however, directed by Arthur Penn, the Vietnam metaphors come thick and fast: vulnerable tepees and animals are torched, an allegory for napalm, while Indian children and young woman are brutally raped or slaughtered by the men in uniform. A simple rural lifestyle is put to death by flames and the barbarism of the so-called 'civilised world'.

Popular perceptions of the American war on communism in Vietnam and Cambodia have been shaped to a considerable degree by the American film industry. In *The Deer Hunter* (1979) disproportionate aerial firebombing of simple agricultural communities provided another vivid picture of the disproportionate might of American air power. The aerial shots in Frances Ford Coppola's *Apocalypse Now* (1979) depict deadly fleets of USAF planes dropping napalm onto a vulnerable jungle landscape. The 'Ride of the Valkyries' sequence in the same movie depicts a swarm of attack helicopters machine gunning many helpless innocent civilians in the coastal villages. In Oliver Stone's *Platoon* (1986) both American and Vietnamese soldiers are victims of an American air strike. The Vietnam war films of the late twentieth century are very different from the early post-war representations of the Second World War from 1939–45, where death and injury was not graphically depicted. Interestingly, the bombing of Vietnamese cities is rarely represented in the genre of Vietnam War films. The more vulnerable, innocent rural landscape is perhaps a more emotive landscape than the city to critique the alleged brutality of American air power.

One of the most compelling films about the Vietnam War, however, was *The Fog of War* (2011), a series of interviews with the former Secretary of Defence Robert McNamara. His emphasis upon the need for air superiority prefaces a sequence of heavy bombing raids from 1965, in which falling bombs and explosions below almost seem detached from their consequences. In his earlier memoir, McNamara accepted some responsibility for errors made in the fog of war, but ultimately placed blame for the terrible death toll on the Cold War and the threat of communism.[370]

From Destruction to Reconstruction

Much of Hanoi, Haiphong and other Vietnamese urban centres lay in varying degrees of desolation as the Americans retreated. But while the USA had been instrumental in the reconstruction of post-1945 Germany and Japan, they were absent from the post-1975 Vietnamese reconstruction. In fact, as William Stewart Logan has argued, the growing Soviet influence in North Vietnam from 1972 was accompanied by urban renewal schemes in Hanoi and other Vietnamese cities hammered by American bombing. Following American withdrawal in 1973 reconstruction began in earnest, but as had so often happened in other countries, the rebuilding of Vietnam was beset with practical problems. The USAF had destroyed about 70 per cent of Vietnamese industrial capacity, and large swathes of infrastructure lay in ruins. Hundreds of thousands of urban homes needed to be built to address the post-war housing shortage. A shortage of materials hampered reconstruction, however, and the country lacked a skilled corpus of architects, planners and civil engineers. The Americans also refused to honour their commitment to financial and practical aid for reconstruction as laid down by the Paris Peace Treaty, and even imposed an economic embargo on Vietnam in 1978.[371]

In common with North Korea some twenty years earlier, the new urban landscape of communist Vietnam was to reflect the ideology of the ruling elite with practical support and ideological input from the USSR. According to a leading Vietnamese social scientist and government advisor in 1980, existing towns and cities were to be transformed and modernised to reflect the communist future, not the past, while bomb-damaged cities, notably Hanoi, were to be constructed to promote worker productivity, while eliminating any Western-influenced 'consumer town aspect.'[372] In addition to Soviet Russian influences, utopian urban designs from the GDR also influenced the rebuilding of post-war Vietnamese cities, bringing into being suburbs of apartment blocks arranged around putatively communitarian spaces and facilities.[373] Ironically, the USAF had once more, as with North Korea, unwittingly assisted in the post-conflict creation of modern socialist cityscapes.

The NATO Bombing of Yugoslavia

The Balkan Wars of the 1990s demonstrated once again that large regions of Europe were politically unstable. As the Former Republic of Yugoslavia disintegrated into nationalist and sectarian conflict between Orthodox Serbs and Muslim minorities, and as news of Serbian atrocities against Muslim men began to be widely reported in 1998–9, international pressure grew for a 'humanitarian' bombing campaign to protect Kosovar Albanians from Serbian aggression. NATO launched an offensive against Serbia on 24 March 1999 which lasted for 78 days. Kosovo was effectively liberated 12 June when NATO and Russian troops moved in from Macedonia, and Kosovo soon regained its autonomy.

In February 2000 the NGO Human Rights Watch (HRW) published its report *Civilian Deaths in the NATO Air Campaign*. Concerned with the targeting of civilians and non-military facilities during the air campaign of 1999, and by the deployment of cluster bombs, HRW felt that a case should be answered by NATO, and of course the USA. It was particularly keen to investigate incidents including the bombing of refugees, of displaced civilians, and raids on a prison and a Serb radio station.[374]

In common with earlier major conflicts, destruction caused reconstruction, and key themes re-emerged. Some fascinating recent historiography on architecture and heritage in the Balkans has uncovered the fact that most people wanted to see a rebuilt urban landscape that reminded them of their home, community and city prior to the destruction. They prefer facsimile rebuilding, an emphasis upon history, an imagined past and familiar traditional structures, to modernity. Hence in Bosnia and Herzegovina many thousands of listed and public buildings that were destroyed in the wars of the 1990s, for example municipal buildings and mosques, were rebuilt 'with these sentiments of continuity and identity in mind.'[375] This rebuilding of historical landscapes was shaped by historical memory, cultural identities, social values, and political conflicts in the Balkan region, but similar influences are germane to all reconstructions in different contexts.[376]

The Middle-East and South Asia Since 1991

Criticism of American bombing in the Middle East began with the Persian Gulf War of 1991, and the American-led coalition campaign to free Kuwait from the murderous Iraqi occupying forces. This was Operation Desert Shield, described by the US Defence Secretary Dick Cheney as 'the most successful air campaign in the history of the world'. Following the liberation of Kuwait from the murderous intentions of Saddam Hussein, the United States attacked Iraqi forces as they retreated. Tragically, many civilians were killed in Iraq as 'collateral damage'. One of the most disturbing events was the loss of over 400 civilian lives in the Amiriyah shelter bombing in February 1991. Human Rights Watch was again on the case, highlighting the 'needless deaths' to non-combatants, not only as a consequence of coalition air attacks, but also the Iraqi Scud missiles launched in Kuwait and Saudi Arabia.[377]

During the present century, American interventions in Iraq, Afghanistan, Libya, Pakistan, Somalia and Syria have all pursued military objectives, claiming to minimise civilian casualties but often wilfully accepting this as an inevitable consequence of aerial warfare.[378] Non-combatant deaths from drone strikes in Afghanistan and Pakistan have caused anti-war activists to question the legitimacy of the bombing, and invite opprobrium against the United States. In Iraq and Syria, Islamic State (ISIS) and other fundamentalist groups also coexisted with (and terrorised) the local population, meaning civilian casualties of bombing were inevitable.[379]

American Criticisms of US Bombing Campaigns

The American bombings during the Vietnam War led to a growing internal criticism of the aggressive so-called 'imperialism' of the United States. The peace protesters during the Vietnam War continued to condemn American military conduct, but increasingly, critical academic interpretations of American air raids during the Vietnam War began to interpret these the latest tragic historical phase in a continuity of American atrocities since the Second World War.

The most famous opponent of American air warfare has been the linguist and Marxist academic Noam Chomsky. His *American Power and the New Mandarins* was first published in 1968 when the air war was raging. Blaming the conflict in no small part on American imperialism, Chomsky bitterly attacked the loss of life caused by the American bombing of Cambodia and Laos, and in the same year the Americans pulled out of Hanoi, he denounced American attacks on Vietnamese society as criminal, an unnecessary aggression in which 'the conduct of war was an indescribable atrocity':

> The US goal was to eradicate the revolutionary nationalist forces which, US officials estimated, enjoyed the support

of half the population. The method, inevitably, was to destroy the rural society. While the war of annihilation partially succeeded in this aim, the US was never able to create a workable system out of the wreckage.[380]

In many articles held on his website, Chomsky views US foreign policy during and since the Second World War as an extension of American geopolitical expansionism for the purposes of economic and cultural hegemony.[381] In his view, the terrorism of 9/11 can in large part be viewed as consequent upon the USA's support for Israel, for condoning the alleged 'terrorism' of the Israeli state, and the wider alienation and anger of Muslims in the Middle East caused by American interventions in the region.[382]

Another passionate and biased critic of American bombing policy is William Blum, an ex-federal government employee and Left-liberal writer who asserts a deadly continuity in US foreign policy and air wars since 1945. His widely-read polemic *Rogue State* bizarrely draws upon the mass society insights of Adolf Hitler to castigate Americans for their 'primitive simplicity' in accepting the legitimacy of the US bombing of Hiroshima.[383] Listing almost all American bombing campaigns since 1945, including Korea, Vietnam, Yugoslavia, South America, the Middle East and Afghanistan, Blum dismisses these as an imperialistic project to dominate the world and choke off communism (Korea and Vietnam) or rid the world of terrorism (the Middle East, Afghanistan) while perpetrating bombing campaigns which he argues were terrorist in and of themselves: 'a terrorist is someone who has a bomb but doesn't have an air force.'[384] Few people would now argue that the Vietnamese bombing campaigns were always proportionate and successful, but for Blum Korea and Vietnam were simply at the worst end of a spectrum of unjustified American aggression. He sees the USA is the biggest terrorist on the planet, and American culpability has been exacerbated by the use of high-tech weapons such as cluster bombs and drones which have killed and maimed many thousands of innocent civilians. However Blum is unable to attach relative weights to those who committed the atrocity in September 2001, Islamist attackers who bomb or gun down civilians, and the US government. The major culprit remains the American military complex.[385]

Continuities between American air raids have been emphasised by younger historians with similar views to Blum and Chomsky. Writing in the *Asia-Pacific Journal* they have attacked American indifference to civilian mortalities and casualties in air raids. Roosevelt's condemnation of the air raids during the 1930s have been mobilised to question the subsequent morality of US bombing campaigns, initially thrown into relief by the role of the B-29 plane in conventional and atomic bombings.[386] The lessons learned by the USAAF were adapted for the Korean War, where American military commanders sought to avoid civilian casualties but tacitly accepted that there would be death and maiming of innocents during air raids on industrial centres. Similar precepts informed the 'Nixon Doctrine' and the bombings of civilians in Cambodia, Laos and Vietnam.[387]

A problem with these arguments can be identified in the following sentence about the Second World War: 'Although Americans were quiet about the harm to civilians resulting from US bombing, they spoke out loudly against German and Japanese atrocities.'[388] This begs a number of questions. Surely, when loved ones and service personnel are fighting for their country, such emotions are easily explained? The Americans were fighting for democracy, moreover, whereas the Axis powers attempted to brutally impose fascism upon the world. The use of bombs was also a far cry from the hand-to-hand atrocities committed by the Germans and Japanese. Yet none of these articles on American bombing policy since the 1940s detail the fact that the USA was fighting enemies whose *conduite de la guerre* was hardly modelled on the Geneva Conventions. American air raids on civilians did not take place in a neutral context, and civilians in fascist dictatorships were often ruthlessly sacrificed by their own side.

Conclusions

Undoubtedly and tragically wasteful of civilian lives, and devastating to towns, cities and villages, the Cold War conflicts and post-1992 wars have been used by critics of the USA as evidence of American imperialism and of a callous indifference to cultures and peoples of which they knew little. Among the most vocal British opponents of American air raids is the Stop the War Coalition (STWC). On its website, the STWC blames the United States for every global conflict from Korea to the bombing of Syria: 'Since the Korean War (1950-53), the United States has controlled vast regions of the world through first establishing and then continuing a military presence.'[389]

This judgement implies there is no consent from 'controlled' countries, which was not the case for millions of people who opposed communism. It also begs counterfactual questions for both Korea and Vietnam: if the USA had not intervened, would the entire Korean peninsula now be a dynastic dictatorship mired in the oppression and poverty that blights the people of North Korea? And had the Americans and the South Vietnamese been victorious, would Vietnam now be a freer and more prosperous country? And how long and in what directions would the

Balkan conflicts of the 1990s have taken without NATO intervention from the air? Yet such questions are hidden behind the terrible images caused by the atrocities against civilians in both conflicts, for which the USA bears the brunt of responsibility. This chapter has, hopefully, provided a more nuanced and historically-informed approach than those offered up by anti-American interpretations aerial warfare since 1945. Yet no account of the American bombings during the Cold War should ignore the terrible legacy of unexploded bombs and the deaths and injuries they have caused since. In 2016 President Barack Obama expressed regret, but offered no apology, for the bombing of Laos during the Vietnam War, and increased compensation for the victims. About 20,000 people have been victims of unexploded ordnance since the war ended. Many were children, fascinated by the small size and shape of unexploded cluster bombs.[390]

Coda

Most readers of this book will be aware of the conflicts in Syria and the Ukraine. In common with the website of the Stop the War Coalition, the online articles by both Chomsky and Blum offer little criticism of the Russian bombing of the Ukraine in 2015 which killed innocent bystanders, and led to an illegal annexation of Ukrainian territory. While in Syria since 2015, air strikes on Aleppo and other cities by the Russians have killed innocent civilians, in order to support a barbaric regime that uses chemical weapons on its own citizens. This raises a serious question mark over the integrity of their arguments.

CHAPTER 8

Commemoration and Controversy: Remembering Air Raids and Their Victims Since 1945

Introduction

Most wars in history have led the victors and the vanquished to create memorials to those who were slain in the course of battle. The terrible casualty rates of the First World War gave rise to nationwide projects to remember those who would not grow old. In Britain, the most famous of the memorials is the Cenotaph in Whitehall, London. Those who died during the Second World War fighting for their country were added to the First World War memorials in the cities, towns and villages where they had once lived. As Amy Helen Bell argues, however, the First World War cast long shadows over the interwar period. The promise of a land fit for heroes was tarnished by economic decline, unemployment and increasing

How to cite this book chapter:
Clapson, M. 2019. *The Blitz Companion.* Pp. 173–228. London: University of Westminster Press. DOI: https://doi.org/10.16997/book26.h. License: CC-BY-NC-ND 4.0

inequality. Mixed emotions over the Armistice Day commemorations, the tragedy of so many lost lives during the 'war to end all wars' and fear of another war during the later 1930s, meant that memorialisation was never a singular and shared national experience.[391]

Yet the twentieth century marked a decisive shift in commemoration. The First World War produced other commemorative emblems, not to those who died in service, but to civilians and cities hit by air raids. It is rare to see a building named after the device that destroyed the previous building on the site, but along the Farringdon Road in East London the Zeppelin Building proudly announces itself to passers-by (See Fig 1). A hundred years later, on the anniversary of the Zeppelin raids, the London Borough of Hackney placed a brown plaque on the wall of a house in Alkham Road, the site of one of the first bombs to be dropped on London during the First World War.[392] All across London, and many other British cities, plaques mark the place where a bomb or an incendiary device caused death and destruction. They are modest, localised sites of memory, or *lieux de memoire*.

Historians of commemoration have drawn a significant distinction between official and 'top down' commemoration events and structures, and those from the 'bottom up', initiated by the social agency of people and groups who are not in government. Across the world many state-led or local-government sponsored memorial fixtures exists to the war dead, and many others reflect the actions of local people, associations of bomb survivors, and non-governmental organisation such as charities, religious initiatives, pacifist groups and veterans organisations. In some important cases, however, both official and public initiatives fused together, hence the distinction between top-down versus social agency approaches can sometimes be misleading.

Memories of war are not confined to those who lived through or endured conflict. As Geoff Eley and Penny Summerfield have argued, 'remembering' the Second World War does not require direct lived experience of it.[393] Those who were born soon after the war, and who grew up during the 1950s and 1960s were socialised into images of the war and a sense of victory by many triumphalist war films. For those born later still, a significant range of sites, spatial, textual and visual, encourage vicarious experiences of the air raids. As Lucy Noakes and Juliette Pattinson have argued, British cultural memory has been strongly influenced by the victory of 1945.

German cultural memory, by contrast, has been troubled by the Allied bombings. In her study of the Dresden bombings of February 1945, Anne Fuchs focuses upon the 'carriers of memory' of the 'impact narrative' of the bombing of Dresden, namely photography, ruins, fine art, architecture, fiction and film.[394] Each of these textual or visual genres may be viewed as presenting Dresden as the most important *lieu de memoire* of German suffering in the Second World War. These sources also remind us that the Second World War was a very visual war, more so than previous major conflicts due to the new popularity of film and photography.

Fuchs' arguments are certainly applicable beyond Dresden. She argues that 'the Holocaust, the bombing of Warsaw, Dresden, Hiroshima and Nagasaki:'

> the Vietnam War, and recently perhaps the Iraq War, are signature events that underline the destructive potential of a modernity that divorced technological progress from ethical reflection.[395]

Some refinements are required to this argument. Comparing the botched and tragic attempt to liberate Iraq from a Ba'athist neo-fascist dictatorship as a 'signature event' alongside the industrialised murder of 6 million Jewish people is fraught with difficult issues. And as previous chapters have shown, the reactions of Churchill to the Dresden bombing, and of the American pilots who dropped the atomic bombs on Hiroshima and Nagasaki, were not devoid of ethical reflection. Yet Fuchs is broadly correct in her view that bombings on other major cities have carried impact narratives. They acknowledge and recall the impact of air raids mostly as urban phenomena with global significance.

Urban Sites of Commemoration in Post-war Britain

Within the context of fixed war memorials in towns and cities, the remembrance of the air war on Britain has been a largely pragmatic affair, mostly relying upon agencies such as interest groups, local activists and charities for their provenance and construction. In 2010 the journalist Peter Watts asked why London, the city that sustained the longest continuing bombing raids in Europe, had no powerful and meaningful memorial to its Blitz victims.[396] The absence of a significant site of active commemoration of the London Blitz was denied to those who have lived through it, and denied a context for subsequent generations to activate historical empathy an imagination. Some years later it is still the case. Within the precincts of St Paul's Cathedral a diminutive circular monument fails to project the scale of the bombing of London, and does little to commemorate the victims of the Blitz and their suffering. The modestly-sized Cenotaph in Whitehall, the memorial to the dead of the First World War, is proof that well-designed memorials do not have to be on a large scale, but a more significant statement commemorating civilian endurance and suffering during the Blitz would make a powerful contribution to the sites of memory in the capital city.

The piecemeal nature of commemoration of air raids in Britain is evident in the random plaques or interpretation boards which adorn the sides of homes and buildings where bombs, or V1 and V2 rockets struck. Yet East London, the first and most heavily battered area of the London Blitz, has been proactive in calling for memorials to those who suffered the air raids. Popular literature has recognised the devastation wrought on East London, and the experiences of women during the Blitz are at the heart of the stories. Sally Worboyes' novel *Over Bethnal Green* (2000) deals with the experiences of a young mother in the East End during the Blitz, while Dee Williams in *Love and War* (2004) explores a young woman and her family's endurance of the Blitz in Rotherhithe in the London Docklands. Worboyes grew up in the East End, and Williams was herself a young girl during wartime London, so the novels contains autobiographical elements. In July 2008 the Hermitage Riverside Memorial Gardens were opened in the Docklands by the Culture Secretary of the Labour government, Hazel Blears. Those in attendance included a local survivor of the bombings and an ex fire warden. Designed by the architect Wendy Taylor CBE, the memorial in the gardens depicts a dove of peace within a marble rectangle set on a stone plinth.[397] Hence both the popular novel and sculpture present East London as a site of memory of wartime air raids.

A modest tribute on the ground in the precincts of St Paul's Cathedral is the memorial to Londoners who lost their lives during the Second World War, and to the many thousands of others in the capital city who endured the conflict. It was paid for by the public following an appeal by the *Evening Standard*. The words around the memorial state 'Remember Before God the People of London, 1939-1945' while the spiral inscription on the top states

'In war resolution, in defeat defiance, in victory magnanimity, in peace goodwill.' These words were used by Winston Churchill in his preface to his history of the Second World War.[398] Dedicated on 1 January 1999, it is rather underwhelming. (See Fig 4)

The heroism of the fire fighters and other members of the emergency services was the subject of some powerful documentary films made during the Second World War, as noted in chapter

Figure 7: National Firefighter's Memorial, St. Paul's Cathedral London (photograph by author, 2017).

three. Just south of the St Paul's Cathedral stands the National Firefighters Memorial, a superior statement to the one in the grounds of St Paul's itself. Commissioned by the Firefighters Memorial Charitable Trust, and opened by the Queen Mother in May 1991, it depicts the kind of action poses seen in documentary war films such as Humphrey Jennings *Fires Were Started* (1943). The monument also lists the names of those killed in the service of their country, as they fought to protect others in London from the conflagrations that engulfed so many buildings and streets. The memorial also hosts the praise from Churchill to the firefighters as 'Heroes with grimy faces', a term revealing the influence of American cinema on British popular culture during the 1930s. The arms pointing towards the cathedral also reference its miraculous survival.[399]

Situated close to St Paul's Cathedral, it is respectful, heroic, yet unboastful, a significantly better memorial than the floor-bound disk to those killed and injured by the London Blitz. St. Paul's Cathedral is therefore commemorated in both film and by the memorials within and just beyond its precincts. This is one of the most significant sites of memory to the dead of wartime London, and particularly to those killed during the Blitz on the capital city.[400]

Close to the Cenotaph in Whitehall is the Monument to the Women of World War II. Unveiled by Queen Elizabeth II in July 2005, just two days after the London bombings, it was a long overdue statement to the contribution of women not only in military uniform but as civil defenders. Its history again highlights the pragmatic culture of commemoration in Britain: it was the product of voluntary lobbying and fund raising by the Memorial to the Women of World War II charitable trust, and it gained support from the National Memorial Heritage Fund. Dame Vera

Lynn, a popular wartime singer, was among many famous women who supported the memorial, including notably Baroness Betty Boothroyd, the patron of the trust. At the unveiling, Boothroyd dedicated the memorial to 'all the women who served our country and to the cause of freedom, in uniform and on the home front.'[401] This was an important moment and monument recognising the role of women in wartime, a mostly male-dominated arena of commemoration. Many other memorials to the bravery and sacrifice of people in wartime came London can be found on the website londonremembers.com.

Beyond London, the National Memorial Arboretum in Staffordshire hosts the Civil Defence Memorial Grove, which recognises

Figure 8: Monument to the Women of World War Two. (Photograph Jane Rix / Shutterstock.com).

the sacrifice and work of Civil Defence workers in the Second World War. It also holds a memorial to animals who helped defend Britain.[402] Across provincial Britain, cities and towns host fixed memorials to the dead of air raids. There are too many to detail here but in Clydebank for example, the memorial contains the names of the 528 people who were killed by the Luftwaffe on 13–14 March 1941. Commissioned by West Dumbartonshire Council, and designed by a local artist, the memorial was unveiled in 2009, and powerfully creates a sense of lost lives among a living city.[403]

Art: Representations and Remembering

Leading artists were commissioned by governments during the Second World War to paint images of the Home Front. Others painted spontaneously in the wake of air attacks. Art is both a representation of the air raids and their impact, as well as reinforcing cities and places as *lieux de memoire*. *Guernica* (1937) by Pablo Picasso is one of his finest and possibly his most famous painting. In London, for example, there are many fine paintings on air raids and their aftermath in the Imperial War Museum, while the City of Westminster Archives in Victoria also contains artwork on the London Blitz, including an amateur depiction of St Paul's Cathedral, one of many paintings of the cathedral completed during the war. Many online websites host representations of air raids, for example, *Premonitions of the Blitz, 1940* by Julian Trevelyan and John Piper's *Interior of Coventry Cathedral* following air raid damage are partcularly haunting images.[404] Many local history museums hold amateur paintings of cities during and after air raids. They may not have the impact of Picasso but they are carriers of imagery of the air raids and depict landscapes forever altered by air raids.

Ruins and *lieux de memoire*

Places of worship destroyed by air raids, and left in preserved ruins, are also spaces of contemplation and of memories. Many churches in London and the City of London were laid waste during the Second World War. Not far from the Fire Service Memorial are the ruins of Christchurch Greyfriars Church, for example. The ruins of this place of worship, designed by Sir Christopher Wren, were left by the City of London Corporation and the Church of England as a visual reminder of the Blitz on the City of London. They are beautifully preserved, as the once covered interior is now open to the elements, and hosts an attractive garden.[405] Although many people eat their lunch there, it is also a place of quiet contemplation about the nature of war.

The shell of the medieval Coventry Cathedral is also an important religious site of commemoration, and this took on global significance when Coventry was twinned with Dresden in 1959. This is discussed further below. These memorials and sites of memory also form some of the places of interest in the guided Blitz walks that are now popular tourist events in London, introducing thousands of people to the palimpsests of bombsites, and to the types of buildings that were built on them during the reconstruction era, or since. Field walks are another carrier of memories, providing informed retrospective impressions of air raids; a number of books and websites are dedicated to them.[406]

Film, Television and Memories of the Blitz

Contemporary documentary films made during the Second World War provide powerful and often moving images of ordinary people and of emergency service workers battling against the air raids. Among the most famous are the films directed by Humphrey Jennings, one of the leading pioneers of the British documentary film movement between the wars. It was Jennings who directed *London (Britain) Can Take It* at the height of the Blitz in 1940, discussed in chapter three. *Listen to Britain* (1942) is a depiction of life on the Home Front, set to music, while *Fires were Started* (1943) sensitively presented the quiet heroism and the stoicism of the AFS during the worst nights of the air raids. These were not filmed *in situ*, but used 'real people' as opposed to actors to stage realistic enactments of the work of the AFS. Jennings also made the end-of-war film *A Diary for Timothy* (1944–5) which looked forward to the democratic future that would emerge from the horrors of war. To the present-day viewer, wartime documentaries, alongside wartime newsreels, provide vivid, if censored, scenes from everyday life. The British Film Institute (BFI) and the Imperial War Museum (IWM) host many films about the Blitz and other air raids.

Not to be confused with contemporary documentaries are historical documentaries. Providing a rich vein of information and interpretations of air raids and their consequences historical documentaries are a synthesis, a combination, of both secondary interpretations and primary sources. Some are specifically about air raids, others view air raids within the wider context of war. Among the best historical documentaries is the award-winning television series *The World at War*, first broadcast in 1974, and available as a box set. Made for Thames Television, a British commercial channel which broadcast on the ITV network, *The World at War* drew upon interviews and oral testimonies, wartime newsreels, propaganda, documentary films, military films and recordings, photographs, and images of newspaper front pages to accompany the narration by the classical actor Sir Laurence

Olivier. A total of twenty-six episodes were overseen by historical adviser Noble Frankland and written by leading historians such as Neal Ascherson, Courtney Browne, David Elstein and David Wheeler. The Blitz on British cities, the Nazi Blitzkrieg across Europe, the Allied bombing campaign against Germany and the War in the Pacific, culminating in the bombing of Hiroshima and Nagasaki, are given balanced treatments, tending not towards pure objectivity or neutrality but a multi-angled narrative from the perspectives of the combatants as well as innocent victims. For example, in the episodes on air raids over Britain and Germany, interviews are held with combatants and civilians from both sides.[407] The series is therefore also very useful in putting the British Blitz into comparative international context.

On the fiftieth anniversary of the ending of the Second World War, the BBC ran a series of mock news reports on the events of the war, reminding viewers of the differences in tone then and now. While encouraging a powerful sense of nostalgia for those who were alive at the time, for younger viewers it 'placed us inside the grand narrative' of the People's War, of a country that had once been fought alone, endured the air raids and other wartime hardships and battles, and ultimately triumphed over the Nazis.[408]

A further television series, broadly within a historical documentary tradition, was the BBC series *Blitz Cities* (2005). Remembering the air raids and the victims of Birmingham, Cardiff, Liverpool, London and Cardiff, each episode was hosted by a celebrity from the city, and included images and films of the bombings, alongside interviews with people who lived through them. The inclusion of famous people was a clever device to encourage people to watch and share in the experiences of seventy-five years ago. That the Blitz remained a popular subject with both audiences and programme makers was further evidenced in the fine BBC series *Blitz: The Bombs that Changed Britain* (2017). Drawing upon oral testimonies, contemporary footage and photographs, the series showed the impact that one bomb or raid could have on individuals, families and communities.[409]

Cinema and television fiction features have also dealt with the impact and legacy of air raids. Earlier post-war films that include images of air raids or their aftermath include the 1955 film *The End of the Affair*, in which an illicit love affair is conducted against the austere background of wartime London. Almost fifteen years after its deadly arrival in London the V2 rocket made a post-war appearance in the BBC science fiction series *Quatermass and the Pit*, written by the acclaimed screenwriter and science fiction author Nigel Kneale, and broadcast live to an awestruck television audience in 1958–9. The story was also made into a movie by Hammer Film Productions during the Sixties. As foundations for an extension to a London Underground station were being dug, construction workers unearthed an alien rocket which the government and military officials claimed was an unexploded German V2, but which was really an ancient Martian spaceship. There is a kind of inverted echo in *Quatermass* of the misleading denials about the existence of the V2 issued by the wartime government. During the war, the V2 was seen by some politicians as too menacing for public awareness; now it was a useful foil to cover up the terrible truth about latent Martian menace lurking beneath the streets of London. The concluding scene in which the devil appears over London might have reminded many Londoners of the first appearance of the Luftwaffe.[410]

In the BBC television series, *Goodnight Sweetheart*, broadcast from 1993–9, which of course coincided with the fiftieth anniversary of 1945, the Home Front in wartime London was imaginatively recreated within the context of a time-travelling

TV repairman who repeatedly enters wartime London through a time portal. His life is one of infidelity to his late-twentieth-century wife and his wartime spouse, the main humorous theme of the series. But *Goodnight Sweetheart* also gently mocks figures of authority in the police service and the ARP, while depicting the humour but also tensions, irritations and privations of the Home Front. Nonetheless, the sense of nostalgia in *Goodnight Sweetheart* is palpable. Rather than invalidating it, the series can be a useful source for social historians in any comprehensive interpretation of the Blitz. Nostalgia is a powerful emotion. As people age, they often feel they have lost something, while many possess a more nuanced and realistic understanding of the past than Calder gives them credit for. It also cleverly creates and depicts the atmosphere of the Home Front with its plot juxtapositions of 'then' and 'now'.

Chapter three drew attention to *Hope and Glory* (1987), a film about childhood during the Blitz. So too was *The Evacuees*, (1975) a television film for the BBC's *Play for Today* series. Written by Jack Rosenthal, it sensitively deals with the experiences of two Jewish boys evacuated from Manchester during the Blitz. Both *Goodnight Sweetheart* and *The Evacuees* also shows how television drama is a carrier of imagined memory.

Among the least obvious yet most evocative representations of the Blitz are drawn and animated images of the air raids and their effects. The air raids on wartime London make a tantalising appearance in Walt Disney's *Peter Pan 2: Return to Never Land*, a children's animation based on the boy hero of J.M. Barry, when Peter and Wendy are hiding in an air raid shelter. Some of the most emotionally moving depictions, however, are literally drawn from the experiences of the artists themselves. The English artist Raymond Briggs has produced a beautiful autobiographical graphic novel of the lives of his parents, and his childhood, which includes a poignant segment on the Home Front. First published in 1998, *Ethel and Ernest* depicts the evacuation of young Raymond from London to the county of Dorset. It evokes the atmosphere in Britain as war is declared, the voluntarism and good humour of ARP wardens such as his father, the impact of bombs on the terraced houses, the searchlights and the bombers, Anderson shelters, the irritations of rationing, the spectre of the doodlebugs, VE Day celebrations, and the election of the Labour Party to government in 1945.[411] In 2016, the BBC and the BFI released *Ethel and Ernest* as an animated film, demonstrating many similarities with the original, but also a couple of subtle but revealing differences that can creep into stories as they transition from one textual format to another. For example, unlike the graphic novel, the opening frames of the film depict a bi-plane flying over London in 1928, an echo of the air-mindedness of the interwar years discussed in chapter two, and a harbinger of the prominence of air raids in the story to come.

Ethel and Ernest also references the momentous events in Japan in August 1945: 'ATOMIC BOMB…HIROSHIMA…100,000 DEAD…' blares the radio. 'Hundred thousand dead from one bomb', repeats Ernest in awe, while Ethel exclaims that 'at least it will put paid to wars'.[412] Briggs also drew and wrote *When the Wind Blows*, a powerful graphic novel about atomic destruction. Made into a film released in 1986, it depicts a nuclear attack on a typical English town.[413]

Air Raid Photography: Creating Images for Memorialisation

Contemporary photographs of air raids, of survivors, victims and of the landscape during and after bombings, were a conscious act of enabling memorialisation during or immediately after the attacks themselves. During the Blitz on London, the *Picture Post* photographer Bert Hardy captured many black and white images of East Enders. Hardy recorded the images for 'East End at War'. In common with the work of documentary film makers, he took photographs of everyday life: of the AFS battling against walls of flames; of working-class people living in their bombed-out streets or sleeping in the tube stations platforms at night; of shop-workers carrying on despite the bomb damage, and of ARP wardens and local clergymen comforting children. This was documentary photography of the highest order.[414] Any memories or imaginary recreations of the London Blitz would be lacking without sight of such images.

Hardy was aware that he and his newspaper were creating a visual record of the air raids, and of the bravery of civilians, ARP volunteers and fire fighters. His photographs are well-known, but less so are the personal experiences which he endured to take them. He accompanied a fireman into the cellar of a burning warehouse, when the roof collapsed, leading to a frantic struggle to escape. 'I must have gone onto the roof of one of the buildings to get pictures of firemen fighting the fire from the tops of ladders', he recalled, 'but I can't remember anything about it.' In common with the British documentary film movement, Hardy's photographic realism was motivated by the bravery and dignity of 'ordinary' people, and of their resilience in adverse circumstances.[415] An impressive collection of photographic images of the Blitz are held at the Imperial War Museum.

Memoirs, Autobiographies and Oral Testimonies as Carriers of Memory

Remembering exists beyond the built environment, and beyond ceremony and symbolism. Memoirs, autobiographies and oral

testimonies enable us to gain insights into the sensory and emotional experiences of air raids. Drawing upon a wide range of
wartime and post-war memoirs for London, Amy Helen Bell
draws attention to the predominant subjective characteristics of
memory among those who survived the air Blitz. Emphasising
the predominance of a British sense of *sangfroid*, a subjectivity
of 'taking it' always with a good dose of humour or stoicism, Bell
argues that 'the memory of the Blitz:'

> helped to create a retrospective vision of civilian collec-
> tivity. In this vision, the fortitude of Londoners during
> the bombing raids assured them of victory, and a new
> post-war social contract. The British war victory, and
> subsequent Labour election victory in 1945, consolidat-
> ed this hindsight vision.[416]

Bell does not seek to deflate the achievement of Londoners and
of the British more widely in withstanding aerial bombardment.
She is more concerned with the nuances of memory, arguing that
the traces of fear and loathing, anger at politicians, and grief at the
loss of home and family, were also important parts of the story.

Oral testimonies also record eyewitness accounts of air raids,
not only from the point of view of those attacked, but also of military personnel. These are some of the carriers of memory of the
Blitz and other air raids. There are however both particular problems as well as distinctive advantages when using autobiographies
and oral testimonies in historical accounts of air raids. Because
memory can be flawed, or selective, oral histories can never be
relied upon solely as an accurate or verifiable version of events.
Statements need to be checked, contextualised and integrated
within a wider apparatus of sources.

Students and anyone wishing to interview people with a living
memory of the past can create their own oral histories. Some

useful guides to undertaking oral history and memory work can be found in Rob Perks and Alastair Thomson's (eds) *The Oral History Reader* (2016). Testimonies of such traumatic events as air raids possesses immense value to the student of modern warfare in general, and of the experiences of civilians in violently disrupted circumstances in particular. Such testimonies are not only gained through interviews conducted by historians and respondents. Invitations to write letters to newspaper or magazines, or the use of autobiography, all count as oral history.

The oral historian Joshua Levine, for example, has collected many testimonies, and drew upon autobiographies and memoirs, of those who lived through the Blitz, and most of the best social histories of wartime Britain include oral testimony for the vivid and often emotional manner in which people relate their experiences, experiences which since 1945 have only really been visited again on London by terrorist bombings. Many of the gobbets of testimony in *Forgotten Voices of the Blitz and the Battle for Britain* (2007) or *The Secret History of the Blitz* (2015) are about bereavement, the killing of friends and family, the loss of home and neighbourhood, illicit sexual relations, sweeping away rubble, disposing of the dead, and tending to the wounded. The pain of disrupted lives, the sense of loss, spontaneous pleasures, and the senselessness of many wartime horrors, are still felt many years after the bombings were over. Two important and accessible collections of Second World War testimonies in Britain are held online by the BBC on the People's War website, the subject of some interesting insights by Noakes, while the British Library Sound Archive is available online in addition to further materials in the collection at the British Library site on the Euston Road in London.[417]

So the picture was by no means one of uncritical triumphalism when looking back on the air raids. Nonetheless, victory for the

British powerfully influenced the national culture of memory as a shared celebration resonant with varying degrees of celebration. British post-war attitudes to Germany have in turn been power-fully influenced by that.[418] International football matches, notably the World Cup Final of 1966, held in London, became occasions to remember and re-fight the Second World War. Moreover, images of the Germans as militaristic and humourless have pervaded post-war British popular culture.[419] As Summerfield argues, how-ever, different generations, while encouraged to 'remember' the Second World War, often respond in complex ways to predomi-nant wartime narratives.[420]

But things were different for the citizens of occupied Euro-pean countries. Their wartime experience was involved with col-laboration, genocide, heroic or tragic resistance, and everyday interactions with the enemy. British celebration may be sharply contrasted with the defeated people of Germany, who endured post-war expulsions, mass rape and looting, and the 'occupation' by American, British and Soviet forces. The significance of violent anti-Semitism and of the Holocaust, furthermore, infused Ger-man memory with the crimes of participation, and the turpitudes of casual racism or wilful indifference to the plight of Jews. Bell points to the highly-charged *Historikerstreit* in Germany dur-ing the 1980s, when leading German historians interrogated the role of the Holocaust in national history and memory.[421] At one end of the argument, historians argued that the Holocaust was not the fault of most Germans then, and certainly not of younger Germans since. Strangely, in a book about the Blitz, Bell avoids mention of the air raids on German and other European cities within her analysis of their cultures of memory. Since the 1980s, however, German historians and many other commentators have increasingly focused upon the aerial bombardment of German cities in order to disrupt notions of German guilt. The most blatant interpretations even implicate the Allies in a 'holocaust' against the German people, wherein memories can be recast within the context of German victimhood and suffering.

Commemoration and Remembering Air Raids in Germany

Acts of commemoration and remembrance in Germany have a controversial and contested history. In West Germany, for much of the 1950s, 1960s and 1970s, the defeat in 1945 was reinterpreted as liberation, while the German post-1945 'economic miracle' brought about an increasingly affluent and comfortable society. As we saw in chapter six, reconstruction led to a significant modernisation of the blasted and burned-out areas of German cities. While the memories of the terrible air raids lived on, much of the mnemonic landscape of destruction and despair was concreted over. The legacy of National Socialism and its ignominious defeat also haunted many who had participated in Nazi Germany and its war. In combination these points explain why the memorialisation of the Allied air raids remained problematic.

Following the end of the Second World War, the Cold War divided commemoration as it divided so many other aspects of German life. The Federal Republic of Germany (FDR) adopted an official version that the Nazi regime had caused the war, and a certain level of penitence was required for German actions during the conflict. Communist East Germany, by contrast, the home of Dresden and other heavily bombed cities, framed the devastating air raids of February 1945 as acts of American imperialism, supported by the lickspittle British, who now existed in a state of confrontation with the German Democratic Republic (GDR).

Commemorative insistence on the Anglo-American bombings as a war crime also served the communist regime's presentation of the Soviets as liberators in 1945.[422]

A study of 'the Allied war and urban memory' compared the politics of memory in Kassel in West Germany with Magdeburg in the communist zone of occupation. Kassel had been heavily bombed in October 1943 while Magdeburg was attacked in January 1945, a month before the Dresden bombings. Both cites experienced what Jörg Arnold has termed 'catastrophic rupture' of both the landscape but also in the subjective memories of the citizens whose life stories were harshly interrupted by aerial bombardment. As Arnold makes clear, however, these air raids were not experienced in a moral vacuum beloved of revisionist interpretations but 'by members of a brutalised society, whose hegemonic voice was Nazism, the very force that had been responsible for the unleashing of a world conflagration in the first place.'[423] The spectre of 'World Jewry' was blamed for the bombing as opposed to the honest, chivalrous Aryan victims of global treachery, and almost immediately tropes of a much-beloved 'home town' wrecked by the British and Americans arose amongst the corpses and ruins that pervaded the town.[424]

In Kassel, following the war, the *Gedentag* or 'day of memory' of 22 October was mostly decontextualized and depoliticised by local political and religious leaders. During the 1950s and much of the 1960s they preferred to present the bombings in terms of Christian forgiveness and reciprocity across borders. In Magdeburg, by contrast, as in Dresden, the communist elites used the anniversaries of the air raids to mobilise sentiment not only against Nazism, but increasingly against the Anglo-American imperialist enemies of the Cold War.[425]

Comparing the commemorations in Hamburg in pre-unification West Germany and Dresden in East Germany, Claudia Jerzak draws out the different groups and actors that sought to commemorate the suffering and destruction wrought by the allies. These included the governments of West and East Germany, civic associations, and the church.[426] In Dresden, the allied bombing was utilised by the communist regime to demonise the Americans as 'imperialist war-mongers' during the Cold War.[427] The 'Florence of the Elbe' was viewed by its citizens and many other Germans as an 'innocent city' undeserving of attack, while Hamburg was presented as an open port city long associated with international trade and a liberal political culture. A strong reluctance after the war to acknowledge the approval of National Socialism there during the 1930s permeated early post-war Hamburg.[428] Yet in Hamburg the culture of commemoration from the late twentieth century increasingly recognised German complicity in aerial warfare, and also sought to be more inclusive towards minority citizens, particularly Jewish groups who had suffered terribly from the mid-1930s to 1945.[429] This may also partly reflect the wider tendency of the West German state to avoid nationalistic memorials to the Second World War after 1945.[430]

The reunification of Germany in 1990, however, began to erode the East-West distinction in the national memory of air raids. More tellingly, literary works encouraged German anger about hostile air raids in the Second World War, notably *Air Raids and Culture* (1999) by the German-born academic and writer W.G. Sebald, later translated into English as *The Natural History of Destruction*. He was heavily critical of what he saw as the collective amnesia of both the German post-war liberal establishment for their failure to acknowledge the Allied bombings.[431] During the late 1990s

Sebald also gave a series of public lectures on the same theme, while the left-leaning novelist Günter Grass also deplored the scale and tragedy of the Allied bombings.[432] The German cultural historian Annette Seidel Arpaci has made some withering criticisms of Sebald, arguing that he contributed to the dubious concept of the *Bombenholocaust* which gained currency in neo-Nazi and far-right circles in Germany, and with many members of the German public.[433] Sebald wilfully drew upon Holocaust tropes, claiming the Allies were responsible for 'German suffering' which was on a scale compatible with the atrocities committed by the Nazis. Yet his key arguments about a complicit silence within the German elites were erroneous, while the extent of consent from millions of Germans to the Nazi war was under-explored. And in choosing to deploy such terms as 'war of annihilation' and 'cultural invasion' by Americanisation, Sebald was drawing upon familiar rhetorical phrases used by the Nazis against their enemies. His 'universalised notion of trauma', moreover, failed to properly weigh the anti-Semitism in wartime Germany and its terrible consequences.[434] The South African social scientist Leo Kuper also argued that the deliberate bombing of the population of Dresden and in other large cities by incendiaries held equivalence with genocide and was an undeniable war crime.[435]

Equating German suffering caused by air raids with the Holocaust was not a new idea, however. During the 1980s the American historian Earl R. Beck clumsily argued that the Allies 'achieved holocaust' in heavily bombed German cities.[436] Beck was writing on the eve of the *Historikerstreit*, the dispute between German historians over the nature and legacy of the Nazi regime in German history, and the place of the Holocaust in the remembrance of the past, and in contemporary German identity. Liberation from a sense of shame and guilt was a key theme of the debates, leading to a striking media and public debate in West German society over the extent to which late twentieth-century Germany should accept or challenge an apologetic view of history. The *Historikerstreit* was less concerned with the Allied and German bombing campaigns, but it was sharply indicative of the shifting cultural attitudes towards the years 1933–45 in German history, and a growing aspiration towards a less black-and-white interpretation of the recent past.

The controversy over commemoration resonated beyond academic and literary spheres. In 2002 the publication of *The Fire* (*Der Brand*) by the anti-establishment writer Jörg Friedrich fanned the flames of public anger about the mass bombings of 1943–5. Friedrich blamed the Allies for hundreds of thousands of unnecessary deaths and injuries. Serialised by a leading German tabloid, *The Fire* was calculated to stir the emotions, for example lambasting Winston Churchill as 'the greatest child-slaughterer of all time. He slaughtered 76,000 children'.[437] Friedrich's follow-up offering *Fire Sites* contained gruesome photographs of charred and skeletal bodies in the charnel houses left by area bombing.[438] Such visuals were deployed explicitly to evoke anger at the Allied bombing and pity for German victims. As Bill Niven has argued, *The Fire* also 'represented a radicalisation of GDR anti-Western rhetoric', contributing to the growing notion in post-1990 Germany that the bombings were a war crime.[439]

Such sympathetic attempts to revaluate the historical commemoration of air raids over Germany in the Second World War led to some predictable responses in Britain and the USA. The left-leaning *Guardian* newspaper carried a couple of articles in the wake of the controversy engendered by the publication of *The Fire* and *Fire Sites* that gave a qualified admission of British and American war crimes. An article in *The Guardian* by the writer Ian Buruma sided with Friedrich claiming 'London in the Blitz was dreadful; Hamburg was worse.'[440]

Similar perspectives were adopted by many German socialists and communists. As Schmitz has further argued, the Left student movement in late twentieth-century and early twenty-first century Germany accepted the view that their grandparents were victims both of Nazism and of Allied atrocities. This 'belated empathy' enabled the German student generations since the 1970s to emphasise victimisation, a seductive and indulgent position that fails to acknowledge wider issues such as complicity.[441] Endurance of mass bombing and the devastation to people and places has furthermore become woven into a narratives that interpret Germany and Germans during the 1940s as a historically mistreated people, bombed blasted and burnt not into democracy but into the genocidal atrocities of mass expulsions and homelessness, and the widespread rape and looting witnessed at the end of the war and in its aftermath.[442] Both Arnold and Tony Joel agree that the post-1968 student movement in West Germany and Western Europe more widely increasingly influenced the politics of memory culture away from culpability and condemnation of Nazism towards Allied conduct during the war.[443]

Yet this revisionist tendency struck a powerful chord with the German public. Many increasingly articulated long-held feelings of anger towards the Allied bombing campaigns. Viewing the cumulative consequences of the air raids as a holocaust enabled Germans, even those with a dubious war record themselves, to adopt the pose of victimhood. This leads to the danger that privileging German suffering may obscure the verifiable causes of the war, and soften the lens when looking back on German genocidal and military atrocities during the Second World War. It also enabled Germans to challenge the notion of collective guilt for the war. As the Israeli historian Gilad Margalit shows, different stages of psychological coping with guilt and bereavement can be identified in both East and West Germany, and in the unified Reich, following the fall of the Berlin Wall. Today, he argues, Germany has difficulty coming to terms with its guilt as a consequence of the growing popularity of cultural sentiments of suffering and victimisation.[444] Margalit deplores the way in which German victims of air raids are depicted 'in ways borrowed from the Jewish narrative of the Holocaust' and the allocation of similar moral responsibility for war crimes to all political elites, despite their politics and global intentions.[445] He argues the discourse of German suffering and victimhood was transmitted from one generation to the next, becoming part of German national identity during the early twenty-first century. This may have influenced the recent growth of anti-Americanism and of anti-Semitism in Germany.[446] Linde Apel is also suspicious of German victimhood, arguing that a key driver of its subjectivity is a desire to exonerate 'ordinary' Germans from the Holocaust and other atrocities.[447]

Friedrich, Sebald and others shared views disseminated by the far-right National People's Party (NPD) in Germany, and neo-Nazi fringe groups. They tried to turn the allied air raids into a 'bombing holocaust', a cynical manoeuvre to 'depict the Germans as hapless victims.'[448] Leaving wreathes on the graves and memorials of the dead, and making their mostly unwelcome presence felt at commemoration ceremonies, NPD interventions have inadvertently served to undermine German claims to victimhood and unnecessary persecution. Such interpretations have been fodder for more extreme positions on commemoration. There is also a rather shadowy web presence by a right-wing German outfit calling themselves *justice4germans.com*. One of their offerings on YouTube depicts the bombing of Dresden explicitly as an unnecessary and disproportionate attack, while failing to highlight the German air campaigns against Britain and other European countries. The Nazi Party, who brought the war upon Germany, is not mentioned.

German television also took up the theme of Allied bombing and its legacy for the Fatherland, reaffirming the media as visual and diverse channels for stirring up emotions. In 2006 the German television channel ZDF broadcast an 'authentic, emotional and moving' two-part television-movie drama entitled *Dresden*.[449] Influenced by Friedrich's *The Fire*, it was hugely popular in Germany. The plot pursued an unlikely romantic affair between a downed British pilot and a German nurse. As Dietmar Süss argues, 'the British-German history of the air war carries the baggage of cultural memory in both countries', and he views *Dresden* partly as an attempt at reconciliation between former enemies still conscious of wartime air aids.[450] While an attempt to show that love could cross the most terrible of divides, the television drama reiterated themes in *The Fire*:

> While the movie painstakingly tries to avoid any simplistic reversal of moral positions and attempts to represent *all* perspectives from a point of empathy – German, British and Jewish – it ultimately relies on a distinction between 'ordinary' Germans and 'evil' Nazis that is redolent of the 1950s. [This] is facilitated by the narrow fo-

cus of the first two hours of the film on the love story between Anna, a nurse working in her father's hospital, and Robert, a British bomber pilot who hides in the hospital cellar after his plane is shot down. The final 40 minutes of high-production-value destruction, horror, suffering and mayhem caused by the bombing is thus visited upon a series of individuals, witnessed mainly through the eyes of the two main characters. This creates a sense of visual immediacy that decontextualizes the suffering, reducing it to a pure spectacle of horror.[451]

The horror of air raids, of course, was experienced no matter which country was suffering them, which may be why *Dresden* decontextualized the Allied bombings. The shared experience of bombing became the basis of reconciliation amongst former enemies.

Reconciliation and Commemoration Since the Second World War

In 1992 Queen Elizabeth, the Queen Mother, unveiled a fairly modest statue of Sir Arthur Harris outside the RAF Church of St Clement Danes in Central London. It was commissioned by the Bomber Command Association (BCA) in recognition of his achievements and the bravery and sacrifice of those who served under him. As Joel wryly observes, St Clement Danes still bears the scars of damage from wartime air skirmishes.[452] The intention of the BCA had been to commemorate the RAF, rather than glorify the death and destruction wrought upon Germany. But protestors who saw the bombing of Dresden as a war crime gathered to disrupt the proceedings, to the extent the Queen Mother was struggling to be heard (See Fig 6).[453]

In October of the same year, 1992, Queen Elizabeth II and her husband Prince Philip, the Duke of Edinburgh, paid the first state visit to newly unified Germany, attending a reconciliation service in the *Kreuzkirche* in Dresden. The Mayor of Dresden Herbert Wagner campaigned against the statue in 1992, arguing it had no place in the Europe of the 1990s, and that the bombing of Dresden had been militarily unjustifiable.[454] Three years later, during an event commemorating the sixtieth anniversary of the Allied bombing of Kassel, a heckler called out to the British ambassador, 'Ambassador, when are you going to pull down the statue to Bomber Harris'? He then went on to shout about the absence of any permanent fixture to the memory of Herman Goering.[455] Unlike the fascist leader Goering, however, Harris was fighting for democracy. Nonetheless, the event at Kassel was one of many episodes in the 'media tumult' that surrounded the statue to Bomber Harris.[456] The protests, and also the notion of Germans as victims, attracted international attention. *The New York Times,* for example, viewed Dresden as symbolic of unjustifiable mass destruction.[457] Surviving members of Bomber Command who had bravely flown over Germany, including Dresden, were upset at what they perceived as a lack of appreciation for the risks they and their dead comrades had taken.[458]

Yet attitudes began to soften. In June 2012 the memorial to Bomber Command was unveiled by Queen Elizabeth. This was another long overdue recognition of the bravery and sacrifice demonstrated by the aircrew who flew night raids over Germany during the Second World War. Surviving members of Bomber Command and relatives of those who were killed celebrated the memorial, and although there was some concern in Germany at the memorial, an acceptance that Britain deserved to honour its war dead prevailed, indicating further reconciliation between

Figure 9: The Bomber Command Memorial, Green Park London. In addition to the 55573 air crew killed, the memorial also commemorates 'those of all nations who lost their lives in the bombing of 1939–1945'. Hence it reflects the globalisation of memorialisation (photograph by author, 2018).

former enemies. It received less condemnation than the statue to Arthur Harris.[459]

During the war, even as beautiful old churches were reduced to ruins by air raids, many British Christian leaders had expressed concerns about the Allied bombing of German cities. Once the war was over, Christian principles of forgiveness and reconciliation would surface sooner or later, to greater or lesser degrees, in Britain and across Europe. Religion was thus a driver of reconciliation. The ruins of the *Frauenkirche* in Dresden served a strongly similar purpose to the shell of the old cathedral in Coventry. And in 1959 Coventry was twinned with Dresden. During the 1960s, Christians in both Coventry and Dresden worked for reconciliation between Britain and Germany. Young Germans helped to build an International Centre for Reconciliation in the ruins of the old cathedral in Coventry, while young British believers assisted with repairs to the *Frauenkirche*.[460] Local and national governments in the GDR however increasingly positioned the bombing of Dresden as one of many acts of American imperialist aggression that led to the Cold War. Every 13 February, 'the day of remembrance or commemoration' was an occasion not simply to remember and mourn the 25,000 victims of the Dresden bombing, but to stage demonstrations against the West. Every tenth anniversary was particularly charged with passion and anger towards the Allied bombings as an expression of hatred toward capitalism, but as Joel shows, the first post-Cold War day of memory in 1995, when Germany was no longer divided, posed hugely significant questions for national identity. The process of accommodating different political positions within Germany towards the Allied bombings while inviting once adversarial opponents to the commemorations was fraught with potential problems.

In 1995, on the fiftieth anniversary of the ending of the Second World War, a service of Thanksgiving, Reconciliation and Hope was held at St Paul's Cathedral, a symbolic act that came with commemorative memorabilia such as postal stamps depicting the cathedral surrounded by anti-aircraft searchlights.[461] Both

St Paul's and Coventry cathedrals are Anglican places of worship, one razed to the ground by bombing, the other miraculously surviving. Despite the impossibility of knowing God's will in the outcome of the war, the increasingly liberal establishment within the Church of England would come to suggest moral equivalence between British and Nazi complicity in air warfare. In 2009 the Bishop of Coventry, the Right Reverend David Cocksworth, apologised for the bombing of Dresden in February 1945. Speaking at the newly rebuilt *Frauenkirche,* he deplored the violence visited upon both Coventry and Dresden, praised the two cities for their forgiveness, and looked forward to a future of hope and cooperation, and of course, peace.[462] A further act of reconciliation and commemoration, modest yet moving, is the dedication by Frederick Taylor of his book on the bombing of Coventry to his dear departed friend, a teenage survivor of the 1945 raids on Dresden.[463]

In a passage that neatly links German memories of air raids to those in Japan, Joel argues that Dresden became 'a highly visible memory politics asset' for international peace campaigners. Its destruction served 'as a warning and an obligation to pursue and promote world peace' and to prevent an atomic 'Euroshima'.[464]

Memorialisation and Commemoration in Japan

A complex welter of emotions, dominated by anger, grief and the physical and mental wounds from the atomic bombings emerged to dominate memorialisation of the air raids in post-war Japan. Yet tendencies for cultural self-condemnation and guilt were moderated by cultural and political pressures.[465]

The attacks on Hiroshima and Nagasaki created consecutive phases of the grieving process for the many thousands who were directly bereaved and deprived of their homes. The initial post-war response to the attacks was rage, enabling the Japanese to view themselves as the victims of a terrible war deed. The humili-ation of resounding defeat led to widespread revulsion towards the bombings but that anger had to be tortuously negotiated with the prevalence of denial about atrocities committed by Japanese forces against unarmed civilians and uniformed com-batants.[466] Hence places of commemoration, beautifully designed, and accompanied by thoughtful interpretation and information, where reflection can be situated within a human response rather than one conditioned by nationalistic attributions of blame, can be such places to come to terms with the horror of aerial warfare. The Hiroshima Memorial Peace Park (HMPP) is the most famous site of memory in Japan. And together, Hiroshima and Nagasaki are the most powerful *lieux de memoire* in the world.

The visitor to the city of Hiroshima today cannot really avoid the reminders of those terrible events in August 1945. The Industrial Promotional Hall, which was situated beneath the hypocentre of the Atom Bomb, is now a poignantly preserved ruin labelled the 'Peace Dome'. A number of plaques mark the places where civil-ians were incinerated. The Peace Dome is an essential but by no means the only symbolic and experiential space, connected as it is to the Hiroshima Memorial Peace Park in 1955. The opening of the HMPP on the tenth anniversary of the atomic bombings was an official or 'top-down' project. Designed by the leading Japanese architect Kenzo Tange, 'it was a simple concept':

> The centrepiece was a long pavilion raised on Corbusian pilotis and set across the axis which connected the Me-morial Monument, a saddle-like structure based on the Haniwa funerary house of the 3rd to 6th century AD, with the torn and melted Gembaku, or Atomic Dome.[467]

Figure 10: Peace Dome, Hiroshima (Photograph, Shutterstock.com).

The Pavilion was a fusion of both modern architecture with influences from Le Corbusier, and traditional motifs drawn from Japanese culture.[468] In a sense it encapsulates the modern-traditionalist tension in many other reconstruction projects, yet resolves them, unlike many other major undertakings. The HMPP has been the major national and international focus of remembrance of the victims of atomic bombing in Japan, drawing hundreds of thousands of visitors every year.

Yet the emotional experience intended by interpretation boards, and the information and images offered at the Peace Park, has increasingly been questioned. It may sound strange to argue that a beautiful and moving memorial to those killed and affected by nuclear bombing and its aftereffects could be criticised, but the sensory and emotional experiences at the heart of the HMPP have been attacked by critics as manipulation, exercises in stimulating American and Western guilt, de-contextualised from the bitter context of war in which the bombs were dropped.[469]

Ending all wars, as well as remembering victims of the atomic bombings, and in preventing another atomic cataclysm, merged to become combined intentions of the *hibakusha*. As Pierre Nora has argued, for sites of memory to even exist 'there must be a will to remember'.[470] The *hibakusha* themselves became increasingly proactive in creating an apparatus of commemoration and memorialisation to those who had perished. Susan Southard argues in a chapter entitled 'Against Forgetting' that the *hibakusha* of Nagasaki were motivated by an overwhelming desire to tell their stories in order that the world might learn from their terrible ordeal and decommission the global arsenal of nuclear weapons. Rage at the violence and pain done to them was certainly a powerful driving force, but so too was a strong sentiment of 'reconciliation not revenge.' The bomb-affected survivors of Nagasaki formed organisations to deliver their message across Japan and to the world. As a way of reclaiming their history, they also fought for the repatriation from the United States of captured Japanese footage of Hiroshima and Nagasaki in the immediate wake of the bombings. This was broadcast on Japanese television in 1968 but censored by the government to remove images of suffering.[471]

For one elderly and ill man in Nagasaki, bereavement was not simply about the loss of family and friends, although his emotional pain was palpable. He was also grieving for the loss of his familiar landscape, for the homes and the community with which he was intimately associated until *Fat Man* wiped them away. He attempted to reclaim their lives from 'the darkness of history', by remapping the community in which he had lived. Initiating a 'restoration project' that drew upon survivor memories to recreate the pre-August 1945 layout of the settlements in his valley, cemeteries were searched for names of those killed by the bomb; people put names to homes, and homes to streets; they recalled where shops and public buildings were, and drew maps of remembered landscapes: 'one house, shop, and ration station at a time':

> they filled in a comprehensive map of Matsuyama-machi, rendering back into historical existence the immediate hypocentre area and nearly all of the people who had lived and worked there.[472]

Such commemorative work is an imaginative example of *hibakusha* agency. There are also fascinating unconscious similarities to the mind-mapping urban research undertaken by Kevin Lynch. In his seminal work *The Image of the City* (1960), Lynch defined five elements that influenced individual perceptions of their surroundings in the city they lived in. These were *paths*, for example, streets, roads, canals; *edges*, such as walls, streets, shorelines or spaces where people felt their community ended; *districts* which people entered into and out of during their everyday life; *nodes*, such as the town and city centres, where local people migrated to for regular or commonplace interactions; and external *landmark*s that served as common points of reference for all, such as mountains and hills, or even the sun.[473]

Southard is disappointed that *hibakusha* testimonies have been mostly marginalised from the American war story, and points to the commemoration of the atom bomb raids at the Smithsonian's National Air and Space Museum (NASM) in Washington DC as proof. During the late 1980s curators at the NASM began planning for an exhibition on the *Enola Gay* as a historically important military artefact. This led to lobbying from the Japanese who wished to include the consequences of the bombs on the *hibakusha*, and thence to a conundrum for the NASM curators who felt compelled to recognise the bravery of the pilots. It proved impossible to achieve the acquired balance to satisfy both American and Japanese audiences, so a pared down exhibit of the *Enola Gay* was presented to the public in 1995, the fiftieth anniversary of the atomic bombings.

Disappointment felt by the *hibakusha* was supported by some Americans who wanted the full story of the atomic bombs to be told in the exhibition. Other Americans, however, pointed to Pearl Harbor and the cruelty of Japanese hand-to-hand combat against civilians, to justify the exhibition, and through that, the bombings.[474]

Ultimately, sadly, the *hibakusha* have not accomplished their mission to rid the world of nuclear weapons. And while they have succeeded in helping to keep alive the flickering flames of anti-nuclear and anti-war movements, a significant irony permeates their actions: the concept of Mutually Assured Destruction, and images and memories of the hell on earth that the *hibakusha* suffered, have served together in an unlikely alliance to prevent nuclear catastrophe.

Nonetheless, the simple fact that the message of the *hibakusha* was being heard around the world evidences what Zwigenberg terms 'a global memory culture', a truly international effort to promote memories of suffering to ensure that humanity never again imposes such suffering upon itself.[475] As the Japanese-American cultural historian Yuki Miyamoto argues, reconciliation drove the attempts to internationalise the *hibakusha* experience, to ensure that nuclear catastrophe would never happen again.[476] This is one theme amongst many in the NHK channel programmes about the *hibakusha*. NHK is the leading national public broadcasting channel of Japan, with a worldwide distribution via satellite television and the internet. One of its many programmes focused upon US journalist Henry Hersey's early post-war book *Hiroshima* (1946), which told the stories of survivors of the bomb. Both regret and reconciliation coursed through the programmes. As a satellite television channel, NHK has also helped to create a global memory culture.[477]

Hence, the bomb survivors were not acting alone. Although they had formed collective self-help groups in both Hiroshima and Nagasaki in the aftermath of the Second World War, their worldwide dissemination of commemoration and reconciliation messages was aided by some hugely influential organisations, including leading religious institutions, the Japanese government, and the United Nations and the World Health Organization, among the largest NGOs in the post-war world. The cause of the *hibakusha* was also taken up by pacifist movement such as the World Federalist Association (WFA) and the Campaign for Nuclear Disarmament (CND).[478] Formed in Britain in 1957, the CND became a well-known pressure group in Western Europe, marching against nuclear research establishments and using the media to promote its cause.[479] CND personnel have included many pacifists who have visited Hiroshima and Nagasaki, and propagated the cause of the *hibakusha*. Here is another reminder that sharp distinctions between state-led or top-down initiatives, and social-agency or bottom-upwards movements, are not always helpful. Equally importantly, it demonstrates how different agencies and organisations can adapt a message of reconciliation for their own agendas.

The moral relativism of commemoration, that views all bombing raids and their victims as essentially state crimes, regardless of the nature of the state, and without due recognition of historical context, has increasingly attached itself to the commemoration of the Hiroshima-Nagasaki survivors. One unwitting expression of such relativism was the explicit connection between the atomic bombings and the memorialisation of Auschwitz, evidenced in the Hiroshima-Auschwitz Peace March during the early 1960s, as Cold War tensions rose sharply. This emanated from a genuine if sometimes naïve desire by four Japanese peace campaigners to

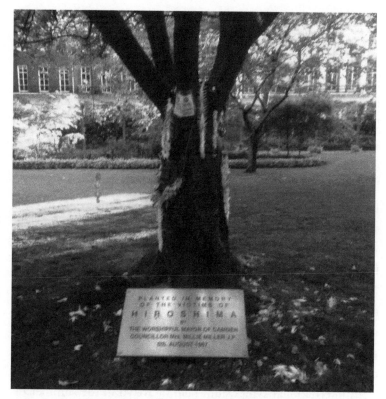

Figure 11: Hibakusha Memorial Tree, 1967, Tavistock Square, London, another symbol of the global presence of hibakusha memorialisation in a world city (photograph by author, 2017).

unite the different sites of commemoration that stemmed from the tragedies of the Second World War.[480] Yet the equation of the atomic bombings with the deliberate industrialised incineration, gassing and torture of 6 million Jewish people by the Nazi regime was by no means convincing. And of course, both Germany and Japan were former Axis partners.

The politics of the *hibakusha* were by no means monopolised by the Left, and indeed the atomic bombings have also contributed to a strong sense of victimhood coursing through Japanese memory culture. This is evident, for example, in the commemoration of the war dead, be they civilians or soldiers, cobblers or kamikaze pilots, at the Yasakuni Shrine in Tokyo. A place of worship for followers of the Shinto religion, the shrine is also a space for a 'dialogue with the dead' rather than the apportionment of blame.[481] The Buddhist and Christian religions have tended to frame the atomic bombings in terms of forgiveness and reconciliation, but some in the Japanese Roman Catholic Church appropriated the atomic bombings as a message of punishment from God for sins committed on Earth. Equally troubling to the secular mind was the notion that bombings played a part in some Divine Plan for the ending of the war.[482] In the Japanese fiction feature film *Matouquin Nocturne* (2007), the Fountain of Miracles at Lourdes, a sacred Catholic space, is abstractly juxtaposed with the searing apparition of light of the Nagasaki bombing. If spiritual transcendence towards the afterlife is the message, no atheist will be convinced.

An international symposium held in Tokyo in the summer of 1978 self-consciously drew upon the language of the *Communist Manifesto*, linking it with apocalyptic images of urban destruction in the call for an international decommissioning of nuclear weapons:

> Women and men, young people and children of the world, unite! You have nothing to lose but the chains that bind you to the increasing armaments and war. Unless you break these chains, we may lose our jobs, our homes, our schools, our playgrounds, our culture, our civilisations, our world.[483]

Supported by UNESCO and the WHO, the symposium comprised pacifists and academics from many different countries, as well as the victims of the bombings. It issued a powerful declaration that 'hibakusha should be made an international word and find its way into every language of the world.'[484]

For Miyamoto, as for Southard, the efforts of the hibakusha are still being ignored in the USA, where the discourse of the atomic bombings as 'necessary' has predominated.[485] She argues that a wider failure to really listen to the voices of the hibakusha partly explains the disconnection between a nuclear arms-free world and the culture of memory. While this is mostly true, it is not the complete picture. The website miningawareness.com contains testimonies and actions by Japanese-American hibakusha who have tried to tell their story to the USA in recent years.[486]

Film and 'Remembering' the Atomic Bombings in Japan

In the episodes on Japan in the television series *The World at War*, fascinating newsreel and propaganda footage depicts everyday life on the Home Front, provides glimpses into the Air Raid Precautions. The episodes on Japan contain interviews with leading members of the Japanese wartime government, and with hibakusha; talking heads of General Curtis LeMay and the pilots who dropped the bombs on Hiroshima and Nagasaki, and documentary, military and newsreel film of the conventional as well as atomic bombings of Japan.[487]

Beyond historical documentaries, some of the most powerful representations and carriers of memory of the atomic bombings have been Japanese movies. They tell stories of the hibakusha within a fictional frame, or use metaphor to remind their viewers and the world of the horrific nature and consequences of the attacks on Hiroshima and Nagasaki. Looking at cinema, moreover, enables historians to explore 'popular culture responses' to the atomic bombings and their victims within the prevailing 'political, social, psychological and cultural milieu' during the post-war decades.'[488]

During the American occupation and until 1952, Japanese films made about the events in August 1945 tended to treat them as a' tragedy', while in the West there was gathering criticism of them as an 'atrocity'.[489] Films such as *The Bells of Nagasaki* (1950), *I'll Never Forget the Song of Nagasaki* (1952) and *Children of Hiroshima* (1952) reflected a sense of wistful realism: this is not how we would wish it to be, but how it is.[490] *The Bells of Nagasaki* tells of the fate of the 10,000 Catholic *hibakusha* partly through the allegorical suffering of Christ, and the resurrection after the catastrophe.[491]

Once the Americans left, Japanese film directors became a little more critical of their nuclear legacy. In the science fiction film *Godzilla* (1954), a sleeping prehistoric monster is awoken from millions of years of slumber under the seabed by American atomic testing in the Pacific. Just like the bombs that fell on Hiroshima and Nagasaki, the monster wreaks havoc on the environment, killing people indiscriminately, and devastating the Japanese metropolis. *Godzilla* was initially distributed by an American company, and edited to remove its anti-American and anti-nuclear messages. The version released by the BFI in 2005, however, is the original film, with the often crude anti-American sentiments re-introduced.[492] The aforementioned *Children of Hiroshima* was directed by Shindo Kineto, whose concern for the atomic bomb survivors was also evident in the ironically-titled *Lucky Dragon Number 5* (1958). This also dealt with the effects of radioactive contamination from American atomic testing, but this time on a Japanese fishing boat, its fishermen and their haul. He also dealt with the theme of radiation-induced impotence in male *hibakusha* in *Lost Sex* (1966).

The theme of 'remembering', at the heart of commemoration, forms the meta-narrative of the French film *Hiroshima Mon Amour* (1959). Written by Marguerite Duras and directed by Alain Resnais, who also made a film about the Holocaust, a multi-layered story focuses upon an affair during the late 1950s between a French actress in Hiroshima and a married Japanese architect whose family were killed in August 1945. She is acting in an anti-war film, but their relationship is troubled by memories of their haunted pasts – she had been in love with a German soldier during the war – and images and flashbacks of the bombings. *Hiroshima Mon Amour* plays with the intensity and fragility of romantic attachment, the imminence of forgetting, and tragedy as possessing both a personal and global dimension. At one point the French actress declares 'I'm forgetting you already' as their relationship comes to its end. In another scene, the Museum in the Hiroshima Memorial Peace Park becomes a site of contested memory between the two lovers.

A key moment in the filmic representation and commemoration of the bomb-affected people was *Black Rain* (*Kuroi Ame*, 1967) originally a novel by Ibuse Masuji within the canon of *gembaku bungako*, or 'atomic bomb literature'.[493] Subsequently adapted into film by the renowned director Shohei Imamura, *Black Rain* (1989) depicts horrifying images of the death and injuries caused by the bomb. The title refers both to the filthy torrent of radioactive rain that falls upon the desolated landscape of Hiroshima and its victims during the fallout, and to the erosion of the lives affected by radiation sickness in the following decades. Set in the 1950s, a beautiful young woman who had moved to Nagasaki prior to the bombing finds she has leukaemia. Her beauty declines as her health deteriorates.[494] A key theme in both novel and film include the often difficult relationship between non-sufferers and the female *hibakusha*: some detested their own victimhood, while many unaffected people viewed the bomb victims as pathetic or shameful, and turned their eyes away from their appearance.

Possibly better known to Western audiences is the film *Rhapsody in August* (1994) an American-Japanese production starring Richard Gere. Directed by Akira Kurosawa, starring a mainly Japanese cast, and released on the eve of the eve of the fiftieth anniversary of the bombings, the film was attacked by some movie critics, for example such as Leslie Halliwell, whose blunt unenthusiastic summary hardly does justice to the profundity of the issues:

> A grandmother, prompted by her grandchildren and a visit from her Japanese-American nephew, recalls the death of her husband when the atomic bomb was dropped on Nagasaki.
> *A small-scale but ponderous plea for an understanding of the past.*[495]

Its subject matter is directly within the canon of memorialisation, however. The film can also be interpreted as a genuine even cathartic attempt at reconciliation between Japan and the USA around the central figure of a female bomb survivor. The lead actor Richard Gere apologises to the grandmother for the tragedy inflicted upon her by the bomb. The grandmother also unwittingly represents the gendered nature of interpretations of the suffering caused by the bombings. In *Black Rain, Rhapsody in August, Women in the Mirror* (2002) and in the television series

Yumechiyo's Diary (1985) a popular Japanese television melo-drama from the 1980s, women are at the centre of narratives of sorrow. In *Yumechiyo's Diary*, for example, the central character is both a geisha and an atom bomb survivor, a beautiful woman whose life, in common with the young woman in *Black Rain*, ends prematurely as a consequence of irradiation. On one reading, such films remind both Japanese and international film audiences of the human stories, the seemingly-endless suffering of the heroic women survivors. But in another interpretation, the feminist cultural critic Mayo Todeschini argues that the declining beauty of Yumechiyo is insensitively handled, almost a mocking essay on the ephemerality of youth and female good looks. Hence within the context of atomic bomb memory culture, *Black Rain* and *Yumechiyo's Diary* expose the often difficult relationship of vulnerable female *hibakusha* to the more conservative patriarchal cultural forces in Japanese society.[496]

Filmmakers rarely consulted the survivors when making their movies.[497] This was not the case with the work of Kenji Nakazawa. Like Raymond Briggs he lived through the Second World War as a little boy, but in Hiroshima. Nakazawa authored the graphic novel series *Barefoot Gen* (*Hadashi no Gen*) first serialised during the 1970s republished thereafter, and later made into an anime film and a television series. Nakazawa was about a kilometre from the epicentre of the explosion. Protected from the searing blast by a concrete wall, he was not incinerated to death or torched into agonies as were so many of his school friends.[498] His illustrations are in the Japanese manga tradition, narrating stories over many frames, and relying heavily upon symbolism. The burning morning sun is a recurring motif, a comment on the flag of Japan, the Land of the Rising Sun, ruled over by a divinely ordained

Emperor. The sun is also a metaphor for the atomic conflagration, while the strong wheat underfoot, growing back after the devastation, symbolise survival and renewal.[499] That the bomb that detonated over Hiroshima was called *Little Boy* and that Nakazawa was a little boy is no coincidence.

Nakazawa's father objected to the war and was attacked locally as a traitor before his death in August 1945. Nakazawa agreed with his father that 'Japan had been stupid and reckless to start the war'.[500] Such autobiographical details partly explain the hostile responses to *Barefoot Gen*. As in Germany, Japan possesses no victorious myth of the Blitz which allows for a heroic and patriotic narrative of civilian behaviour during either the conventional or the atomic bombings. The martial code of Japan, however, and powerful sentiments of militaristic nationalism, led to criticisms that Nakazawa was a traitor, dishonouring the dead and shaming the history of the Japanese military. *Barefoot Gen* was removed from the shelves of school libraries in 2013.[501]

Barefoot Gen is not the only manga about the effects of the A-bomb on children. A more recent and intensely powerful anime representation of life before the atomic bombings, *In This Corner of the World* (2016), is a beautiful anime film 'remembering' how life was before the cataclysm, and how people coped with destruction and loss. Again, the centre figure was a young woman, Suzu, who moves to be with her husband's family in the port city of Kure, Hiroshima. In common with *Barefoot Gen*, the ominous sight of bombers in the beautiful blue skies prefigures the tragedy to come. The film depicts the Japanese Home Front, including rationing, making-do-and-mending with fabric, air raid alerts and actual raids. The thriving city and the devastation that follows are symbolically contrasted in the central image, drawn by Suzu, of the Industrial Promotional Hall, now the Peace

Dome, before and after the attack. The emotional narratives create a colourful, romantic and tragic imaginal representation of loss and survival, and a return to the themes of transient youthful beauty.

Remembering the Victims of Conventional Bombing in Japan

The focus on the nuclear attacks has tended to obscure the history and remembrance of the conventional bombings suffered by Japanese cities and their civilians in 1944 and 1945. Yet conventional bombing killed many more people due to its sustained and intensive nature, and the firestorms it created.[502] For those who were not there, wartime photography enables imaginal memories of the conventional bombings of Japan and its consequences. At the instruction of the Chief of Police for the Metropolitan Police Department, and at great risk to himself, the police photographer Ishikawa Koyo ranged around the city during the Great Tokyo Air Raid in March 1945. His testimony bears strong similarities with survivors in many different countries, including vivid details of speeding fire trucks, wailing sirens, streams of people trying to run from the fires, charred corpses of women and children, and the gallant efforts of fire fighters. Koyo was caught up in a collapsing building:

> As the blizzard of sparks and embers blew down over me, I wondered how long I could last. I was prepared for death. But to die there like that without a struggle was just intolerable. [I] told myself I must not die. In that deadly whirlwind of flames, my police colleagues were still making desperate efforts to save as many people as they could, under this fierce attack by the barbaric enemy.

In the sky above, as if they were mocking us, the B-29s were still flying serenely through the black smoke at such low altitude that it seemed you could hold out your hand and touch them. [In] my fury at being unable to grab them and throw them to the ground, I yelled 'You bastards! But no sound came from my mouth.[503]

In common with Bert Hardy in London, he was not going to let his fear get the better of him. The social historian Arthur Marwick

Figure 12: Anti-war sculpture in the plaza of the Tokyo Metropolitan Government Building, designed by Kenzo Tange. The inscription reads 'An appeal for peace by the citizens of Tokyo' (photograph by author, 2017).

has written of the unwitting testimony of documents and contemporary accounts of the past.[504] Here the unwitting testimony
is that sense of defiance, but he also reveals something of the
indefatigable spirit of the Japanese that so frustrated the Allies.
His testimony can also be viewed as complementary to the photographs he took, bringing some of them to life many years later.

The terrible suffering and loss caused by the conventional bombing of Japanese cities became increasingly acknowledged since
the late 1960s. Over twenty years after the Great Tokyo Air Raid
of 1945, painful and vivid memories of the raids were increasingly articulated. In June 1967, construction workers unearthed a
group of human skeletons in a Tokyo subway station. Once pub-
licised, the sad story behind the skeletons was revealed by a man
who recalled losing most of his family during the air raid. Some
twenty-two years later, they were found huddled together in what
was left of the air raid shelter in which they sought safety. This
was the beginning of the end of the 'public amnesia' about the fire
bombings in Japan during 1945. However, it took until 1970 for
the 'critical turning point in public awareness of the firebombing
of Tokyo to emerge. That year saw the carpet-bombing of civilians in Vietnam, and continuing student protests in the streets of
Japan against the US-Japan Security Treaty signed after the Second World War. In a letter published in the *Asahi Shinbun* newspaper on 10 March 1970, the twenty-fifth anniversary of the Great
Tokyo Air Raid, a victim described his 'harrowing experience of
escaping from the inferno as the incendiary bombs rained down
around him':

> Should not those of us who experienced the raids, at
> least on this day, just for one day, speak of what war is
> really like? And shouldn't we also think about the bombs
> indiscriminately falling on Vietnam?[505]

The author of the letter was Saotome Katsumoto, a pacifist and critic of the United States. In common with the German Left and extreme Right, anti-Americanism was a key theme in Japanese commemoration and remembering. So many accounts of the raid were sent to the newspaper offices that Katsumoto and a group of academics established the Society for Recording the Tokyo Air Raids in 1970. The testimonies have been collated into a number of collections by Katsumoto, and a significant sample of them was republished on the seventieth anniversary of the Tokyo Raid by the *Asia-Pacific Journal* in March 2015.[506] Subsequently, Japanese-American oral historians have explored the experiences of survivors of both atomic and conventional weapons in Japan.[507]

Anime movies also represent victims of conventional bombing raids. The Studio Ghibli film *Grave of the Fireflies* (1988) is a deeply emotional animation about the struggle to survive malnutrition, homelessness and ill-health of a young boy and his sister; a struggle which the young girl (it is so often a girl) loses in an intensely moving scene. Fireflies, of course, live fleeting, forgotten lives.

The Applied Globalisation of Victimhood Narratives

Both Germany and Japan, the major aggressors against democracies during the Second World War, have suffused their national cultures of commemoration with a sense of victimhood that has diluted national blame for martial malpractice and even national consent for fascism. As Healy and Tumarkin argue, cultures of victimhood can provide 'both identity and considerable power from their sense of a shared traumatic past'.[508] The victims of Allied bombing raids on Germany from 1943–5, and the *hibakusha* of

Hiroshima and Nagasaki are obvious examples of groups who have fought to promote an identity based upon shared suffering, and to confront cultural amnesia.

Such positioning has led to considerable ethical compromises and a pernicious relativism when the *hibakusha* and German victims of bombing are compared with the dead of other conflicts during the late twentieth and early twenty-first centuries. For example, in an insightful and critical essay on the German Peace Movement, Andreas Huyssen argues that extensive pacifist sentiment in post-1990 Germany allowed for a selective interpretation of the Nazi regime and the German war to emphasise German suffering as a consequence of Allied air raids.[509] This in turn allowed for a spurious identification with the victims of the Iraq War from 2003, and its accompanying anti-Americanism on the German Left.

The Israel-Palestine conflict has led many Arab and anti-American critics of the Jewish state to liken those killed by Israeli air raids and other military occupations as innocent victims of an unjust and imperialistic aggressor. The victimization narrative thus transferred to the Arab-Israeli conflict. As Zwigenberg argues, for example, during the Lebanese Civil War from 1975–90 Israel was held responsible for massacres it did not commit. Following his visit to the Hiroshima Peace Memorial in 1983 the Tunisian Ambassador likened the suffering of the Lebanese people to the Japanese in 1945, while the Syrian ambassador, 'conveniently forgetting his own government's massacre of 10,000 civilians in Hama' stated that 'the slaughter of non-combatants is what brings Hiroshima and Israel's genocide in Lebanon together.'[510] Ran Zwigenberg notes the attempts by Palestinian leaders and other dignitaries from Middle Eastern countries to equate the Israeli attacks on the Gaza Strip in Palestine not only with the American bombing of Japan but with the Holocaust.[511] Yet the scale of suffering, calculated mass murder and torture involved in German genocide bears little comparison. It is also noteworthy that the Israeli Air Force issues warnings to Palestinians, known as 'roof knocking', when an air raid is imminent.[512] The Nazis made no such gestures to the victims of air raids.

The use of the noun 'genocide' raises hugely important issues, because if the atomic bombings of Japan and the Israeli air raids on the Gaza Strip are indeed genocides, then the Allied bombings of Germany can also be defined as genocidal. At first sight, the United Nations Convention on Genocide, passed in December 1948, would appear to support such claims:

> Article II
> In the present Convention, genocide means any of the following acts committed with intent to destroy, in whole or in part, a national, ethnical racial or religious group, as such:
> a) Killing members of the group;
> b) Causing serious bodily or mental harm to members of the group;
> c) Deliberately inflicting on the group conditions of life calculated to bring about its physical destruction in whole or in part;
> d) Imposing measures intending to prevent births within the group;
> e) Forcibly transferring children of the group to another group.[513]

As Chalk and Jonassohn pointedly argue, however, 'the UN definition is of little use to scholars' for many reasons, not least because of a wider failure to differentiate between violence intended to eradicate a group as opposed to brutality directed against the group. Moreover, the UN Convention 'intentionally excluded the deliberate annihilation of political groups and social classes from its definition of genocide.'[514] Chalk and Jonassohn offer an alternative definition:

> Genocide is a form of one-sided mass killing in which a state or other authority intends to destroy a group, as that group and membership in it are defined by the perpetrator.[515]

This definition allows for the fact there is no reciprocity between victim and perpetrator. This means, furthermore, that casualties of aerial warfare are not victims of genocide, because of the control that belligerent states have over their own territory and its population. In a total war, civilians can be regarded as combatants if their governments control their cities, a principle true for most aerial bombings (with exceptions such as Guernica in 1937 and Aleppo from 2015–17).[516] Given that the Germans and Japanese attacked the Allies, and vice versa, and that civilians were active participants in total warfare, commemorations to the *hibakusha* and to the German war dead cannot be accurately described as memorials to victims of a genocidal programme of bombing. Reciprocity to greater or lesser degrees was possible. The Armenians in the First World War, and Jews, Roma and gays in the Second World War, had no way of fighting back against an ideological and state-sponsored process of extermination directed at their group. They are examples of genocide. Allied air raids from 1940–5 are not.

Coda: Air Raids and Cultures of Memory: Some Wider Conclusions Post 9/11

Total war as both catalyst and context for retrospection gave rise to global similarities of experience that transcended national borders, but also to local and national variations in how the war was remembered. Sites of commemoration were also intertwined with a wider multi-dimensional culture of memory that involved people's memoirs of the war, autobiographies and diaries, film and television, and the growing use of oral history from the 1970s. Commemoration was a personal and public act, local, national and international. This can be further understood within the context of a twenty-first century atrocity.

The terrorist air attacks in September 2001 led to a passionate national debate about the nature of commemoration of the victims. Nearly 3,000 people were killed at the World Trade Centre, and at the Pentagon in North Virginia. The dead reflected a diverse range of American middle-class society. At least 270 Jewish people and thirty American Muslims also died. Many fire fighters and paramedics lost their lives, and foreigners were also killed. The attacks were almost immediately compared with the Blitz on London, despite huge differences in the scale, duration and casualty rates of the events. The fortitude of New Yorkers was compared with that of Londoners during the Second World War, and the Republican Mayor, Rudy Giuliani, likened himself to Winston Churchill.[517]

The United States has a grand monumental commemorative tradition, evident in the haunting and powerful symbols in Washington DC to the dead of the major wars in which it has fought. The National World War II Memorial was constructed in the aftermath of 9/11, and dedicated by President George W. Bush in 2004. One literary critic has argued that the memorial reinforces 'a singularly heroic reading of the American past and a unilateral approach to world history' which celebrates the imposition of American values on other countries.[518] It also follows that 'this message' can be identified in American foreign policy since the events in September 2001.[519] Interpreting the American contribution to the Second World War within an attempt to impose American 'ideals and ideologies', however, does not fully acknowledge the US and Allied war against German, Italian and Japanese fascism, violent ideologies pursuing brutal transnational dictatorships.

Various writers have contended that the use of the term 'Ground Zero' for the site of the Twin Towers borrows from the term used for devastation wrought at Hiroshima and Nagasaki, viewed unequivocally as an American atrocity.[520] Suggesting that the adoption of the label 'Ground Zero' might be a cynical attempt to convert the image of the USA from aggressor to victim, nothing is offered in the way of either historical context or debate about the causes, nature and consequences of the atomic bombings in drawing the Japanese war to an end.

The attack on New York also raised the spectre of the Holocaust for many American Jews, as another fascist ideology, this time associated with extremist Islamism rather than Nazism, targeted a city heavily populated by Jewish Americans. It must have been incredibly difficult for Jewish citizens of New York to disassociate the attacks on the Twin Towers from anti-Semitism, an evil at the heart of both Islamism and Nazism. This partly explains the controversy over the calls for a Muslim prayer room to be included in an Islamic Centre near the site of Ground Zero. As Zwigenberg argues, 'many pundits claimed that building a mosque so close to the site would be an affront to the memory of 9/11' while others viewed this as a victory for tolerance and American democracy.[521] The issue polarised opinion across the USA, but the debate was nuanced. Many American Christians and Jews were unhappy at the othering of Muslims and at the nascent or overt Islamophobia in many religious protests against the Islamic Centre.[522] At the time of writing, however, the mosque project had been deemed a failure. Both alleged corruption and inadequate funding were blamed. Apartments alongside a museum were proposed instead.[523]

The controversy in New York highlighted some of the key themes in commemoration and memorialisation: bereavement, catharsis and the drive for recognition of the dead; a synthesis of both private and public grief in memorial events; powerful emotions of anger and revenge towards the enemy; and the desire for reconciliation and forgiveness. These were defining characteristics in the global culture of commemoration since 1945.

CHAPTER 9

Archives and Online Resources

Introduction

The history of aerial warfare on civilians and urban areas has left us with a vast and diverse range of primary sources. This chapter is essentially a general guide to the most accessible sources further research. Beginning with a summary of the strengths and issues associated with the major types of sources available, it then provides an introduction to the major archival repositories in Britain, Germany, Japan and the United States. Other archives are indicated for cities and towns where significant air raids and civilian casualties occurred.

How to cite this book chapter:
Clapson, M. 2019. *The Blitz Companion*. Pp. 229–224. London: University of Westminster Press. DOI: https://doi.org/10.16997/book26.i. License: CC-BY-NC-ND 4.0

Primary Sources

Primary sources are defined by historians as any source generated during the period under study. This includes artefacts such as aeroplanes, bombs and the remnants of air raid shelters or pieces of shrapnel. It covers political documentation such as committee minutes at local and national government levels, or governments reports into morale, surveys of destruction, and of course the various forms of official propaganda. The term 'primary sources' further embraces a wide range of *contemporary* documents including newspapers and magazine articles and reports published at the time, different genres of films and photography made during the historical era under study, radio and sound recordings, maps, and contemporary writings in the form of letters and diaries.

Visual Sources: Documentary Film, Newsreels and Photography

Documentary films on the British Blitz and on other air raids are held at the British Film Institute (BFI). Based in London, the BFI is the major repository of key films and television programmes of the twentieth and twenty-first centuries. Two BFI websites contains links to many free-to-view documentary and propaganda short films about the Blitz and wartime Britain, and also reconstruction. Pay-per-view streaming is available, as is a facility to purchase different genres of film, and also books about the Blitz and air raids during the Second World War.

Four main search categories cover the wartime experience in London and many provincial towns and cities: 'Blitz'; 'Life under Fire'; 'Air raids' and 'Fire damage'. Film content includes instruction about putting on gas masks, ARP, evacuation, anti-aircraft measures, air raids, secret royal visits to bomb damaged cities, auxiliary and fire services, and reconstruction. Some are silent, some are spoken. Fiction feature films and documentary are prominent: the BFI adjunct website *screenonline.org* contains a wealth of information about the content, actors, producers and directors of wartime films.

Moreover, the BFI also hosts the instruction film *Protect and Survive* (1976) issued to the British public to inform them about protective behaviour in the event of a nuclear attack. Anyone watching will be reminded that the chilling information on the bomb and its effects came from the events in Japan in August 1945. Classic Vietnam War films are among other relevant genres introduced online.

Anyone interested in film and air raids, and in representations of the Blitz, the Home Front, reconstruction and war from the air during the twentieth century, should begin with the BFI Websites: www.bfi.org.uk/education-research and www.screenonline.org.uk

American documentaries are held at the National Archives and Records Administration (NARA) and on a number of online websites, discussed later in this chapter. The context of censorship during wartime needs to be accounted for when understanding the use of films as primary sources. All films were edited, and contain biases. Nonetheless, bias can be very useful for understanding the values of the filmmakers, and of the context in which they were operating. Newsreels were also edited for domestic consumption and often to boost morale as well as inform the public. Two richly varied online archives are www.movietone.com and www.britishpathe.com.

Contemporary photographs can be found in a wide variety of publications, from newspapers and magazines, many of which were censored, many of which were not, to official histories that utilised photography to record the consequences of air raids. The United States Strategic Bombing Survey (USSBS) was initiated on 3 November 1944 'to establish a basis for evaluating the importance and potential of air power as an instrument of military strategy and for planning the future development of the armed forces.'[524] It was wound up in 1947, leaving an incomparable resource for historians of the Allied bombings in Europe and Japan. The USSBS records at the National Archives, College Park, Maryland, hold over 18,000 photographs taken during its operations, providing a visual dimension to the detailed textual descriptions and analyses of the impact of bombing on people, buildings, infrastructure and landscapes. Many of these images along with sections of the survey are available online. Harrowing images of the dead huddled in ineffectual air raid shelters; pictures of survivors picking their way through the rubble; and compelling photographs of huge urban landscapes reduced to smoking ruins by carpet bombing or the atom bomb provide visual evidence of American air power, and by extension of the heart-rending consequences of all air raids. The J. Paul Getty Museum holds many photographs of twentieth-century conflicts, and the Getty Images website also provides a number of Blitz and air raid photographs from the twentieth century: www.gettyimagesgallery.com.

The Japanese public broadcasting channel NHK also hosts an online archive with photographs about the bombing of Japan: www.nhk.or.jp/peace/english/chrono/chrono_08.html.

National Archives and Libraries

Thanks to the internet we now have almost instantaneous access to nothing less than an online global archive covering the history of air wars. Myriad examples of all of the primary source formats given above can be found on the internet, but not everything is posted online. Many other sets of materials are still un-digitized: they are in hard copy formats, and stored in libraries, museums and archives. All of the key libraries, museums and archives get around this access issue by providing websites which offer samples of the riches contained there, and content summaries of their in-house collections which the interested historian or member of the public can peruse prior to their research visit. Other websites authored by historians also offer contemporary sources alongside secondary interpretations of the history of air raids in particular, and of aerial warfare in general.

Deutsches Historisches Museum (Germany)

The website of the Deutsches Historisches Museum holds eyewitness accounts of Germans who lived through the Second World War, including testimonies of those who experienced bombing raids. Many photographs of damage and destruction are available, along with wartime posters, images of artefacts, biographies of both important and 'ordinary' Germans. The website has a prominent and easy-to-use search engine. Try typing in 'Dresden' or 'weltkreig' and many fascinating results become available. Website: www.dhm.de/fileadmin/lemo/suche/search/index.php?q=*&f[]=seitentyp:Zeitzeuge&f[]=epoche:Zweiter%20Weltkrieg

Imperial War Museum (IWM)

The IWM is based on a number of sites in Britain, the largest at Kennington in South London. While not strictly a repository of printed materials, it does house the instruments of total war. Visitors to the IWM in Kennington can see at first hand some of the fighter and bomber planes that terrorised cities across Europe, the V1 flying bomb and the V2 flying rocket, and many other military artefacts. The IWM also places considerable emphasis on every-day life during the Second World War. Domestic interiors, air raid shelters, and the experiences of war work are represented through contemporary paraphernalia, photographs, newspaper cuttings, artwork, maps and models. Website: www.iwm.org.uk/

The IWM at Duxford in Cambridgeshire hosts many materials on the Battle of Britain that preceded and overlapped with the onset of the Blitz. Fighter and bomber planes are a core element of the conservation project at Duxford, along with photographs and materials relating to planes, pilots and stories of bravery and heroism. The IWM at Duxford also holds a permanent American Air Museum (AAM) exhibition. Both the AAM and its web-site present key aspects of the American history of flight, the US contribution to the winning of the Second World War, notably the bomb groups and squadrons, and the pilots, that played a vital role in the defeat of Germany and the liberation of Europe from fascism. The website includes interactive maps depicting the American presence in Britain and Europe, including military sites, cemeteries and crash sites. Websites: www.iwm.org.uk/visits/iwm-duxford; www.americanairmuseum.com

Mass Observation Archive, 'The Keep', University of Sussex, Brighton

Mass Observation (MO) was established in 1937 by the social anthropologist Tom Harrisson and the social scientist Charles Madge. The movement attracted many middle-class people who fancied themselves as writers and observers of popular culture and everyday life in 'mass society'. Volunteer personal writers kept diaries, while investigators made detailed observations in everyday situation, noted 'overheards' and recorded responses from questionnaires. These all went into the 'file reports' held at the MO archives, and formed the raw materials for Mass Observation publications.

From the mid-1980s archivists at the MO collection at the University of Sussex set about increasing awareness of the materials there and accessibility to them. A number of booklets for secondary schools were produced on the Blitz in Britain, still available on the MO website: www.massobs.org.uk/images/booklets/Blitz.pdf

National Archives and Records Administration (NARA; United States)

Based in College Park, Maryland, the National Archives II building holds records of the USAAF/USAF and wider sets of materials on the two world wars, and American involvement in other conflicts during the twentieth century, notably the Korean and Vietnamese Wars. The NARA website has a very easy-to-use search engine. Record Group 243 (RG243) holds the extensive collection of the United States Strategic Bombing Survey from 1944–6 so is an invaluable resource for the Allied bombings of Europe and Japan: www.archives.gov/research/guide-fed-records/groups/243.html. A sense of the depth and range of materials on the Korean War can be found here: www.archives.gov/research/alic/reference/military/korean-war.html while a search for 'Vietnam War bombings' produced not only materials held at NARA but also at the presidential libraries: https://search.archives.gov/search?query=vietnam+war+bombings&submit=&utf8=&affilia

te=national-archives. Further records on American involvement in Vietnam can be found at www.archives.gov/research/military/ vietnam-war. Additionally, USAAF/USAF records are listed here: www.archives.gov/research/military/air-force. Some materials are digitised hence available online. Students can spend many hours pursuing the NARA website, just to gain a sense of the richness of the materials held there. Website: www.archives.gov/research

The National Archives, Kew, London (TNA)

Wartime records form a significant part of the twentieth century materials held at the British National Archives. These can be searched using key terms in the catalogue 'Discovery', while other web pages for TNA provide information and links to many of the important aspects of the air raids and the Home Front, including teacher's notes. Online webpages provide useful introductions to the zeppelin and Gotha raids, for example. The materials on the Second World War however are naturally more extensive, and include bomb census maps, air raid damage files, records of the civilian war dead including names of individual casualties, sources for the National Fire Service and ARP, and records from the key government ministries. The files on the Ministry of Home Security and Ministry of Information are invaluable sources for the historical study of morale and of the official importance of monitoring it. TNA holds home intelligence reports for wartime Britain but also for Germany from 1945, as it was defeated and became occupied. Propaganda, illustrations and artistes collectively labelled as 'the Art of War' form part of the Ministry of Information deposits, while the Ministry of Supply records detail the practical problems and solutions facing the government from aircraft production to the delivery of essential goods for wartime production. The website also contains links to local and regional collections held elsewhere in the UK, and to websites dealing with air raids in specific towns and cities. Some government records of British RAF and army operations since 1945, notably the Korean War and the air attacks in the Falklands War, are also held at Kew.

The National Archives also hold materials on post-war reconstruction in the Housing and Local Government (HLG) record group, incorporating many records from the Home Front. Other record groups contain materials on health, military operations, etc. Website: http://discovery.nationalarchives.gov.uk

National Diet Library, Japan

The National Library of Japan, based in Tokyo, contains repatriated materials, and also records of the American 'occupation' of Japan from 1945–52, which will be valuable to historians of reconstruction. Leading newspapers such as the *Asahi Shinbun* are also held there. Some of these materials are digitised and available online. Website: www.ndl.go.jp/en

Royal Air Force Museums in London and Cosford, Shropshire

The RAF museums hold over 100 aircraft from the previous century, and hundreds of thousands of objects drawn from over a century of aerial warfare. The RAF museum website offers some fascinating exhibitions on the First and Second World Wars in the skies above Britain. Naturally, the 'finest hour' of the RAF, namely the Battle of Britain, features prominently on the website, which prefaces web pages on the Blitz and air defences. It is good to see the brave and often neglected contribution of the Polish

Air Force to the defeat of the Luftwaffe. Women in the history of the RAF and the contribution of the USA to the aerial defence of the United Kingdom are also featured. Website: www.rafmuseum.org.uk

The Smithsonian National Air and Space Museum, Washington DC

The Smithsonian is the oldest research and museum complex in the world, and the National Air and Space Museum is one of nineteen museums and galleries in the Washington DC Metro area. The website is very user-friendly, and the collections, exhibitions and artefacts it links to mostly covers the history of flight and technological progress that enabled the exploration of space. Yet using the search engine to type in relevant key words can yield some fascinating results on air campaigns from the point of view of the USAF and its personnel. These include the Second World War, and the Korean and Vietnam conflicts. Website: www.si.edu/Museums/air-and-space-museum and https://airandspace.si.edu

Local Archives in the United Kingdom

Beyond the national libraries and archives, a great many town and city libraries and archives host valuable sources for historians of the Blitz. In London for example, the London Metropolitan Archives (LMA) based in Finsbury holds London County Council (LCC) records and borough council records of the air raids, and of wartime planning and post-war reconstruction schemes. These are in the form of committee minutes, for example, the Housing and Town Planning committee and the Architect's Department of the LCC, in addition to the borough council committee minutes held at the LMA. The archive also holds bomb damage maps for London, photographs and art works depicting bomb damage, and plans for reconstruction schemes at borough level. Website: www.cityoflondon.gov.uk/things-to-do/london-metropolitan-archives/Pages/search.aspx

The City of London suffered heavy damage during the Blitz of 1940–1, although it mostly escaped the V1 and V2 attacks towards the end of the war. Many records of the Blitz are held there. During the conflict a large-scale plan for the reconstruction of the City was drawn up by Charles Holden and William Holford, and published in 1947. The City was not part of the LCC administrative area, however, being governed by the Corporation of London. Photographs, Corporation records of bomb damage and destruction and primary materials relating the reconstruction plans are held at the Guildhall Library near Liverpool Street Station in Bethnal Green. Website: www.cityoflondon.gov.uk/things-to-do/guildhall-library/Pages/default.aspx

The City of Westminster Archives in Victoria, South London, possesses some fascinating sources from the air raids on Westminster between 1940 and 1945. An impressive bomb survey map for almost all the bombing events on Westminster is held there, but is also available along with any photographs and accompanying descriptions, on the www.westendatwar.org.uk website. This provides an excellent online introduction to the materials available at the City of Westminster Archives, which in addition to many photographs and artworks includes contemporary artefacts from the Battle for London, for example ARP materials, including a helmet and gas masks, along with incendiary devices and collections of wartime photographs and correspondence.

Across Britain, almost all cities and large towns with a local history library hold some information on the air raids of the Second World War. Many records also held in County Records Offices. There are too many to list here but the examples of two provincial cities will suffice. For Manchester in north-west England the following link provides a clear introduction to local materials held at the Manchester Central Library and the University of Manchester: https://manchesterarchiveplus.wordpress.com/2012/12/14/manchester-blitz/. Manchester Central Library holds photographs, correspondence and oral history collections on the Manchester Blitz. Websites: www.manchester.gov.uk and www.gmlives.org.uk.

In Belfast the **Public Record Office of Northern Ireland** (PRONI) is a great example of the richness of archives beyond London. Its extensive collection on one of the last air raids during the Blitz of 1940–1 includes many files of the Ministry of Public Security on air raids the bombing of the shipyards, the waterside complexes and nearby housing areas; the Public Security War Room War Diary which contains warning messages about bombings; a Ministry of Home Affairs files on publicity surrounding the war effort, and on Civil Defence; records on Civil Defence organisations and ARP; the WVS; a record of the damage to Harland and Wolff and Short and Harland ship-builders; Ministry of Public Service intelligence summaries of air raids on Belfast; casualty lists, and collections of contemporary photographs and diaries of the Belfast Blitz. PRONI also contains records of the Northern Ireland Housing Trust, one of the government-funded agencies established in 1945 to address the housing shortage in Belfast and other towns and cities in the Six Counties. The Housing Trust was a major provider of social housing during Reconstruction. Website: www.nidirect.gov.uk/proni

Taking Care with Online Searches and Their Results

Countless websites about air raids and their consequences can be found online. They vary hugely in the quality of their presentation and user-friendliness. Some are academically quite rigorous and cite information given, others less so. Many such as www.westen-datwar.org.uk/ and www.bombsight.org are fully researched and presented by professional archivists or historians. A plethora of websites offered by amateur enthusiasts is also available, and can be useful for images, sounds and film clips. A good example is www.flyingbombsandrockets.com/ on the V1 and V2 attacks on London from 1944–5. All such websites should have their details checked if used in essays or research-based work.

Many websites aimed at school students and university under-graduates contain pages on the Blitz and other air raids of the twen-tieth century. A good example is www.historylearningsite.co.uk/ set up by a highly-respected history teacher, whose untimely death led to his family maintaining the site online. Based on the History Channel, www.history.com has both American and British web-sites, with some fascinating and useful articles on both countries at war. The www.bbc.co.uk learning websites can be searched for useful information on the Blitz and other air raids. Intended for school students, they are also useful as a way-in for the general reader, but not really academically extensive enough to amount to more than a few references in a thoroughly-researched essay.

There is also the question of bias: many websites are simply online portals for highly tendentious or politically warped inter-pretations of air raids during the twentieth century and since. Using websites during the course of research should be under-taken with as much, possibly more, critical awareness than when consulting primary sources of historical information. What follows is not an exhaustive coverage, but a focus on a couple of websites to serve as a kind of health warning to users.

Take the strident anti-Allied bombing campaign website www.revisionist.net, established under another name by the now deceased Linda Schaitberger, a right-wing German-American Republican. Prior to her death the site was taken over, revised and is now maintained online by her enthusiastic successor Simon Sheppard who has been convicted of several race-related offences. The historical perspective of revisionist is straightforward: Germany was the traumatised and historically persecuted victim of the First World War, hence the Second World War was caused by the mistreatment of the Fatherland, when the Germans were bombed into submission by the American, British and Soviet forces. Subsequently a successful post-war *kulturkampf* reduced German history and identity to a deracinated condition of shame and guilt for the two world wars of the last century. 'It does not disturb the modern German', states the introduction to the website:

> that his homeland was bombed into rubble. [It] makes them uncomfortable to realize that their families, as civilians, were intentionally burned alive in violent, unnecessary residential fire bombings, or fiendishly drowned by the thousands when dams were calculatedly destroyed, or purposely shot at when they were running for their lives.[525]

While revisionist.net does contain some comparative Allied and German bombing statistics, the glaring absence of the airborne atrocities committed by the Luftwaffe, combined with a wilful silence on German war crimes and the Holocaust, reveals the specious and unreliable content of the website.

Many similarly dubious websites were created in the aftermath of 9/11. For example, www.911truth.org is a forum for the so-called 'truthers' who claim that terrorism was not to blame for the airborne destruction of the Twin Towers and the death of 3,000 people on that terrible day. Many Americans believe that 9/11 was brought upon the USA by itself, either as an inside job by a maniacal President Bush and his cadre of crazies, or as divine retribution for secular degeneration. While it appears to have scholarly credentials, and links to articles in respected publications, the site mostly draws its strength from the view that President Bush and Vice President Cheney were culpable in a terrible conspiracy to demonise Islam and provide justification for a violent phase of American intervention in the Middle East. Conspiracy theories permeate much of the content, including the view that Osama Bin Laden was dead long before the US Navy Seals took him out in 2013. An anti-Israeli perspective fuels many articles while veiled hints about Jewish involvement in 9/11 are not far from the surface in some pieces. This Jewish conspiracy trope reeks of the long-standing historical fabrication of *The Protocols of the Elders of Zion*. Many Islamist websites, in common with Nazi-inspired sites, sadly perpetuate both the lie that Israel and the American Jewish lobby have blood on their hands within the wider context of a global Jewish conspiracy. Even adversaries such as A. C. Grayling and Christopher Hitchens agree that 9/11 was indubitably a terror attack on civilians with similar intentions to the area bombing of cities during the twentieth century. Yet those air campaigns were conducted by states that had declared war on each other, while the attack on the Twin Towers was by a religious fundamentalist organisation seeking a global caliphate.[526]

As for secondary sources …

Finally, a useful way to grasp the extent and the fascinating historiography of air raids is to go to www.history.ac.uk, the website of the Institute of Historical Research (UK), and enter your search terms, from 'Blitz' to 'Korean War' to 'Vietnam' to take but three examples. You will then be presented with pages of reviews of books which highlight key themes in the historiography of your chosen subject within the broader history of air raids. While relying on reviews is no substitute for reading the books themselves, looking at reviews also gives you a fascinating and wide-ranging insight into how historians see their work, and those of others.

Bibliography and Sources

Articles, Books and Book Chapters

Adams, David and Larkham, P.J. 'Bold Planning, Mixed Experiences: The Diverse Fortunes of Post-War Birmingham', in Clapson, Mark and Larkham, P.J. (eds) *The Blitz and its Legacy: Wartime Destruction to Post-War Reconstruction* (Farnham: Ashgate, 2013)

Adams, David and Larkham P.J. *The Post-War Reconstruction Planning of London: A Wider Perspective* (Birmingham: Birmingham City University, Centre for Environment and Society Research Series; Working Paper No. 8 (2011))

Adey, Peter, Cox, D.J. and Godfrey, Barry *Crime Regulation and Control during the Blitz* (London: Bloomsbury, 2016)

Anon 'East End at War', *Picture Post*, 8 September 1940

Anon, 'News of the Week', *The Spectator*, 1 October 1937

Anon, Report in *Polytechnic Magazine*, September, 1939

Anon, Report in *Polytechnic Magazine*, December, 1939

Apel, Linde 'Voices from the Rubble Society: "Operation Gomorrah" and its Aftermath', *Journal of Social History* 44:4 (2011)

Arnold, Jörg *The Allied War and Urban Memory* (Cambridge:
Cambridge University Press, 2011)

Baruma, Ian 'Germany's Unmourned Victims', *Guardian*, 26
November 2002

Beaven, Brad and Griffiths, John, 'The Blitz, Civilian Morale and
the City: Mass Observation and Working-Class Culture in
Britain, 1940–41', *Urban History* 26: 1 (1999)

Beck, E.R. *Under the Bombs: The German Home Front, 1942-45*
(Lexington, Kentucky: University Press of Kentucky, 1986)

Bell, Amy Helen *London Was Ours: Diaries and Memoirs of the
London Blitz* (London: I.B. Tauris, 2011)

Betjeman, John 'Slough', in Skelton, Robin (ed.) *Poetry of the Thirties* (Harmondsworth: Penguin, 1985)

Bevan, Robert *The Destruction of Memory: Architecture at War*
(London: Reaktion Books, 2006)

Blum, William *Rogue State: A Guide to the World's Only Super-
power* (London: Zed Books, 2014)

Bold, John and Pickard, Robert 'Reconstructing Europe: The
Need for Guidelines', *The Historic Environment: Policy and
Practice* 4:2 (2013)

Bold, John, Larkham, P.J and Pickard, Robert (eds) *Authentic
Reconstruction: Authenticity, Architecture and the Built Heritage* (London: Bloomsbury, 2017)

Bond, Lucy *Frames of Memory after 9/11: Culture, Criticism, Politics and Law* (London: Palgrave Macmillan, 2015)

Bosworth, Patricia *Jane Fonda: The Private Life of a Public Woman*
(London: The Robson Press, 2011)

Boyer, Paul *By the Bomb's Early Light: American Thought and
Culture at the Dawn of the Atomic Age* (New York: Pantheon,
1985)

Briggs, Raymond *Ethel and Ernest* (London: Jonathan Cape, 1999)

—— *When the Wind Blows* (London: Penguin, 1982)

Broderick, Mick 'Introduction' in Broderick, Mick (ed.) *Hibakusha Cinema: Hiroshima, Nagasaki and the Nuclear Image in
Japanese Film* (London: Kegan Paul International, 1996)

Calder, Angus *The Myth of the Blitz* (London: Pimlico, 2008)

Campbell, Christy *Target London: Under Attack from the V-Weapons* (London: Little, Brown, 2012)

Chalk, Frank and Jonassohn, Kurt *The History and Sociology of Genocide* (New Haven, CT and London: Yale University Press, published in cooperation with the Montreal Institute for Genocide Studies, 1990)

Chinnery, Phil *Vietnam: The Air War over South-East Asia* (Stamford, Lincolnshire: Key Publishing, 2015)

Churchill, Winston *The Second World War* (London: Pimlico, 2002)

Clapson, Mark 'Destruction and Dispersal: The Blitz and the "Break up" of Working-Class London', in Clapson, Mark and Larkham, P. J. (eds) *The Blitz and its Legacy: Wartime Destruction to Post-War Reconstruction* (Farnham: Ashgate, 2013)

—— 'From Garden City to New Town: Social Change, Politics and Town Planners at Welwyn, 1920-1948', in Meller, Helen and Porfyriou, Helen (eds) *Planting New Towns in Europe in the Inter-War Years: Experiments and Dreams for Future Societies* (Cambridge: Cambridge Scholars Publishing, 2016)

—— *Invincible Green Suburbs, Brave New Towns: Social Change and Urban Dispersal in Post-War England* (Manchester: Manchester University Press, 1998)

—— *Working-Class Suburb: Social Change on an English Council Estate, 1930-2010* (Manchester: Manchester University Press, 2012)

Clodfelter, Mark *The Limits of Air Power: The American Bombing of North Vietnam* (New York and London: Macmillan, 1989)

Clout, Hugh 'Destruction, Revival and Reconstruction across Alsace and Lorraine, 1939-1960', in Clapson Mark and Larkham, P.J. (eds) *The Blitz and its Legacy: Wartime Destruction to Post-war Reconstruction* (Farnham: Ashgate, 2013)

Conway-Lanz, Saul 'The Ethics of Bombing Civilians After World War Two: The Persistence of Norms Against Targeting Civilians in the Korean War', *Asia-Pacific Journal: Japan Focus*, 12:37 (2014)

Cook and Cook, *Japan at War: An Oral History* (London: Phoenix Press, 1992)

Corrigan, Gordon *The Second World War: A Military History* (London: Atlantic Books, 2010)

Cowan, Susanne 'The People's Peace: The Myth of Wartime Unity and Public Consent for Town Planning', in Clapson, Mark and Larkham P. J. (eds.) *The Blitz and its Legacy: Wartime Destruction to Post-War Reconstruction* (Farnham: Ashgate, 2013)

Croft, Hazel 'Rethinking Civilian Neuroses in the Second World War', in Leese, Peter and Crouthamel, Jason (eds) *Traumatic Memories of the Second World War and After* (Basingstoke: Palgrave Macmillan, 2016)

Cumings, Bruce *The Korean War: A History* (New York: Modern Library, 2010)

Dale, Robert 'Divided We Stand: Cities, Social Unity and Post-War Reconstruction in Soviet Russia, 1945-53', *Contemporary European History* 24:4 (2015)

Denham, Scott and McCulloh, Mark *W.G. Sebald: History, Memory, Trauma* (New York: Walter de Gruyter, 2006)

Dodd, Lindsey 'La Ville Entrée, or How Bombing Turned the City Inside Out', in Clapson, Mark and Larkham, P. J. (eds) *The Blitz and its Legacy: Wartime Destruction to Post-War Reconstruction* (Farnham: Ashgate, 2013)

Dorsey, J.T. and Matsuoka, Naomi 'Narrative Strategies of Understatement in *Black Rain* as a Novel and Film', in Broderick, Mick (ed.) *Hibakusha Cinema: Hiroshima, Nagasaki and the Nuclear Image in Japanese Film* (London: Kegan Paul International, 1996)

Diefendorf, J. M. 'America and the Rebuilding of Urban Germany', in Diefendorf, J. M., Frohn, Axel and Rupieper, Hermann-Josef (eds) *American Policy and the Reconstruction of West Germany, 1945-1955* (Cambridge: Cambridge University Press, 1993) 331-52

—— *In the Wake of War: The Reconstruction of German Cities after World War Two* (New York and Oxford: Oxford University Press, 1993)

—— 'War and Reconstruction in Germany and Japan', in Hein, Carola, Diefendorf, J.M. and Yorifusa, Ishida (eds.) *Rebuilding Urban Japan* after 1945 (Basingstoke: Palgrave Macmillan, 2003)

—— 'Reconstructing Civic Authority in Post-War Germany', in Clapson, Mark and Larkham, P.J. *The Blitz and its Legacy: Wartime Destruction to Post-War Reconstruction* (Farnham: Ashgate, 2013)

Doherty, Ben 'France Launches "Massive" Airstrike on ISIS Stronghold of Raqqa', *Guardian*, 16 November 2015

Dominscsak, Jacek 'Warsaw and Gdansk as Two Distinctive Approaches to Post Second World War Reconstruction', in Barakat, Sultan, Calame, Jon and Charlesworth, Esther (eds) *Urban Triumph or Urban Disaster? Dilemmas of Contemporary Post-war Reconstruction* (York: Post-War Reconstruction and Development Unit, 1996)

Eiserman, F.A. *War on Film: Military History Education* (Fort Leavenworth, Kansas: Combat Studies Institute, 1987)

Eley, Geoff 'Finding the People's War: Film, Collective Memory and World War Two', *American Historical Review*, 106:3 (2001)

Farrington, Karen *The Blitzed City: The Destruction of Coventry, 1940* (London: Aurum Press, 2016)

Felton, Monica *What I Saw in Korea* (Watford: Mrs Monica Felton, 1951)

Ferguson, Niall *The War of the World: Twentieth-Century Conflict and the Descent of the West* (New York: Penguin, 2006)

Flinn, Catherine 'Reconstruction Constraints: Political and Economic Realities', in Clapson, Mark and Larkham P. J. (eds.) *The Blitz and its Legacy: Wartime Destruction to Post-War Reconstruction* (Farnham: Ashgate, 2013)

Forrester, Helen *Lime Street at Two* (London: HarperCollins, 2012)

Gardiner, Juliet *The Blitz: The British under Attack* (London: HarperCollins, 2010)

Garnett, Mark and Weight, Richard *Modern British History: The Essential A-Z Guide* (London: Pimlico, 2004)

Gibbons, Duncan 'Bishop of Coventry Apologises for Dresden Bombing', *Coventry Telegraph*, 17 February 2009

Gilbert, Martin *The Dent Atlas of American History* (London: J.M. Dent, 1993)

Goldstein, Richard 'Charles Sweeney', *New York Times*, 19 July 2004

Grayling, A.C. *Among the Dead Cities* (London: Bloomsbury, 2014)

Grayzel, Susan *At Home and Under Fire: Air Raids and Culture in Britain from the Great War to the Blitz* (Cambridge: Cambridge University Press, 2012)

Griffith, Robert *Major Problems in American History since 1945* (Lexington, MA.: D.C. Heath and Co., 1992)

Ham, Paul *Hiroshima Nagasaki: The Real Story of the Atomic Bombings and Their Aftermath* (London: Doubleday, 2013)

Haapamaki, Michele *The Coming of the Aerial War: Culture and the Fear of Airborne Attack in Interwar Britain* (London: I.B. Tauris, 2014)

Hane, Miso *Japan: A Modern History* (London: One World Publications, 2015)

Harding, Luke 'Germany's Forgotten Victims', *Guardian*, 22 October 2003

Harnden, Toby 'Churchill Spirit inspires Bush and Giuliani', *Daily Telegraph*, 27 September 2001

Hasegawa, Junichi, 'Problems of Blitz Reconstruction in Japan: The Case of Sendai', in Clapson, Mark and Larkham, P.J. *The Blitz and its Legacy: Wartime Destruction to Post-War Reconstruction* (Farnham: Ashgate, 2013)

Halliwell, Martin 'Hiroshima in December', *Spectator*, 11 January 1946

Harris, Clive *Walking the London Blitz* (Barnsley: Pen and Sword, 2006)

Hashimoto, Akiko *The Long Defeat: Cultural Trauma, Memory and Identity in Japan* (Oxford: Oxford University Press, 2016)

Hastings, Max *Bomber Command* (London: Pan, 2010)

—— *Nemesis: The Battle for Japan, 1944-45* (London: Harper-Collins, 2014)

—— *The Korean War* (London: Pan Macmillan 2010)

—— 'What Would You Have Done?' *Guardian*, 30 July 2005

Healy, C. and Tumarkin M., 'Social Memory and Historical Justice: Introduction' *Journal of Social History* 4: 44 (2011)

Hebbert, Michael 'The Street as Locus of Collective Memory', *Environment and Planning D: Society and Space*, 25, (2005)

Hein, Carola, Diefendorf, J.M. and Yorifusa, Ishida (eds.) *Rebuilding Urban Japan* after 1945 (Basingstoke: Palgrave Macmillan, 2003)

Hitchens, Christopher *Orwell's Victory* (London: Allen Lane Penguin, 2002)

Hogan, M.J. (ed.) *Hiroshima in History and Memory* (Cambridge: Cambridge University Press, 1996)

Holman, B. *The Next War in the Air: Britain's Fear of the Bomber, 1908-1941* (Farnham: Ashgate, 2014)

Holmes, Richard *Falling Upwards: How We Took to the Air* (London: William Collins, 2013)

Houghton, Frances 'The "Missing Chapter": Bomber Command Aircrew Memoirs in the 1990s and 2000s', in Noakes, Lucy and Pattinson, Juliette (eds) *British Cultural Memory and the Second World War* (London: Bloomsbury, 2014)

Hunt, Michael *A Vietnam War Reader: American and Vietnamese Perspectives* (London: Penguin, 2010)

Huyssen, Andreas 'Air War Legacies: From Dresden to Baghdad', in Niven, Bill (ed.) *Germans as Victims: Remembering the Past in Contemporary Germany* (Basingstoke: Palgrave Macmillan, 2006)

Irving, David *The Destruction of Dresden* (London: William Kimber and Co., 1963)

Jackson, Neil 'Tradition and Modernity: Architecture in Japan after Hiroshima' in Clapson, Mark and Larkham P.J. *The Blitz and its Legacy: Wartime Destruction to Post-War Reconstruction* (Farnham: Ashgate, 2013)

Janis, I.L. *Air War and Emotional Stress: Psychological Studies of Bombing and Civilian Defence* (Westport, CT: Greenwood Press, 1951)

Jerzak, Claudia 'Memory Politics: The Bombing of Hamburg and Dresden', in Gerstenberger, Katharina and Nusser, Tanya (eds) *Catastrophe and Catharsis: Perspectives on Disaster and Redemption in German Culture and Beyond* (Rochester, NY: Camden House, 2015)

Joel, Tony *The Dresden Firebombing: Memory and the Politics of Commemorating Destruction* (London: I.B. Tauris, 2013)

Jones, Harriet '"This is Magnificent": 300,000 Houses a Year and the Tory Revival after 1945', *Contemporary British History* 14: 1 (2000)

Kim, Mina and Jung, Inha 'The Planning of Microdistricts in Post-War North Korea: Space, Power and Everyday Life', *Planning Perspectives: An International Journal of History, Planning and the Environment* 32:2 (2017)

Kamada, Nanao *One Day in Hiroshima: An Oral History* (Hiroshima: International Physicians for the Prevention of Nuclear War and Hiroshima Prefectural Medical Association, 2007)

Kamm, Oliver 'Catastrophic Visions Formed in Dresden', *Times*, 14 April 2007

Katsumoto, Saotome and Sams, Richard 'Saotome Katsumoto and the Firebombing of Tokyo: Introducing the Great Tokyo Air Raid', *Asia-Pacific Journal: Japan Focus*, 13:10 (2015)

Kinzer, Stephen 'Honor to RAF Leader Wakes Dresden's ghosts', *New York Times*, 6 January 1992

Kusmarov, Jeremy 'Bomb after Bomb: Air Power and Crimes of War from World War Two to the Present', *Asia-Pacific Journal: Japan Focus*, 10:1 (2012)

Kynaston, David *Austerity Britain, 1945-51* (London: Bloomsbury, 2007)

Ladd, Brian 'Double Restoration: Rebuilding Berlin after 1945', in Vale L.J. and Campanella T.J. (eds) *The Resilient City: How Modern Cities Recover From Disaster* (Oxford and New York: Oxford University Press, 2005)

Larkham, P.J. and Lilley, Keith *Planning the 'City of Tomorrow': British Reconstruction Planning, 1939-1952; An Annotated Bibliography* (Pickering: Inch's Books, 2001)

Law M.J. *The Experience of Suburban Modernity* (Manchester: Manchester University Press, 2014)

Leese, Peter and Crouthamel, Jason (eds) *Traumatic Memories of the Second World War and After* (Basingstoke: Palgrave Macmillan, 2016)

Levine, Joshua *Forgotten Voices of the Blitz and the Battle of Britain* (Harmondsworth: Penguin, 2007)

—— *The Secret History of the Blitz* (London: Simon and Schuster, 2015)

Logan, W.S. 'Hanoi after the Bombs: Post-war Reconstruction of a Vietnamese City under Socialism', in Barakat, Sultan, Calame Jon and Charlesworth, Esther (eds) *Urban Triumph or Urban Disaster? Dilemmas of Contemporary Post-war Reconstruction* (York: Post-war Reconstruction and Development Unit (1996)

MacGregor, Neil *Germany, Memories of a Nation* (London: Allen Lane Penguin, 2014)

Mackay, Robert *Half the Battle: Civilian Morale in Britain during the Second World War* (Manchester: Manchester University Press, 2002)

Maddox, R. J. *Weapons for Victory: The Hiroshima Decision Fifty Years Later* (Columbia and London: University of Missouri Press, 1995)

Maier, C. S. 'Targeting the City: Debates and Silences about the Aerial Bombing of World War Two', *International Review of the Red Cross*, 28:859 (2005)

Mann, Jessica *Out of Harm's Way: The Wartime Evacuation of Children from Britain* (London: Hodder Headline, 2006)

Margalit, Gilad 'Dresden and Hamburg: Official Memory and Commemoration of the Victims of Allied Air Raids in the Two Germanies', in Schmitz, Helmut (ed.) *A Nation of Victims? Representations of German Wartime Suffering from 1945 to the Present* (New York, Rodopi; German Monitor No. 67, 2007)

—— *Guilt, Suffering and Memory: Germany Remembers its Dead of World War Two* (Bloomington, Indiana: Indiana University Press, 2010)

Martin, B. K. *Under the Loving Care of the Fatherly Leader: North Korea and the Kim Dynasty* (New York: Thomas Dunne Books, 2006)

Marwick, Arthur *The New Nature of History* (Basingstoke: Palgrave Macmillan, 2001)

Mason, Tony 'Looking Back on the Blitz' in Lancaster, Bill and Mason, Tony, *Life and Labour in a Twentieth-Century City: The Experience of Coventry* (Coventry: Cryfield Press, 1986)

McNamara R. *In Retrospect: The Tragedy and Lessons of Vietnam* (New York: Random House, 1995)

Messenger, Charles *'Bomber' Harris and the Strategic Bombing Offensive, 1939-1945* (London: Arms and Armour Press, 1984)

Military High Command *German Invasion Plans for the British Isles, 1940* (Oxford: Bodleian Library, 2007)

Ministry of Information for the Ministry of Home Security *Front-Line 1940-41: The Official Story of the Civil Defence of Britain* (London: HMSO, 1942)

Mowat, C. L. *Britain between the Wars, 1918-1940* (London: Methuen and Co., 1976)

Miyamoto, Yuki *Beyond the Mushroom Cloud: Commemoration, Religion and Responsibility after Hiroshima* (New York: Fordham University Press, 2012)

Musgrove, Gordon *Operation Gomorrah: The Hamburg Firestorm Raids* (London: Jane's, 1981)

Nakazawa, Keiji *Barefoot Gen: A Cartoon Story of Hiroshima; Volume 1* (San Francisco: Last Gasp of San Francisco, 2004)

Nakazawa, Keiji *Barefoot Gen: The Day After: Volume 2* (San Francisco, CA: Last Gasp of San Francisco, 2004)

Nead, Lynda *The Tiger in the Smoke: Art and Culture in Post-War Britain* (New Haven, CT and London: Yale University Press, 2017)

Nish, Jan 'Japan' in Noakes, Jeremy (ed.) *The Civilian in War: The Home Front in Europe, Japan and the USA in World War Two* (Exeter: University of Exeter Press, 1992)

Niven, Bill and Paver, Chloe (eds) 'Introduction', *Memorialisation in Germany since 1945* (Basingstoke: Palgrave Macmillan, 2016)

Niven, Bill 'The GDR and Memory of the Bombing in Dresden', in Niven, Bill (ed.) *Germans as Victims: Remembering the Past in Contemporary Germany* (Basingstoke: Palgrave Macmillan, 2006)

Noakes, Lucy '"Serve to Save": Gender, Citizenship and Civil Defence in Britain, 1937-41', *Journal of Contemporary History* 47:4 (2012)

Noakes, Lucy and Pattinson, Juliette '"Keep Calm and Carry On": The Cultural Memory of the Second World War in Britain', in Noakes, Lucy and Pattinson, Juliette (eds) *British Cultural Memory and the Second World War* (London: Bloomsbury, 2014)

Nora, Pierre 'Between Memory and History: Les Lieux de Memoire', *Representations* 26:2 (1989)

Omissi, David *Air Power and Colonial Control: The Royal Air Force, 1919-1939* (Manchester: Manchester University Press, 1990)

Overy, Richard *The Bombers and the Bombed: Allied Air War Over Europe, 1940-1945* (New York: Penguin, 2014)

—— *The Bombing War: Europe, 1939-1945* (London: Allen Lane; Penguin, 2013)

—— *The Morbid Age: Britain and the Crisis of Civilisation, 1919-1939* (London: Penguin, 2010)

Owen, Taylor and Kiernan, Ben 'Roots of US Troubles in Afghanistan: Civilian Bombing Casualties and the Cambodian Precedent', *Asia-Pacific Journal: Japan Focus*, 8:26 (2010)

Perks, Robert and Thompson, Alastair (eds) *The Oral History Reader*, 3rd edn. (Abingdon: Routledge, 2016).

Perlman, Michael *Imaginal Memory and the Place of Hiroshima* (New York: SUNY Press, 1988)

Piehler, H.A., *Baedeker: Great Britain: Handbook for Travellers* (Leipzig: Baedeker Publishers, 1937)

Probert, Henry *Bomber Harris: His Life and Times* (London: Greenhill Books, 2006)

Purvis, T.L. *A Dictionary of American History* (Oxford: Blackwell, 1999)

Ray, Gene *Terror and the Sublime in Art and Critical Theory: From Auschwitz, to Hiroshima to September 11* (New York: Palgrave Macmillan, 2005)

Ray, John *The Night Blitz: 1940-1941* (London: Cassell and Co., 2000)

Rose, Norman *Churchill: An Unruly Life* (London: I.B. Tauris, 2009)

Rose, S. O. *Which People's War? National Identity and Citizenship in Wartime Britain* (Oxford: Oxford University Press, 2003)

Ryall, Julian 'Japan to Ban 40-Year Old Comic from Schools for Being Too Graphic', *Telegraph*, 23 August 2013

Saint, Andrew '"Spread the People": The LCC's Dispersal Policy, 1889-1965', in Saint, Andrew (ed.) *Politics and the People of London: The London County Council, 1889-1965* (London: Hambledon, 1989)

Schaller, Michael, Scharff, Virginia and Schultzinger, R.D. *Present Tense: The United States since 1945* (Boston, MA.: Houghton Mifflin, 1996)

Schmitz, Helmut 'Introduction: The Return of Wartime Suffering in Contemporary Memory Culture, Literature and Film', in Schmitz, Helmut (ed.) *A Nation of Victims? Representations of German Wartime Suffering from 1945 to the Present* (New York, Rodopi; German Monitor No. 67, 2007)

Scott, J.M. *Target Tokyo: Jimmy Doolittle and the Raid that Avenged Pearl Harbor* (New York and London: W.W. Norton and Company, 2015)

Seidel Arpaci, Annette 'Lost in Translations? The Discourse of "German Suffering" in W.G. Sebald's *Luftkrieg und Literatur*', in Schmitz, Helmut (ed.) *A Nation of Victims? Representations of German Wartime Suffering from 1945 to the Present* (New York, Rodopi; German Monitor No. 67, 2007)

Schwenkel, Christina 'Traveling Architecture: East German Urban Designs in Vietnam', *International Journal for History, Culture and Modernity* 2:2 (2014)

Sherry, Michael *The Rise of American Air Power: The Creation of Armageddon* (New Haven, CT and London: Yale University Press, 1987)

Sherwell, Philip 'Barack Obama Backs Ground Zero mosque', *Daily Telegraph*, 14 August 2010

Skelton, Roger *Poetry of the Thirties* (Harmondsworth: Penguin, 1985)

Smith, David 'Queen Honours War's Heroines', *Guardian* 10 July 2005

Smith, H.L. *Britain in the Second World War: A Social History* (Manchester: Manchester University Press, 1996)

Smith, Malcolm *Britain and 1940: History, Myth and Popular Memory* (London: Routledge, 2000)

Southard, Susan *Nagasaki: Life after Nuclear War* (London: Souvenir Press, 2015)

Speiser, Peter *The British Army of the Rhine: Turning Nazi Enemies Into Cold War Partners* (Urbana, IL: University of Illinois Press, 2016)

Stamp, Gavin *Britain's Lost Cities* (London: Aurum Press, 2007)

Stargardt, Nicholas *The German War: A Nation Under Arms* (London: Penguin-Random House, 2015)

Storry, Richard *A History of Modern Japan* (Harmondsworth: Penguin, 1982)

Summerfield, Penny 'The Generation of Memory: Gender and the Popular Memory of the Second World War in Britain', in Noakes, Lucy and Pattinson, Juliette (eds) *British Cultural Memory and the Second World War* (London: Bloomsbury, 2014)

Süss, Dietmar *Death from the Skies: How the British and Germans Survived Bombing in World War Two* (Oxford: Oxford University Press, 2014)

Taylor, Frederick, *Coventry, Thursday 14 November 1940* (London: Bloomsbury, 2015)

Thorpe, Andrew 'Britain', in Noakes, Jeremy (ed.) *The Civilian in War: The Home Front in Europe, Japan and the USA in World War Two* (Exeter: University of Exeter Press, 1992)

Thorpe, F.T. 'Demolition Melancholia', *British Medical Journal*, 15 July 1939

Tibbets, P.W. Junior *The Tibbets Story* (New York: Stein and Day, 1978)

Titmuss, R. M. *Problems of Social Policy* (London: HMSO, 1950)

Tiratsoo, Nick, Hasegawa, Junichi, Mason, Tony and Matsumura, Takao *Urban Reconstruction in Britain and Japan, 1945-1955: Dreams, Plans and Realities* (Luton: University of Luton Press, 2002)

Todd, Selina *The People: The Rise and Fall of the Working Class 1910-2010* (London: John Murray, 2014)

Todeschini, Maya Morioka '"Death and the Maiden": Female *Hibakusha* as Cultural Heroines, and the Politics of A-bomb memory', in Broderick, Mick (ed.) *Hibakusha Cinema: Hiroshima, Nagasaki and the Nuclear Image in Japanese Film* (London: Kegan Paul International, 1996)

Tsubaki, Tatsuya '"Model for a Short-Lived future?" Early Tribulations of the Barbican Redevelopment in the City of London, 1940-1982', *Planning Perspectives: A International Journal of History, Planning and the Environment* 27: 4 (2012)

Tucker, S.C. *Encyclopedia of the Vietnam War: A Political, Military and Social History* (Oxford: ABC-Clio, 2000)

USAAF, *United States Strategic Bombing Survey*, 1944-46 (Washington DC: USSBS, 1946)

Vahimagi, Tise *British Television* (Oxford: Oxford University Press/BFI, 1994)

Vale, L.J. and Campanella T.J, 'Cities Rise Again', in Vale L.J. and Campanella T.J. (eds.) *The Resilient City: How Modern Cities Recover From Disaster* (Oxford and New York: Oxford University Press, 2005)

Van Young, Sayre *London's War: A Travelers Guide to World War Two* (Berkeley, CA.: Ulysses Press, 2004)

Victor, S. 'Tempers Flare as Bomber Veterans Honour Harris', *Times*, 1 June 1992

Vonnegut, Kurt *Slaughterhouse 5 or The Children's Crusade* (London: Vintage, 2000)

Walker, John *Halliwell's Film, DVD and Video Guide 2007* (London: HarperCollins, 2006)

Waters, Sarah *The Night Watch* (London: Virago, 2006)

Wheatcroft, Sue 'Holiday Camps, Castles and Stately Homes: The Residential Option for the Evacuation of Disabled Children during World War 2', in Clapson, Mark and Larkham, P.J. *The Blitz and its Legacy: Wartime Destruction to Post-War Reconstruction* (Farnham: Ashgate, 2013)

Ward, Laurence *The London County Council Bomb Damage Maps, 1939-1945* (London: Thames and Hudson, 2015)

Ward, S. V. *Planning and Urban Change* (London: Sage, 2004)

Watson, Janet 'Total War and Total Anniversary: The Material Culture of Second World War Commemoration in Britain', in Noakes, Lucy and Pattinson, Juliette (eds) *British Cultural Memory and the Second World War* (London: Bloomsbury, 2014)

Weiss, Lois, 'Apartments, Islamic Museum to be Built on Site of Failed Ground Zero Mosque', *New York Post*, 19 May 2016

Werrell, Kenneth P., *Blankets of Fire: US Bombers Over Japan during World War Two* (Washington and London: Smithsonian Institution Press, 1996)

White, Jerry *London in the Twentieth Century* (Harmondsworth: Penguin, 2001)

Wilkinson, Colin *Bert Hardy's Britain* (London: The Bluecoat Press, 2013)

Williams, Dee *Love and War* (London: Headline, 2004)

Wilson, Kevin *Blood and Fears: How America's Bomber Boys and Girls in England Won Their War* (London: Weidenfeld and Nicolson, 2016)

Wintour, Patrick, 'Britain Carries out First Syrian Airstrikes after MPS Approve Action against ISIS', *Guardian*, 3 December 2015

Woolven, Robin 'Between Destruction and Reconstruction: London's Debris Clearance and Repair Organisation', in Clapson, Mark and Larkham, P. J. (eds) *The Blitz and its Legacy: Wartime Destruction to Post-War Reconstruction* (Farnham: Ashgate, 2013)

Worboyes, Sally *Over Bethnal Green* (London: Hodder, 2000)

Youde, Kate 'Christopher Hitchens', *Independent*, 7 February 2010

Young, Hugo *One of Us: A Biography of Margaret Thatcher* (London: Macmillan, 1989)

Zeigler, Philip *London at War: 1939-1945* (London: Pimlico, 2002)

Zwigenberg, Ran *Hiroshima: The Origins of Global Memory Culture* (Cambridge: Cambridge University Press, 2014)

—— 'Never Again: Hiroshima, Auschwitz and the Politics of Commemoration', *Asia-Pacific Journal* 13: 3 (2015)

Screen and Audio Materials

Frank, Melvin and Panama, Norman (dirs.) *Above and Beyond* (Metro-Goldwyn-Mayer, 1952)

Anderson, Michael (dir.) *Operation Crossbow* (Metro-Goldwyn-Mayer, 1965)

—— *The Dam Busters* (Associated British Picture Corporation, 1955)

Boorman, John (dir.) *Hope and Glory* (1987)

Browne, Courtney 'Japan, 1941-1945'; episode 22, *World at War* (Thames Television, 1974)

Coppola, F.F. (dir.) *Apocalypse Now* (Zoetrope Studios, 1979)

Douglas-Home, Charles 'Whirlwind', episode 12, *World at War* (Thames Television, 1974)

Elstein, David, 'The Bomb-February-September, 1945'; episode 24, *World at War* (Thames Television, 1974)

Honda, Ishiro (dir.) *Godzilla* (Toho Co. Ltd, 1954)

Hood, Stuart, 'Nemesis', episode 21, Thames Television, *World at War* (Thames Television, 1974)

Korda, Alexander (dir.) *Things to Come* (1937)

Jennings, Humphrey *London (Britain) Can Take It* (Crown Film Unit, 1940)

Katabuchi, Sunao (dir.) *In This Corner of the World* (Mappa, Genco et al., 2016)

Kimura, Takao (dir.) *Matouquin Nocturne* (Project Lamu, 2007)

Kurosawa, Akira (dir.) *Rhapsody in August* (Kurosawa Production Co., 1991)

Mainwood, Roger (dir.) Raymond *Ethel and Ernest* (BBC and BFI, 2016)

Ministry of Information, *London: The Proud City* (Ministry of Information, 1946)

Mori, Masaki (dir.) *Barefoot Gen* (Madhouse et al., 1983)

Morris, Errol (dir.) *The Fog of War: Eleven Lessons from the Life of Robert S. McNamara* (Sony Pictures Classics, 2003)

Ōba, Hideo (dir.) *The Bells of Nagasaki* (Shochiku Co., *et al*, 1950)

Movietone: *City of London. Bombed* (1940): *Story Number:* 39610

Movietone: *Korea: Air Blitz Checks Reds* (1950): *Story Number:* 54232

Movietone: *The Realm Remains Resolute* (1940): *Story Number:* 36231

Movietone: *Vietnam Blitz* (1965): *Story Number:* 20133

Penn, Arthur with Glasner, Matthias and Zinberg, Michael (dirs.) *Little Big Man* (Cinema Center Films, 1970)

Resnais, Alain (dir.) *Hiroshima Mon Amour* (Argos Films *et al*, 1959)

Richter, R.S. (dir.) *Dresden* (ZDF, 2006)

Takahata, Isao (dir.) *Grave of the Fireflies* (Studio Ghibli, 1988)

Thompson, Laurence 'Alone', episode, 24, Thames Television, *World at War* (Thames Television, 1974)

US Army Air Forces, First Motion Picture Unit *Target Tokyo* (USAF, 1945)

US War Department *Tale of Two Cities* (US War Department, 1946)

Yoshida, Yoshishige (dir.) *Women in the Mirror* (Gendaieiga Co. et al., 2002)

Online Resources

http://airminded.org/2007/11/10/the-bomber-will-always-get-through/

https://airandspace.si.edu

www.archives.gov/

www.atomicbombmuseum.org/6_1.shtml
www.bbc.co.uk
www.bbc.co.uk/history/ww2peopleswar/categories/c1161/
www.bfi.org.uk/education-research
www.bombsight.org/
www.britishpathe.com
www.businessinsider.com/japanese-leaders-pressure-shinzo-abe-not-to-apologize-for-pearl-harbor-2016-12?IR=T
www.cartoons.ac.uk
www.centenarynews.com/article/first-zeppelin-raid-on-london-remembered/ https://chomsky.info/19850319/
https://chomsky.info/19700604/
https://chomsky.info/19750612/
https://chomsky.info/20020702/
www.cityoflondon.gov.uk
www.cityoflondon.gov.uk/things-to-do/green-spaces/city-gardens/visitor-information/Pages/christchurch-greyfriars-church-garden.aspx
www.civildefenceassociation.org.uk/page15.html
www.cnduk.org/cnd-media/item/2693-hibakusha
www.dailymail.co.uk/news/article-1190841/Stephen-Whittle-Simon-Sheppard-race-hate-Britons-seeking-asylum-U-S--deported-judge-rejects-free-speech-plea.html
http://www.dailyrecord.co.uk/news/local-news/new-memorial-honour-victims-clydebank-2615181
http://discovery.nationalarchives.gov.uk/
www.dhm.de/fileadmin/lemo/suche/search/index.php?q=*&f[]=seitentyp:Zeitzeuge&f[]=epoche:Zweiter%20Weltkrieg
www.flyingbombsandrockets.com/www.gettyimagesgallery.com/
https://greatwen.com/2010/09/06/where-is-the-statue-for-londons-blitz-spirit/www.ibiblio.org/hyperwar/UN/UK/UK-Civil-Social
www.theguardian.com/film/2015/jan/20/jane-fonda-hanoi-jane-photo-was-a-huge-mistake
www.gutenberg.org/files/780/780-h/780-h.htm

http://hansard.millbanksystems.com/commons/1932/nov/10/
international-affairs

www.historylearningsite.co.uk

www.history.com/this-day-in-history/united-states-resumes-
bombing-of-hanoi-and-haiphong

www.hrw.org/reports/1991/gulfwar/INTRO.htm

www.hrw.org/sites/default/files/reports/natbm002.pdf

http://humanities.exeter.ac.uk/history/research/centres/warst
ateandsociety/

www.ibiblio.org/hyperwar/UN/UK/UK-Civil-Social

www.independent.co.uk/news/world/middle-east/isis-leaders-
syria-conscription-civilians-raqqa-deir-ezzor-us-led-
coalition-forces-syrian-army-iraq-a7876606.html

www.independent.co.uk/news/world/middle-east/israel-gaza-
conflict-israeli-military-using-flechette-rounds-in-gaza-
strip-9617480.html

www.independent.co.uk/news/world/middle-east/mosul-latest-
news-isis-fighters-old-city-remain-control-iraq-forces-sami-
al-aridi-special-forces-a7824956.html

www.iwm.org.uk/history/the-blitz-around-britain

www.iwm.org.uk/history/what-were-the-baedeker-raids

www.legislation.gov.uk/ukpga/1939/31/pdfs/ukpga_
19390031_en.pdf

www.liverpoolmuseums.org.uk/maritime/exhibitions/blitz/blitz.
aspx#

www.londonremembers.com

www.londonremembers.com/memorials/civilian-deaths-
in-ww2-blitz-east-london

www.londonremembers.com/memorials/women-in-ww2

www.massobs.org.uk/images/booklets/Blitz.pdf

https://miningawareness.wordpress.com/2015/08/06/japanese-
american-hibakusha-atomic-bomb-survivors/

www.movietone.com

www.ndl.go.jp/en

http://nypost.com/2016/05/19/apartments-islamic-museum-to-
be-built-on-site-of-failed-ground-zero-mosque/

www.otr.com/murrow.html

www.parliament.uk/about/living heritage/building/palace/
   architecture/palacestructure/bomb-damage/

https://patriotpost.us/pages/80

www.politicsresources.net/area/uk/man/lab45.htm

www.princeofwales.gov.uk/media/speeches/speech-hrh-the-
   prince-of-wales-the-corporation-of-london-planning-and-
   communication

www.rafmuseum.org.uk

www.revisionist.net/hell-introduction.html

www.rollingstone.com/politics/news/joan-baez-in-hanoi-
   12-days-under-the-bombs-19730201

www.sas1946.com/main/index.php?topic=28095.144.

www.screenonline.org.uk

www.smithsonianmag.com/history/untold-story-vengeful-
   japanese-attack-doolittle-raid-180955001/

http://archive.spectator.co.uk/

www.stpauls.co.uk/history-collections/the-collections/collections-
   highlights/st-pauls-watch-papers-ww1-_-ww2

www.si.edu/Museums/air-and-space-museum

http://sounds.bl.uk/Search

www.spiegel.de/international/europe/controversial-memorial-
   to-british-wwii-bombers-to-open-a-840858.html

www.stopthewar.org.uk

www.telegraph.co.uk/history/raf-bomber-command/9363220/
   Bomber-Command-memorial-bloody-marvellous-but-long-
   overdue.html

www.telegraph.co.uk/news/worldnews/barackobama/7945558/
   Barack-Obama-backs-Ground-Zero-mosque.html

www.telegraph.co.uk/news/worldnews/asia/japan/10261210/
   Japan-to-ban-40-year-old-Hiroshima-comic-from-schools-
   for-being-too-graphic.html

www.trumanlibrary.org/kids/poem.htm

www.trumanlibrary.org/whistlestop/hh/locksley.html

www.un.org/disarmament/education/slideshow/hibakusha/

www.westendatwar.org.uk

www.westminster.ac.uk/archives

References

1   Farrington, *Blitzed City*, 8–9
2   Overy, *Bombing War*, 1
3   www.stpauls.co.uk/history-collections/the-collections/collections-
    highlights/st-pauls-watch-papers-ww1-_-ww2 (accessed January
    2017)
4   Ferguson, *War of the World*, 159–66
5   Overy, *Bombing War*, 31, 42
6   Doherty, 'France Launches'
7   Wintour, 'Britain Carries'
8   www.stopwar.org.uk (accessed September 2016)
9   Tennyson, *Locksley Hall*, in www.trumanlibrary.org/whistlestop/
    hh/locksley.htm (accessed July, 2016)
10 Holmes, *Falling Upwards*, 122-55
11 Farrington, *Blitzed City*, 8
12 Wells, *War in the Air*: www.gutenberg.org/files/780/780-h/780-h.
    htm (accessed January, 2017)
13 Ibid.
14 Overy, *Bombing War*, 9–10

15   Adey, Cox, Godfrey, *Crime, Regulation and Control*, 33; White, *Zeppelin Nights*, passim

16   Zeigler, *London at War*, 10

17   Grogan, *Shell Shocked Britain*, 112–21

18   Grayzel, *At Home and Under Fire*, 20-63

19   www.cartoons.ac.uk (accessed November 2016)

20   Gardiner, *Thirties*, 752, 755

21   Eliot, *Waste Land*, 41

22   Omissi, *Air Power*, 20–2

23   Ziegler, *London at War*, 10–11

24   Law, *Experience of Suburban Modernity*, 59–61

25   Hastings, *Bomber Command*, 37

26   Ibid., 34–6

27   Adey, Cox, Godfrey, *Crime, Regulation and Control*, 35

28   http://hansard.millbanksystems.com/commons/1932/nov/10/international-affairs (accessed September 2016)

29   Clapson, *Suburban Century*, 53-54

30   Betjeman, 'Slough', in Skelton, *Poetry of the Thirties*, 74

31   http://hansard.millbanksystems.com/commons/1932/nov/10/international-affairs (accessed September 2016)

32   Cited in http://airminded.org/2007/11/10/the-bomber-will-always-get-through/ (accessed July 2016)

33   Gardiner, *Thirties*, 498–9

34   Mowat, *Britain Between the Wars*, 476

35   Ibid.

36   Sherry, *Rise of American Air Power*, 64–5

37   Rose, *Churchill*, 224

38   Clapson, *Suburban Century*, 27–8

39   Overy, *Morbid Age*, 224–52

40   Overy, *Bombers and the Bombed*, 232–3

41   Süss, *Death from the Skies*, 39

42   Holman, *Next War*, 159–60; 203–19; Haapamaki *The Coming of the Aerial War*

43   Ibid., 203–4

44   http://archive.spectator.co.uk/ (accessed September, 2016); Anon, 'News of the Week'

45   Ham, *Hiroshima Nagasaki*, 26

46   Hastings, *Nemesis*, 226; 588

47   Simons, *Scourging of Iraq*, 208

48   Holman, *Next War*, 204
49   Ibid., 211–19
50   www.legislation.gov.uk/ukpga/1939/31/pdfs/ukpga_19390031_
      en.pdf (accessed January 2017)
51   Quoted in Holman, *Next War*, 208
52   Noakes, 'Serve to Save', 743
53   Gardiner, *Thirties*, 728
54   Mann, *Out of Harm's Way*, passim; Wicks, *No Time*, passim
55   Wheatcroft, 'Holiday Camps', 31–3
56   www.westminster.ac.uk/archives: *Polytechnic Magazine*, Septem-
      ber, 1939, 206 (Held at the University of Westminster Archives,
      Little Titchfield Street, London)
57   www.westminster.ac.uk/archives: *Polytechnic Magazine*, Decem-
      ber, 1939, 235 (Held at the University of Westminster Archives,
      Little Titchfield Street, London)
58   Gardiner, *Blitz*, 125–9
59   Overy, *Morbid Age*, 314–62
60   Churchill, *Second World War*, 353–4
61   Military High Command, *Invasion Plans*, 46
62   Ibid., 58
63   Gardiner, *Blitz*, 17
64   Hastings, *Bomber Command*, 236
65   Ministry of Home Security, *Home Front*, 4
66   Cited in Zeigler, *London at War*, 113
67   White, *London*, 38
68   Ibid.
69   Ibid.
70   Woolven, 'Between Destruction and Reconstruction', 61–2
71   Churchill, *Second World War*,
72   www.otr.com/murrow.html (accessed September, 2016)
73   Anon 'East End at War'
74   www.cartoons.ac.uk (accessed October 2016)
75   www.cartoons.ac.uk (accessed January, 2016)
76   Gardiner, *Blitz*, 174, 323; Zeigler, *London at War*, 121
77   www.parliament.uk/about/livingheritage/building/palace/architecture/
      palacestructure/bomb-damage/ (accessed September, 2016)
78   Young, *London's War*, 152–3
79   Waters, *The Night Watch*, 360
80   Ward, *London County Council*, passim

81 White, *London*, 39
82 Jennings (dir.) *London Can Take It*
83 Bell, *London Was Ours*, 86–7
84 Military High Command, *Invasion Plans*, 47
85 Ibid., 68
86 Ray, *Night Blitz*, 108–19
87 Smith, *Britain and 1940*, 86–88
88 Ministry of Information for the Ministry of Home Security, *Front Line*, 82–127
89 Mason, 'Looking Back', 321
90 Ibid., 323
91 Taylor, *Coventry*, 196
92 Ibid., 196, 210
93 Adey, Cox, Godfrey, *Crime, Regulation and Control*, 184
94 www.iwm.org.uk/history/the-blitz-around-britain (accessed December 2016) www.liverpoolmuseums.org.uk/maritime/exhibitions/blitz/blitz.aspx# (accessed December 2016)
95 Forrester, *Lime Street*, 62
96 Adams and Larkham, 'Bold Planning' 138-39
97 www.iwm.org.uk/history/the-blitz-around-britain (accessed December 2016)
98 Ray, *Night Blitz*, 184–5
99 Ibid., 185
100 www.iwm.org.uk/history/the-blitz-around-britain (accessed December 2016)
101 Ray, *Night Blitz*, 213
102 Ibid.
103 Zeigler, *London at War*, 178
104 Harrisson, *Living Through the Blitz*, 63
105 Beavan and Griffiths, 'The Blitz', 77
106 Croft, 'Rethinking Civilian Neuroses', 95–116
107 Noakes, 'War on the Web', 36
108 Harrisson, *Living Through the Blitz*, 305
109 Todd, *The People*, 119–73
110 Titmuss, *Problems of Social Policy*, passim: www.ibiblio.org/hyperwar/UN/UK/UK-Civil-Social (accessed September 2016)
111 www.politicsresources.net/area/uk/man/lab45.htm (accessed December 2016)
112 Ministry of Information for the Ministry of Home Security, *Front Line*, 71

113   Ibid.
114   Calder, *Myth of the Blitz* 128
115   Ibid., 65–89
116   Grayzel, *At Home and Under Fire*, 224–94; Noakes, *War and the British*, passim; Rose, *Which People's War*, passim; Smith, *Britain in the Second World War*, 51–74
117   Rose, *Which People's War*, passim; Smith, *Britain in the Second World War*, passim
118   Calder, *Myth of the Blitz* xiii
119   Ibid., xiv
120   Ibid., 172–3
121   Ibid., 173
122   Clapson, 'Bowling Along', passim; Clapson, *Working-Class Suburb*, 107–8
123   Porter, *London*, 407; White, *London*, 38–45
124   Gardiner, *Blitz*, 366
125   Mackay, *Half the Battle*, 258–9; Thorpe, 'Britain', 17
126   Mackay, *Half the Battle*, 258–9
127   Smith, *Britain and 1940*, 29–51; 55–69; 70–90
128   Joel, *Dresden Firebombing*, 50
129   Bevan, *Destruction of Memory*, 78
130   Piehler, *Baedeker's Handbook*, 116–17.
131   Ibid, 109–11
132   Ibid., 26–8
133   Ibid., 320
134   Ibid., 443–7
135   Ibid., p. vi
136   Bevan, *Destruction of Memory*, 70–80; see also www.iwm.org.uk/history/what-were-the-baedeker-raids (accessed January, 2017)
137   Bevan, *Destruction of Memory*, 70–80
138   Hebbert, 'Street as Locus', passim
139   Thorpe, 'Demolition Melancholia', 127–8
140   See for example Crouthemel, J. and Leese, P. (eds) *Traumatic Memories*
141   Zeigler, *London at War*, 267–81
142   Ibid., 282
143   Campbell, *Target London*, 16, 127–9
144   Zeigler, *London at War*, 283
145   Campbell; *Target London*, 337; Zeigler, *London at War*, 293–5
146   Zeigler, *London at War*, 294

147   Ibid., 299
148   Ibid., 297–8
149   White, *London*, 39–40
150   Bell, *London Was Ours*, 203
151   Campbell, *Target London*, 408-9; Overy, *Bombing War*, 121, 340, 603
152   Adey, Cox, Godfrey, *Crime, Regulation and Control*, 192
153   Overy, *Bombing War*, 63–4
154   Irving, *Destruction of Dresden*, 19
155   Overy, *Bombing War*, 204
156   Ibid., 216–23
157   Ibid., 231–2
158   Dodd, *La Ville Entrée*, 17
159   Ibid.
160   Clout, 'Destruction, Revival', 172
161   Dodd, *La Ville Entrée*, 18
162   Dodd, *La Ville Entrée*, 19
163   Overy, *Bombing War*, 561, 565–6
164   Dodd, *La Ville Entrée*, 19 http://humanities.exeter.ac.uk/history/research/centres/warstateandsociety/projects/bombing/italy/ (accessed May 2017)
165   http://humanities.exeter.ac.uk/history/research/centres/warstateandsociety/projects/bombing/italy/ (accessed May 2017)
166   Farrington, *Blitzed City*, 236–7
167   Overy, *Bombers and the Bombed*, 91
168   Ibid., 92
169   www.raf.mod.uk/history/bombercommandthethousandbomberraids3031may.cfm (accessed December 2016)
170   Beck, *Under the Bombs*, 155–6; 174–5; 185
171   Ibid., 47
172   Ibid.
173   Stargardt, *German War*, 349
174   Beck, *Under the Bombs*, 59
175   Stargardt, *German War*, 349
176   Beck, *Under the Bombs*, 59
177   Cited in Gardiner, *Blitz*, 263
178   Goldhagen, *Hitler's Willing Executioners*, passim
179   Grayling, *Among the Dead Cities*, 80
180   Cited in Musgrave, *Operation Gomorrah*, vii

181   Ibid.

182   Cited in Ibid., viii

183   Ibid., 82

184   Ibid., 88–9

185   Overy, *Bombers and Bombed*, 259–61

186   Niven, 'GDR and Memory', 110

187   Vonnegut, *Slaughterhouse 5*, 18

188   Overy, *Bombing War*, 394–5

189   Kamm, 'Catastrophic Visions'; Irving, *Destruction of Dresden*, 237

190   Overy, *Bombing War*, 395

191   Quoted in Irving, *Destruction of Dresden*, 229

192   Wilson, *Blood and Fears*, 399

193   Beck, *Under the Bombs*, 87

194   Stargardt, *German War*, 361

195   Stargardt, *German War*, 361Ibid.

196   Howard, *Studies in War*, 192

197   Hastings, *Bomber Command*, 163–4; 311–12

198   Messenger, *'Bomber' Harris*, 213–14

199   Ibid.

200   Probert, *Bomber Harris*, 328

201   Hane, *Japan*, 60

202   Ibid, 137–53

203   Scott, *Target Tokyo*, passim

204   Ibid., 95; www.smithsonianmag.com/history/untold-story-vengeful-japanese-attack-doolittle-raid-180955001/ (accessed December 2016)

205   Cumings, *Korean War*, 149–50

206   USAAF, *Target Tokyo* (italics added)

207   Katsumoto and Sams, 'Saotome Katsumoto', 1

208   Cook and Cook, *Japan at War*, 343–53

209   Jackson, 'Tradition and Modernity', 113

210   Ibid.

211   Ham, *Hiroshima Nagasaki*, 127–8

212   Quoted in Griffith, *Major Problems*, 57

213   Ham, *Hiroshima Nagasaki*, 147

214   Griffith, *Major Problems*, 54

215   www.trumanlibrary.org/kids/poem.htm (accessed August 2016)

216   Griffith, *Major Problems*, 49–50

217   Cited in Griffith, *Major Problems*, 57

218   Ham, *Hiroshima, Nagasaki*, 26

219   Ibid.; Hastings, 'What would you?'

220   Corrigan, *Second World War*, 569

221   Hane, *Japan*, 174; Kamada, *One Day*, 13

222   Grayling, *Among the Dead Cities*, 253

223   Maddox, *Weapons for Victory*, 149

224   Hane, *Japan*, 174–5

225   Hastings, *Nemesis*, 548–60

226   Cited in Maddox, *Weapons for Victory*, 1

227   Hane, *Japan*, 174

228   Quoted in Ham, *Hiroshima, Nagasaki*, 584 (italics added)

229   Storry, *Modern Japan*, 182

230   Werrell, *Blankets of Fire*, 241

231   Boyer, *Bomb's Early Light*, passim

232   Hastings, *Nemesis*, 519

233   www.atomicbombmuseum.org/6_1.shtml (accessed August 2016)

234   http://news.bbc.co.uk/onthisday/hi/witness/august/9/newsid_4720000/4720807.stm (accessed August 2016)

235   Nakazawa, *Barefoot Gen*, passim; see above

236   Ham, *Hiroshima, Nagasaki*, 480-508

237   Ibid., 480–2

238   Nish, 'Japan', 17

239   Janis, *Air War*, 53–5

240   Harrisson, *Living Through*, 333–4

241   US War Department, *Tale of Two Cities*

242   Goldstein, 'Charles Sweeney'

243   Tibbets, *Tibbets Story*, 223

244   Kamm, 'Catastrophic Visions'

245   Young, *One of Us*, 272

246   Hastings, *Nemesis*, 551

247   http://archive.spectator.co.uk/article/11th-january-1946/8/december-in-hiroshima (accessed September 2016) Halliwell, 'December in Hiroshima', 8

248   Hastings, 'What Would You'

249   Anon, 'Japan PM'; McCurrie, 'Japanese PM'

250   www.businessinsider.com/japanese-leaders-pressure-shinzo-abe-not-to-apologize-for-pearl-harbor-2016-12?IR=T (accessed January 2016)

251   Tiratsoo and Tomlinson, *Missionaries and Managers*

252   Hein, Deifendorf, Yorifusa, *Rebuilding Urban Japan*
253   Hashimoto, *Long Defeat*, passim
254   www.princeofwales.gov.uk/media/speeches/speech-hrh-the-prince-of-wales-the-corporation-of-london-planning-and-communication (accessed August 2017)
255   Tiratsoo, Hasegawa, Mason, Matsumura, *Urban Reconstruction*, 1
256   Flinn, 'Reconstruction Constraints', 87-98
257   Jones, 'This is Magnificent', 223
258   Clapson, 'Destruction and Dispersal', 99-112
259   Saint, 'Spread the People', 215-36
260   Rose, *Which People's War*, 23
261   Adams and Larkham, 'Post-war Reconstruction', 1–59
262   Larkham and Lilley, *Planning*, 12–30
263   Clapson, 'Garden City to New Town', 5–8, 17–20
264   Clapson, *Invincible Green Suburbs*, 47
265   Ward, *Planning*, 23–4
266   Clapson, *Working-Class Suburb*, 21–41
267   Ibid.
268   Ward, *Planning*, 22–3, 47–52
269   Quoted in Clapson, *Invincible Green Suburbs*, 161
270   Cowan, 'People's Peace', 73
271   Kynaston, *Austerity Britain*, 102
272   Clapson, *Working-Class Suburb*, 101–3
273   Tsubaki, 'Model for', passim
274   Quoted in Tiratsoo, Hasegawa, Mason, Matsumura *Urban Reconstruction*, 17
275   Stamp, *Britain's Lost*, 52
276   Tiratsoo, Hasegawa, Mason, Matsumura *Urban Reconstruction*, 17–24
277   Essex and Brayshay, 'Planning the Reconstruction', 153
278   Ibid., 151–67
279   Adams and Larkham, 'Bold Planning', 137-50
280   Ibid.
281   Nead, *Tiger in the Smoke*, 55–65
282   Ibid., 59
283   Clapson, *Invincible Green Suburbs*, 6
284   MacGregor, *Germany, Memories*, 495
285   Speiser, *British Army*, passim;
286   Diefendorf, 'War and Reconstruction', 216

287   Diefendorf, 'Rebuilding Urban Germany', 331

288   Ibid., 335

289   Ibid., 225

290   Ibid., 351

291   Ibid., 340

292   Gilbert, *Dent Atlas*, 96

293   Diefendorf, 'Rebuilding Urban Germany', 342–5

294   Diefendorf, *Wake of War*, 176–7

295   Bold and Pickard, 'Reconstructing Europe', 105–28

296   Diefendorf, 'Reconstructing Civic Authority', 123–33

297   Ibid.

298   Diefendorf, *Wake of War*, 96–7

299   Ladd, 'Double Restoration', 117–18

300   Diefendorf, 'Rebuilding Urban Germany', 350–1

301   Ladd, 'Double Restoration', 126–7

302   Diefendorf, 'War and Reconstruction', 218

303   Ibid., 219

304   Ibid., 225

305   Diefendorf, *Wake of War*, 147–50

306   Hane, *Japan*, 177

307   Tiratsoo, Hasegawa, Mason, Matsumura, *Urban Reconstruction*, 49

308   Hein, 'Rebuilding Japanese', 1

309   Ibid., 2

310   Ibid., 3

311   Tiratsoo, Hasegawa, Mason, Matsumura, *Urban Reconstruction*, 50

312   Ibid., 54–5

313   Diefendorf, 'War and Reconstruction', 227

314   Tiratsoo, Hasegawa, Mason, Matsumura, *Urban Reconstruction*, 66–7

315   Diefendorf, 'War and Reconstruction', 227

316   Tiratsoo, Hasegawa, Mason, Matsumura, *Urban Reconstruction*, 71–7

317   Matsumoto, 'Reconstruction of Nagaoka', 108–25

318   Tiratsoo, Hasegawa, Mason, Matsumura, *Urban Reconstruction*, 82–92

319   Hasegawa, 'Problems of Blitz Reconstruction', 179–89

320   Hein, 'Rebuilding Japanese', 3–4

321   Jones, '"This is Magnificent"', passim

322   Clout, 'Destruction, Revival', 170

323   Ibid.

324 Ibid., 177
325 Dale, 'Divided We Stand', 493–516
326 Goldman, 'Warsaw', 135–58
327 Dominiczak, 'Warsaw and Gdansk', 18
328 Ibid.
329 Vale and Campanella, 'Cities Rise Again', 5
330 Cumings, *Korean War*, 3–35
331 Ferguson, *War of the World*, 594
332 www.movietone.com: story number: 23432: *Korea: Air Blitz Checks Reds* (1950)
333 Cumings, *Korean War*, 149
334 Ibid., 149–50
335 Ibid., 152–5
336 Conway-Lanz, 'Ethics of Bombing', 12
337 Hastings, *Korean War*, 392
338 Felton, *What I Saw*, 5-6
339 Ibid., 5
340 Clapson, 'Rise and Fall', 211
341 Martin, *Under the Loving*, 85
342 Ibid.
343 Cumings, *Korean War*, 35
344 Kim and Jung, 'Planning Microdistricts, 199-223
345 Martin, *Under the Loving*, 184–5; 408–9; 623
346 Hitchens, *Orwell's Victory*, 52–4
347 Kim and Jung, 'Planning Microdistricts', 199–224
348 Purvis, *Dictionary*, 422
349 Chinnery, *Vietnam*, 98
350 Ambrose, *Rise to Globalism*, 199-200
351 www.movietone.com: story number: 90133 *The Vietnam Blitz* (1965)
352 Spencer, *Encyclopaedia*, 358
353 Drew, *Rolling Thunder*, 13
354 Kuzmarov, 'Bomb after Bomb', 1
355 www.rollingstone.com/politics/news/joan-baez-in-hanoi-12-days-under-the-bombs-19730201 (accessed February 2017)
356 Drew, 'Rolling Thunder 1965', 1–16; Spencer, *Encyclopaedia*,, 360
357 Spencer, *Encyclopaedia*, 358–60
358 Tucker, *Encyclopaedia*, 264–5
359 Kuzmarov, 'Bomb after Bomb',
360 Hunt, *Vietnam War*, 112

361   www.history.com/this-day-in-history/united-states-resumes-bombing-of-hanoi-and-haiphong (accessed April 2017)

362   Hunt, *Vietnam War*, 113

363   Quoted in Clodfelter, *Limits of Air Power*, 182

364   Ibid., 195

365   Ibid., 195

366   Schaller, Scharff, Schulzinger, *Present Tense*, 346–7

367   https://patriotpost.us/pages/80;https://www.theguardian.com/film/2015/jan/20/jane-fonda-hanoi-jane-photo-was-a-huge-mistake (accessed February 2017)

368   Bosworth, *Jane Fonda*, 375

369   Clodfelter, *Limits of*, x

370   McNamara, *In Retrospect*, 333

371   Logan, *Hanoi*, 191–2

372   Ibid., 192–3

373   Schwenkel, 'Travelling Architecture', 155–74

374   www.hrw.org/sites/default/files/reports/natbm002.pdf (accessed June 2017)

375   Bold, Pickard, 'Reconstructing Europe', 107

376   Bold, Larkham, Packard, *Authentic Reconstruction*, passim

377   www.hrw.org/reports/1991/gulfwar/INTRO.htm (accessed June 2017)

378   Kuzmarov, 'Bomb after Bomb', 7-12; Owen, Kiernan, 'Roots of US troubles', 1–10

379   www.independent.co.uk/news/world/middle-east/mosul-latest-news-isis-fighters-old-city-remain-control-iraq-forces-sami-al-aridi-special-forces-a7824956.html (accessed July 2017); www.independent.co.uk/news/world/middle-east/isis-leaders-syria-conscription-civilians-raqqa-deir-ezzor-us-led-coalition-forces-syrian-army-iraq-a7876606.html (accessed August 2017)

380   Chomsky, *Meaning of Vietnam*: https://chomsky.info/19750612/ (accessed December 2016); see also Chomsky, *Cambodia*: https://chomsky.info/19700604/ (accessed December 2016)

381   Chomsky, *American Foreign Policy*: https://chomsky.info/19850319/ (accessed December 2016)

382   Chomsky, *Terror*: https://chomsky.info/20020702/ (accessed December 2016)

383   Blum, *Rogue State*, 14

384   Ibid., 123

385   Blum, *Rogue State*, 122–6

386   Conway-Lanz, 'Ethics of Bombing', 2
387   Kuzmarov, 'Bomb after Bomb', 7–12
388   Conway-Lanz, 'Ethics of Bombing', 3
389   www.stopwar.org.uk (accessed June 2016)
390   www.bbc.co.uk/news/world-asia-37286520; www.theguardian.com/
      world/2015/jan/31/laos-deadly-aftermath-us-bomb-campaign-
      vietnam-air-attacks (accessed October 2017)
391   Bell, *London Was Ours*, 179
392   www.centenarynews.com/article/first-zeppelin-raid-on-london-
      remembered (accessed August 2016)
393   Eley, 'People's War', 818; Summerfield, 'Generation of Memory',
      39–40
394   Fuchs, *After the Dresden Bombing*, xiii
395   Ibid., 9
396   https://greatwen.com/2010/09/06/where-is-the-statue-for-
      londons-blitz-spirit/ (accessed August 2016)
397   www.londonremembers.com/memorials/civilian-deaths-in-ww2-
      blitz-east-london_(accessed November 2017)
398   www.londonremembers.com/memorials/people-of-london
      (accessed December, 2017)
399   www.londonremembers.com/memorials/national-firefighters-
      memorial (Accessed December 2017)
400   www.londonremembers.com (accessed November 2017)
401   Smith, 'Queen Honours'; www.londonremembers.com/memori-
      als/women-in-ww2 (accessed December 2017)
402   www.civildefenceassociation.org.uk/page15.html (accessed Janu-
      ary 2018)
403   *Daily Record*, 'New Memorial'
404   www.sas1946.com/main/index.php?topic=28095.144. (accessed
      December 2016)
405   www.cityoflondon.gov.uk/things-to-do/green-spaces/city-
      gardens/visitor-information/Pages/christchurch-greyfriars-
      church-garden.aspx (accessed December 2016)
406   Harris, *Walking the London Blitz*, passim; Van Young, *London's
      War*, passim
407   Laurence, 'Alone'; Douglas-Home, 'Whirlwind'; Hood, 'Nemesis'
408   Eley, 'People's War', 818
409   www.bbc.co.uk/programmes/b09gtbh2 (accessed January 2018)
410   Walker, *Halliwell's Film Guide*, 74; Vahimagi, *British Television*,
      939

411 Briggs, *Ethel and Ernest*, 31–57

412 Ibid., 57

413 Briggs, *When the Wind Blows*; for the film see Walker, *Halliwell's Film Guide*, 1277

414 Wilkinson, *Bert Hardy's Britain*, 33–47

415 Ibid., 34

416 Bell, *London Was Ours*, 176

417 www.bbc.co.uk/history/ww2peopleswar/categories/c1161/; Noakes, 'Warontheweb', 47-65; http://sounds.bl.uk/Search (accessed January 2017)

418 Noakes, Pattinson '"Keep Calm and Carry On"', 10–13

419 Garnett and Weight, *Modern British History*, 228–9

420 Summerfield, 'Generation of Memory', 40

421 Bell, *London Was Ours*, 193–4

422 Niven, 'GDR and Memory', 114

423 Arnold, *Allied War*, 310–11

424 Ibid., 311

425 Ibid., 311–13

426 Jerzak, 'Memory Politics', passim

427 Joel, *Dresden Firebombing*, 179

428 Jerzak, 'Memory Politics', 54

429 Ibid., 63–4

430 Niven and Paver, 'Introduction', 3

431 Denham, McCulloh *W.G. Sebald*, 335

432 Joel, *Dresden Firebombing*, 30–3

433 Seidel Arpaci, 'Lost in Translations?', 161–2

434 Ibid., 161–75

435 Joel, *Dresden Firebombing*, 9

436 Beck, *Under the Bombs*, 57-82

437 Harding,' Germany's Forgotten Victims', *Guardian*, 22 October 2003

438 Apel, 'Rubble society', 1019; Joel, *Dresden Firebombing*, 30–5

439 Niven, GDR and Memory', 128–9

440 Baruma, 'Germany's Unmourned Victims'

441 Schmitz, 'Historicism, sentimentality', 197–216

442 Jansen, 'Wahreit und Erinnerung', 181–2

443 Arnold, *Allied War*, 313; Joel, *Dresden Firebombing*,

444 Margalit, *Guilt, Suffering*, 42

445 Ibid., 293–4

446 Margalit, *Guilt, Suffering*, 294

447   Apel, 'Rubble Society', 1030

448   Joel, *Dresden Firebombing*, 272

449   Apel, 'Rubble Society', 1019

450   Süss, *Death from the Skies*, 1

451   Schmitz, 'Historicism, Sentimentality', 205

452   Joel, *Dresden Firebombing*, 186

453   Victor, 'Tempers Flare'

454   Kinzer, 'Honor to RAF leader'

455   Arnold, *Allied Bombing*, 319

456   Houghton, '"Missing Chapter"', 165; 167–8

457   Kinzer, 'Honor to RAF leader'

458   Houghton, '"Missing Chapter"', 165; 167–8

459   www.telegraph.co.uk/history/raf-bomber-command/9363220/
       Bomber-Command-memorial-bloody-marvellous-but-long-overdue.
       html (accessed December 2017); www.spiegel.de/international/
       europe/controversial-memorial-to-british-wwii-bombers-to-open-
       a-840858.html (accessed December 2017).

460   Joel, *Dresden Firebombing*, 104

461   Watson, 'Total War and Total Anniversary', 186

462   Gibbons, 'Bishop of Coventry'

463   Taylor, *Coventry*, 343

464   Joel, *Dresden Firebombing*, 269

465   Hashimoto, *The Long Defeat*, passim

466   Hogan, 'Hiroshima in History', 7

467   Jackson, 'Tradition and Modernity', 116

468   Ibid., 115–17

469   Miyamoto, *Beyond the Mushroom Cloud*, 2

470   Nora, 'Between Memory', 19

471   Southard, *Nagasaki*, 237

472   Ibid., 241

473   Lynch, *Image of the City*, passim

474   Southard, *Nagasaki*, 263–9

475   Zwigenberg, *Hiroshima*, passim

476   Miyamoto, *Beyond the Mushroom Cloud*, 13

477   www3.nhk.or.jp/nhkworld/en/special/episode/201708120810/
       (accessed October 2017)

478   Zwigenberg, *Hiroshima*, 250–4; www.cnduk.org/cnd-media/item/
       2693-hibakusha(accessedMarch2017);www.un.org/disarmament/
       education/slideshow/hibakusha/ (accessed March 2017)

479   Kynaston, *Modernity Britain*, 124–7

480   Zwigenberg, *Hiroshima*, 176–7
481   Miyamoto, *Beyond the Mushroom Cloud*, 76–7
482   Ibid., 130–1
483   Japan National Preparatory Committee, *Call from hibakusha*, v
484   Ibid., vii
485   Miyamoto, *Beyond the Mushroom Cloud*, 178
486   https://miningawareness.wordpress.com/2015/08/06/japanese-american-hibakusha-atomic-bomb-survivors/ (accessed July, 2017)
487   Browne, 'Japan, 1941-1945'; Elstein, David, 'The Bomb-February-September, 1945'
488   Broderick, 'Introduction', 2
489   Ibid., 4–5
490   Ibid., 5
491   Southard, *Nagasaki*, 170-71
492   Ishiro, *Godzilla*
493   Dorsey, Matsuoka, 'Narrative Strategies', 204
494   Walker, *Halliwell's Film Guide*, 128; Todeschini, 'Death and the maiden', 225–6
495   Ibid., 969
496   Todeschini, 'Death and the Maiden', 225–30
497   Broderick, 'Introduction', 6
498   Nakazawa, *Barefoot Gen*, Note to Volumes 1 and 2
499   Nakazawa, *Barefoot Gen*, Volumes 1 and 2, *passim*
500   Nakazawa, *Barefoot Gen*, Note to Volumes 1 and 2
501   www.telegraph.co.uk/news/worldnews/asia/japan/10261210/Japan-to-ban-40-year-old-Hiroshima-comic-from-schools-for-being-too-graphic.html (accessed February 2017)
502   Maier, 'Targeting the City', 429
503   Katsumoto, Sams, 'Saotome Katsumoto', 16
504   Marwick, *New Nature of History*, 172–9
505   Katsumoto, Sams, 'Saotome Katsumoto', 2
506   Ibid., 6–30; Katsumoto, *Great Tokyo*, *passim*
507   Cook and Cook, *Japan at War*, 343–3
508   Healy, Tumarkin. 'Social memory', 1007–10
509   Huyssen, 'Air War Legacies' 181–93
510   Zwigenburg, *Hiroshima*, 274–5
511   Ibid., 276–7
512   www.independent.co.uk/news/world/middle-east/israel-gaza-conflict-israeli-military-using-flechette-rounds-in-gaza-strip-9617480.html (accessed February 2017)

513   Cited in Chalk and Jonassohn, *History and Sociology*, 10
514   Ibid., 11
515   Ibid., 23
516   Ibid., 24
517   Harnden, 'Churchill Spirit'
518   Bond, *Frames of Memory*, 63
519   Ibid., 64
520   Ibid., 126–7; Ray, *Terror and the Sublime*, 51–60
521   Zwigenburg, *Hiroshima*, 298
522   McGreal, 'Ground Zero Mosque'
523   www.telegraph.co.uk/news/worldnews/barackobama/7945558/Barack-Obama-backs-Ground-Zero-mosque.html(accessed,February 2017)   http://nypost.com/2016/05/19/apartments-islamic-museum-to-be-built-on-site-of-failed-ground-zero-mosque/ (accessed February 2017)
524   www.archives.gov/research/guide-fed-records/groups/243.html (accessed September 2016)
525   www.revisionist.net/hell-introduction.html (accessed January 2017)
526   Grayling, *Among the Dead Cities*, 255

Index

Jennings, Humphrey   48,
      179, 183
Joel, Tony   197, 200, 203, 204
Johnson, President
      Lyndon B.   156, 158

K

Kassel, Germany   193–194,
      201
Katsumoto, Saotome   222
Kineto, Shindo   214
Kissinger, Henry
      158–159, 160
Kneale, Nigel   185
Kobe, Japan   138
Korea   6, 10
   history of   148
*Korea: Air Blitz Checks
      Reds* (1950)   149
Korean War, the (1950–53)   9,
      147–154, 171
   casualties in   152
Kosovo   166
Koyo, Ishikawa   219
Kurosawa, Akira   216
Kuwait   167

L

Labour League of Youth   27
Labour Party, the   4, 62,
      64, 121, 123–124,
      128, 187
Lancaster Bombers   89, 92
Laos   158–159, 168, 170, 172
League of Nations, the   3, 27

Lebensraum   79
Le Corbusier   129, 144
LeMay, General Curtis
      101, 213
Leningrad, USSR   80
Letchworth, England   124
Libya   1–2, 2, 7–8, 10,
      148, 167
lieux de memoire   174,
      181–183, 205
   cities as   7
Lille, France   81
Listen to Britain (1942)   183
Little Big Man (1970)   163
Liverpool, England   54–56
Living Through the Blitz
      (1976)   59
Locksley Hall (poem,
      1835)   13, 15, 104
London   9, 16, 19–21, 31
   Barbican scheme   126
   bombing of (1944)   72–75
   Christchurch Greyfriars
      Church   182
   Christmas Blitz   46, 49
   Churchill Gardens,
      Pimlico   123
   City of London   182
   County of London Plan
      (1943)   121
   decentralisation of
      housing   122, 124
   East End and East
      London   19, 41–43,
      59–60, 60, 177, 188

Lightning Source UK Ltd.
Milton Keynes UK
UKHW021306200520
363495UK00007B/199

9 781911 534488